W9-CEU-211

THE
SERPENT
GRAIL

Philip Gardiner is a marketing specialist and company director. He has spent the last 16 years reading and researching the history of man, science, religion and philosophy, and believes that much of orthodox history is based upon propaganda in one form or another. His search for the truth has led him to uncover historical evidence which had previously gone unrecognized. He is the author of the highly successful *The Shining Ones: The World's Most Powerful Secret Society Revealed.* For more information on Philip Gardiner please go to www.philipgardiner.net or www.gardinerosborn.com

Gary Osborn, managing director of a family business, has been a writer on mysticism and esoteric traditions for over 10 years. He describes himself as an 'initiate into the mysteries'. He has written articles on subjects related to ancient mysteries, esoteric traditions, alchemy, mysticism, ancient shamanism and the nature of human consciousness, and has also been involved in projects related to some former members of the Esalen Physics of Consciousness Group.

Philip will be doing international Tours through www.powerplaces.com visiting many of the places mentioned in this book. If you would like to join him on a unique Grail Journey, find out more on the Power Places website.

Also by Philip Gardiner:
Proof? Does God Exist?
The Shining Ones

THE
SERPENT
GRAIL

THE TRUTH BEHIND
THE HOLY GRAIL,
THE PHILOSOPHER'S STONE
AND THE ELIXIR OF LIFE

PHILIP GARDINER *with* GARY OSBORN

WATKINS PUBLISHING

LONDON

This edition published in the UK in 2005 by
Watkins Publishing, Sixth Floor, Castle House,
75–76 Wells Street, London W1T 3QH
Distributed in the USA and Canada by Publishers Group West

© Philip Gardiner and Gary Osborn

Philip Gardiner and Gary Osborn have asserted their right under the Copyright,
Designs and Patents Act, 1988, to be identified as authors of this work.

1 3 5 7 9 10 8 6 4 2

Designed and typeset by Brian Cockburn-Smith
Printed and bound in Great Britain

British Library Cataloguing in Publication data available
Library of Congress Cataloging in Publication data available

ISBN 1 84293 129 6

www.watkinspublishing.com
www.gardinerosborn.com

Contents

To my long-suffering wife Julie, who stood by me the whole time
and journeyed from one 'quarry' to another

Philip Gardiner

My contribution to this book is dedicated to my parents,
Eric Osborn and June Day and my daughter Li

Gary Osborn

Acknowledgements

First to my parents, who have encouraged me to 'seek happiness' in all that I do – thank you.

To Michael Mann, who believed in us right from the start.

To Penny Stopa and all the superb and professional editorial team at Duncan Baird/Watkins. Thank you for your help, advice, the great cover and understanding.

To Juliette Humble of Duncan Baird, for your help and advice.

To John Baldock, who edited our book like the true Gnostic that he is. John, there simply are not enough men like you in the world.

To the authors Andrew Collins, Graham Hancock, Robert Bauval, Dominic O'Brien, Paul Devereux, Graham Philips, Alan Butler, Christopher Knight, Acharya S and a whole host of others.

To all those silent unsung people who have helped us with this book – we thank you all.

Philip Gardiner

I would like to thank everyone at Watkins Publishing for their help and support.

My gratitude to John Baldock.

Special thanks to my brother Paul Osborn and to my wife, friend and companion Jacqui, for her unfailing support of me and our children Ben, Victoria, Cameron, Freya and Angel.

Gary Osborn

The authors would like to acknowledge the documents received from the following and used with their permission: Scientologists, Jehovah's Witnesses, Mormons, Jewish Pentecostal Mission, Rosicrucians, Freemasons, Inner Light, Webster's Encyclopaedia, Encarta Encyclopaedia, The Unexplained (Focus), Encyclopaedia of History (Dorling Kindersley), the staff at Lichfield Cathedral, The New Scientist (21 March 1998 and 11 July 1998), Bible Explorer (expert software), Faith in Every Footstep (The Church of Jesus Christ of Latter-Day Saints press information CD-Rom).

List of Illustrations

The publisher would like to thank the following people and museums for permission to reproduce their material. Every care has been taken to trace copyright holders. However, if we have omitted anyone, we apologize and will, if informed, make corrections to any future editions.

Plates

Photographs taken by Philip Gardiner

1. The Grail Chalice in a stained-glass window. St Mary's Church, Scarborough, England.
2. Naga serpent deity. Temple of Manipur, India.
3. Ouroboros encircling the Holy Spirit as a dove. Lichfield Cathedral inner wall, England.
4. The Uffington White Horse. England.
5. Statue of Hygeia. York Minster, England.
6. Male and female stones. Avebury Stone Circle, England.
7. Sculpture of a Neolithic snake goddess (c.4500BC). Heraklion Museum, Crete.
8. Relief of serpent on a doctor's tomb. Cimetière de Montmarte, Paris.
9. Station of the Cross. The Dome Chapel, Paris.
10. Carving on a tomb of Egyptian stylized winged orb of enlightenment with protective serpents. Cimetière de Montmarte, Paris.
11. Adam, Eve and the serpent in a stained-glass window. Lincoln Cathedral, England.
12. St John with dragon chalice in a stained-glass window. Winchester Cathedral, England.
13. Adam, Eve and the serpent with a human head in a stained glass window. York Minster, England.
14. Serpent-headed column. The Pantheon, Rome.
15. Author Philip Gardiner with human skulls. Capela dos Ossos (Chapel of Skulls), Faro, Portugal.
16. Statue of a Grail Maiden with a broken chalice revealing the inside of the Lorraine Cross. Sainte Chappelle, Paris.
17. The Green Man stone carving. York Minster, England.
18. Fifteenth-century Armenian wall painting showing St George killing the dragon. Byzantine Museum, Nicosia, Cyprus.
19. Wall fresco of the Baptism within the Grail. Kykkos Monastery, Cyprus.
20. Bronze relief of St John the Baptist's head on a platter or chalice. Kykkos Monastery, Cyprus.
21. The front of the statue of Prudence. Winchester Cathedral, England.
22. The reverse of Prudence (as above).
23. Obelisk, Paris.
24. Isis, Queen of Heaven, holding the sistrum. *Mosaize Historie der Hebreeuwse Kerke.*
25. Stone carving of the Asp and the Mirror on a building in Paris.
26. The sacred chalice of the Eucharist. Lichfield Cathedral, England.
27. Angels with the Grail chalice collecting the blood of Christ in a stained-glass window. Lichfield Cathedral, England.
28. The serpent gnawing at the roots of the world tree, with Christ crucified, in a stained-glass window. Lichfield Cathedral, England.
29. Stone relief of the shapeshifting serpent Melusine. Newstead Abbey, England
30. Tomb decoration of the serpent Ouroboros encircling the image of time. St Giovanni, Rome.
31. Carving on a tomb of the Ouroboros with rose at the centre. Cimetière de Montmarte, Paris.
32. St Patrick eradicating the serpents from Ireland in a stained-glass window. Salisbury Cathedral, England.

Preface

This book has its own story, which began when I was reading in bed one night. The warm glow from the bedside lamp dispelled any idea of time. The dim red blinking light of the digital clock-radio revealed that it was 1a.m., yet both my wife and I were wide awake, deeply immersed in what we were reading. During our night-time reading sessions we often tell each other about the fruits of our research, and on this particular night I was reading through the final proofs of my second book, *The Shining Ones*. I was totally absorbed in the history and mythology of ancient civilizations when my wife brought me back to the present with a comment about T-cells and how snake venom could assist in their production. Since she is a prolific amateur medical historian, this was not an unusual comment. But to me T-cells meant nothing, so I asked her to explain.

'T-cells,' she replied, 'are part of our immune system. They help people to heal faster.' As she said this I experienced a bizarre sensation that I can only liken to what is known as the shamanic 'enlightenment experience'. It was as if, in a moment of profound illumination, I had received an insight into some ancient secret. And then, without warning, my mind began to race. Jumping out of bed at a speed that surprised my wife and even myself considering the late hour, I ran down the darkened stairs and into my library. I switched on the light and headed straight for three reference books in which I instinctively knew I would find confirmation of the insight I had just received. Grabbing the books off the shelves, I ran back up the stairs to explain my strange behaviour to my wife. As I read out the relevant passages from the books, her look of disbelief mirrored my own growing sense of incredulity. Neither of us slept that night.

The insight I had received in that moment of 'enlightenment' concerned the mysterious phenomena known as the Elixir of Life, the Philosopher's Stone and the Holy Grail. Over the next few days I scrambled my way through hundreds of books, searching until late every night for the inevitable flaw in the theory that was now taking shape in my mind. And yet everything merely seemed to confirm it, and more.

Shortly afterwards, I happened to meet writer and researcher Gary Osborn, who had uncovered some ancient secrets pertaining to shamanism, the enlightenment experience, the Great Pyramid of Giza and what we would come to call the 'cult of the serpent'. This chance meeting led to our collaboration in what was to become a joint quest to find the truth behind the enigmatic Holy Grail. Together we researched, cross-referenced and collated the mounting evidence to support our theory that the Elixir of Life, the Philosopher's Stone and the Holy Grail were not only 'ideals' but had real substance. Moreover, they worked in precisely the way described in ancient myths and legends. Indeed, they were one and the same thing.

According to traditional myths and legends, these three mysterious phenomena cured all manner of illnesses and brought great riches. They were also said to be the source of profound knowledge, enlightenment and even eternal life. As we were to discover, these three mythical objects were the result of humankind's earliest association with one of the most poisonous and dangerous creatures on the planet – the snake. This creature, which in ancient times was worshipped, has since been demonized by Western religion. But this was just one of the many contradictions we came across as our quest for the truth behind the Elixir, the Stone and the Grail led us to the very origins of civilization and the root of our modern belief systems.

We hope you enjoy reading about the discoveries we made during our many years of research. In addition to the information given here, regular updates can be found on our website, *www.gardinerosborn.com*, along with many related articles.

We wish you an enlightening Grail journey. *Qui on en servoit?*

Introduction

If you have bought this book, you are doubtless already intrigued by the Holy Grail and the many myths that surround it. Perhaps you see the Grail as an esoteric or mystical symbol, a key to the secrets of self-discovery. You may also have formulated some ideas about the Philosopher's Stone and the Elixir of Life.

There are many ways of perceiving these mysteries. We may see the Grail as being a historical object, for example, such as a vessel or cup. Or our vision of it may derive from this traditional description, but be influenced by our personal focus in life. For a mystic or alchemist, this 'ace of all cups' represents the spiritual perfection of man. For an archaeologist, it might be the sacred vessel excavated from the tomb of Joseph of Arimathea. For a Formula One racing driver, it could be the 'victory cup' from which he quaffs champagne, while for a soccer player or fan, it would be the World Cup. Some marketing gurus would have us believe that it is a simple pint glass containing a certain brand of 'amber nectar'.

For many of us, the words 'Holy Grail' express supreme perfection or ultimate discovery and can be applied to just about anything and everything, whether spiritual or mundane. In a quick search of the Internet, we found that the words are even used by teenage computer programmers to describe some pre-eminent computer language. So it seems that there is no end to the usage of the term: whatever field we are working in, the Holy Grail is the ultimate goal.

Perhaps it is the inherent ambiguity of the Grail that has captured our imagination. One thing is certain, however: recent interest in the Grail reveals a deep-seated desire to break free from the constraints imposed by orthodox traditions and institutions. For whatever its real secret may be, the Grail has come to symbolize self-empowerment.

Before we go any further, we would like you to picture the Holy Grail in your mind. Close your eyes and allow yourself to travel back through history. Fly over Norman-conquered territory, over Anglo-Saxon fields to Roman Britain and back through Celtic lands to a time that remains a mystery. Let the mystery clear and see your own vision of the Grail before you.

What have you visualized?

A plain and simple cup, made from clay or wood?

A golden chalice, inlaid with jewels and sparkling in the sunlight? Does a glowing mist surround this magical, almost musical chalice?

A plate or dish, edged with Celtic knotwork? Or perhaps a platter that once held the head of John the Baptist?

A cauldron, with images of dragons and mythological beasts prancing around its outer face that recall Celtic tales from ages past?

A blood-red lance that once pierced Christ's side and was sought after by Napoleon, Hitler and others who aspired to rule the known world?

An Eastern sacrificial cup containing the Vedic *Soma*, the Mazdean *Haoma* or the Greek *Ambrosia*? Or does it contain the blood of Christ?

These examples are how many of us in the Western world visualize the Grail. Most of us, however, are inclined to think of it as a cup or chalice that once held the blood of Christ, and we tend to look no further.

The reasons for this are simple. Our image of the Grail derives from popular folk tradition, mass-market books or the silver screens of cinema and television. And now, with the proliferation of the worldwide web, all manner of wonderful new ideas are streaming into popular and cult circles – a veritable cornucopia of modern folklore and modern confusion.

However, there are those for whom the answers to the deeper mysteries of the Grail are to be found instead in esoteric or mystery schools. Finding these answers involves a journey into the unknown – a journey that leads to eternal life, which is itself the Grail.

Our initial research led us to conclude that the Grail had emerged from several different sources, all of which derived from the same generic source, if not from the same geographical location. In our quest we searched through ancient texts, etymology, history, religion and science, and considered them from every possible viewpoint. We also made a conscious decision not to accept the conventional interpretations of the myths we encountered, since we wished to avoid going down the same old road that others had travelled before us and that many more keep travelling.

Although the Holy Grail is now fundamentally a European ideal, we discovered that it was originally a worldwide phenomenon. The familiar Celtic and Christian Grail legends were simply adaptations of the original story, new ideas overlaid on old truths. Whether by design or accident, they served to bury the real facts ever deeper.

In our search for the real meaning of the Grail, we could not help but touch upon the esoteric explanation of the Grail myth as a spiritual quest of self-fulfilment and discovery, and it is perhaps this interpretation that the modern reader can most relate to. However, the origins of the Grail myth lie in a different age, when such ideas were the remit of a select few: the priests and 'masters of the craft'. This élite employed an arcane and symbolic language to hide the real identity of the Grail in much the same way that 'practical' alchemical texts concealed the path to spiritual transformation and enlightenment.

In the end, whichever particular image we personally have of the Grail, they all point to one unique and simple conclusion: *we can obtain eternal life through the Grail.*

Philip Gardiner and Gary Osborn [May 2005, London]

PART ONE

The Grail, the Elixir and the Stone

CHAPTER ONE

Alpha-Omega

The very nature of myth is such that one level of meaning leads to yet deeper levels. Therefore whether we are simply reading a mythical story or researching its origins, a myth has the potential to take us on a journey.

The mythical journey we have come to know as the 'quest for the Holy Grail' belongs in part to the mystical tradition, a tradition that conceals its knowledge of enlightenment and other mystical experiences behind symbolic images and enigmatic language. If this knowledge were expressed in more literal language, it would be met with misunderstanding or even hostility. Also, it cannot be disclosed directly, because this would be to reveal the goal of the journey before the journey had even begun. It is therefore little wonder that many of us have difficulty understanding the mystical aspect of the Grail. Moreover, the popular themes surrounding the Holy Grail date from a time when life revolved around religion, fuelled by the spiritual impulse that seems to be an intrinsic part of human nature.

History and propaganda have also contributed to the story of the Grail. At any given point in history, it is always the most popular stories that are grafted onto an original legend. Sometimes stories are popularized for propaganda purposes. At others, stories that are either unpopular or suppressed by those in power are forgotten, cast upon the funeral pyre of time. Just as we today are persuaded to vote for certain political parties by the mass media, so in ages gone by our ancestors were persuaded to follow certain beliefs. It is in this way that the Grail came to be seen as the vessel that caught the blood of Christ as he hung from the tree. It was also said to be the cup used by Christ at the Last Supper. Known as the 'relic of passion',[1] it has become more important than the original message. But these interpretations share a common symbolism in that they associate the Grail with the blood of Christ.

The most frequently quoted medieval author on the subject of the Grail is Helinand (c.1150–c.1227), a Cistercian abbot from Froidmont in the diocese of Beauvais. However, we noted that Helinand was one of the most ardent preachers of the Albigensian Crusade (1209–44), a crusade in southern France against the Cathars (from the Greek *καβαποι*, meaning 'Pure Ones'), a Gnostic sect who were regarded as heretics by the Church. This must surely have influenced anything Helinand had to say about the Grail, since the Cathars were said to possess the secret of the Holy Grail and to have spirited it away from the town of Montségur before it fell to the Crusaders. They are supposed to have then deposited it in the Ornolac caves in a valley in the Ariège before they themselves became victims of the crusade launched on the orders of Pope Innocent III.

Helinand presupposes the Grail to be a real object, like a chalice or cup. But the secret spirited away from Montségur by the Cathars is more likely to have been written texts that contained the real knowledge of the Grail, or perhaps ritual accoutrements and other paraphernalia associated with this knowledge. These could very well have included a symbolic cup or chalice.

Others believe that the Grail is the platter or Paschal Dish which was present at the Last Supper. In this case we should not look to Christianity or Celtic mythology for the blood element associated with the Grail, but to Judaism. This idea can be proven incorrect, however, although in the story of the Grail there is truth in all.

For Dr Linda Malcor, 'The connection between the Grail and the Eucharistic chalice is generally implicit and often explicit. One exception to this occurs in the metrical Joseph [Joseph of Arimathea] where … the poet describes the Grail as containing the "blood of the slain god" and compares this vessel to the Eucharistic chalice.'[2]

The Holy Eucharist, which is one of Seven Sacraments of the Christian Church, is celebrated during the Mass or Holy Communion. The ritual involves the distribution of white bread and red wine. In some variations, the bread or circular communion wafer is dipped into the red wine contained in a large cup or chalice before being given to each communicant to eat. The bread is said to represent the body of Christ and the wine his blood. The connection between the Grail and the Eucharist is particularly interesting in that the ritual symbolizes the individual's communion with the Christian God, thus revealing how one can establish a personal and conscious connection with that collective centre of intelligence to which all of us are theoretically already linked.

While opinions may vary about the identity of the Grail as an object, the meaning of the word 'Grail' has itself provoked a surge of theories.

In early manuscripts, the Grail is referred to as the *Sangraal*. Helinand claims that the word *graal* comes from *gradalis* and sets the date of a hermit's vision of the Grail as 717–19 (*see* Speculum Historiaie, *by Vincent of Beauvais*). Helinand's *gradalis* is said to resemble a dish on which fish are served, while the Grail scholar Dr Bergmann points out that the medieval Latin noun *gradail* (masculine) or *gradale* (neuter) translates as 'vase', 'goblet' or 'basin'.

Sir Thomas Malory, author of the fifteenth-century *Morte d'Arthur*, was the first to use the words 'Holy Grail' and said that the *Sangkreal* was the blessed blood of Christ. But in his *English Etymology*, Walter Skeat (1835–1912), one of the greatest investigators of the roots of the English language, states that the etymology of the Holy Grail 'was very early falsified by an intentional change from San Greal (Holy Dish) to Sang

Real (Royal Blood)'.[3] This is a perfect example of how the original information surrounding the Grail was later twisted and corrupted by those hoping to further their own ends, usually the pursuit of power. We found that such misinterpretations, or deliberate falsifications, have appeared ever since the Grail's ancient origins.

The change of meaning from 'Holy Grail' to 'Royal Blood' has led various authors and researchers to suggest that the secret of the Holy Grail is that the royal bloodlines of Europe stem directly from the bloodline of Jesus.[4] Like people of ancient Egypt, who saw their pharaohs as the sons of God, we are now encouraged to believe that the royal families of Europe are descended from a divinity. But in our view, the secret of the Holy Grail could just as easily lie in the fact that this addition to the Grail myth provides a further mystery.

Wolfram von Eschenbach, one of the earliest and most famous of Grail writers, was 'bought' by the Templars and Cistercians to ensure that they were written into this then new propaganda myth. More recently, the authors of *The Holy Blood and the Holy Grail* were approached by an alleged secret society, the Priory of Sion, which had decided that it was time to reveal this ancient secret.[5] We have to ask ourselves, what kind of secret society reveals its secrets to the world? Surely such secrets would be highly questionable.

As to what the Grail really is, there are many explanations. There may also be more than one Grail, as Graham Philips, author of *The Search for the Grail*, observed:

> In each romance the Grail or Grails are kept by the family of Perceval, the direct descendants of Joseph of Arimathea... Here lies the Grail's importance – it is a visible, tangible symbol of an alternative apostolic succession. [6]

The idea that there could be more than one Grail matched our own growing conviction of the underlying truth of the Grail story. We would go further than Graham Philips, however, and say that the Grail is guarded by this 'apostolic succession', not that they themselves are the Grail. And it has been guarded well. So much so that misinformation – for example, the stories surrounding the Priory of Sion – has been employed to mislead people and send many Grail researchers on a wild goose chase.

The fact that so many images have been attributed to the Grail also gives the impression that it is many things, when in reality all these images are devices to hide and protect it.

We are told, for example, that the Grail is a vessel of some kind containing the *resurrecting* blood of Christ which was brought by Joseph of Arimathea, the supposed uncle of Jesus, to Glastonbury, England. Yet the Grail is also considered to be the Pagan cauldron of Celtic and Sarmation mythology – the symbol of fertility, transformation and rebirth. This cauldron, which is mentioned in the stories of the *Cauldron of Ceridwen* (a Celtic goddess) and the *Cauldron of Annwn* (the Celtic Underworld) had many uses. It was similar to the Void of Eastern tradition, from which everything in the universe originates, in that it would spew forth copious amounts of 'wondrous food and drink' for the victors of battle. It would also resurrect the dead soldiers of the victorious side, albeit taking a part of each as an offering – either his eyesight or his speech, so that he could either not look upon the cauldron or not talk about it. It was thus impossible for him to impart its secrets to others.

Like the Celtic cauldron, the Grail is associated with fertility, regeneration and the cycle of life-death-rebirth as expressed in the never-ending cycle of the seasons. Within this yearly cycle, followers of religions from around the world celebrate the Spring or Vernal Equinox which falls on or around 21 March. This is one of only two days in the year when day and night are equal in length, the other being the Autumnal Equinox, which falls exactly six months later, on or around

21 September. These celebrations are said to be Pagan in origin, but are more likely to have a shamanic foundation. For many of us, the Spring Equinox represents the victory of light over darkness – of good over evil. For others, this time marks the conception of the Son of God, whose coming to Earth or physical birth takes place at the Winter Solstice in December. For Pagans, it marks the annual death-rebirth of the 'slain god' or 'vegetation god' – gods such as the Egyptian Osiris, the Roman Attis, the Assyrian/Babylonian Tammuz or Sumerian Damuzi and the Celtic Green Man. This time in the yearly cycle is also the death-rebirth of Jesus Christ, which is celebrated at Easter.

In this annual conception or rebirth of the 'resurrecting god', we find a correspondence to the rebirth and resurrection of the dead soldiers of Celtic myth. Furthermore, we find that this resurrecting god also provides the yearly harvest, which corresponds to the 'wondrous food' produced by the Celtic cauldron. The Grail is similarly said to produce an abundance of food and drink, and to appear suddenly, as if from nowhere.

The Grail and the Alpha-Omega

The connection of the Grail with the resurrecting god led us to examine more closely the natural phenomenon of cycles and especially the crucial point in each and every cycle: the beginning-and-end point, the point at which one cycle ends and a new cycle begins, which is by implication the moment of death-rebirth and of resurrection. This point is represented by the ancient circular symbol of the *Ouroboros* ('tail devourer'), the snake that is swallowing or biting its own tail (*see figure 1*). A universal symbol, the Ouroboros first appeared in Egypt around 1600 BC, but is probably much older. It carries the simple message that Creation is a cyclical process – creation, destruction, recreation, or birth, death, rebirth – in which patterns repeat themselves in a series of never-ending cycles, from the slowly changing patterns of the

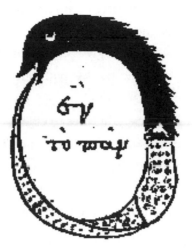

Figure 1: Ancient Graeco-Byzantine Ouroboros

revolving galaxies to the more rapid spin activity that occurs at the sub-quantum level.

The Ouroboros and other ancient symbols like it, such as the Egyptian Shen Ring (a rod and circle combined, also evident in Sumerian art), draw our attention to the most important point in the cyclical process. In the Ouroboros, this point is the place in the circle at which the snake is biting its own tail. This is the beginning-end instant known as the Alpha-Omega after the first and last letters of the Greek alphabet, *A* (Alpha) and Ω (Omega). The significance of this point is emphasized in the words attributed to Jesus Christ, 'I am the Alpha and the Omega, the first and the last, the beginning and the end' (Revelation 22:13). These words have a remarkable parallel in an inscription found in the temple of the Egyptian goddess Isis at Sais in Egypt: 'I am all that has been, that is, and that will be.' The letters Alpha and Omega were also frequently applied to Goddess worship, for it was the Goddess who united us in birth and death.

The few examples given here and the many others we discovered suggested to us that the Grail was itself associated with the crucial point in every cycle at which opposing forces – for example, life–death, winter–summer, day–night – are momentarily joined, fused together and cancelled out, thus allowing a seemingly spiritual third state or third force to manifest. This is personified by the symbolic annual appearance of the resurrecting god or 'Christed one'.

This crucial point in the cycle applies to all opposites and is the *zero-point* at which positive crosses into negative and vice versa, as shown in simple wave phenomena and all periodic systems.

If we take the Spring and Autumn Equinoxes as an example, these two points in the yearly cycle – known in the ancient Pagan Wicca tradition as the 'in-between times' – are 'where' and 'when' the opposites are in balance. It was believed that at these two points a portal opened between the Earth and the heavenly realm, through which radiated the Infinite, the life-force, providing sustenance and nourishment. In the words of the mythologist C. Austin:

In that time of suspended activity, the conduit between the worlds yawns, the 'veil becomes thin'. As the contents of both worlds mingle, the resulting tumult offers an opportunity for a renewed relationship with the unseen.[7]

As we were to discover, the significance of this particular point in the dynamic of the cycle is far-reaching. Every cycle has *three phases*, as can be seen in a simple sine wave (*see figure 2*). These three phases are: positive (peak), negative (dip) and the neutral point we would call the *Transliminal Phase*. 'Transliminal' is a term often used in psychology and consciousness research to describe what is known as the 'Transliminal State' or 'Transliminal experience', however applying it to the dynamic in the cycle enables us to see the deeper connections between consciousness and cyclical phenomena. The neutral point or Transliminal Phase is crossed over twice, where each half of the cycle crosses over into the

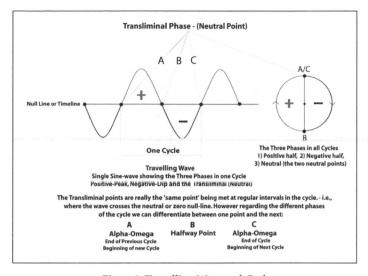

Figure 2: Travelling Wave and Cycle
A travelling wave is really a continuous cycle of energy-information stretched out linearly in time.
Illustration by Gary Osborn

other, and is therefore the point at which both opposites are momentarily united or cancelled out – that is, they are *neutralized*.

We discovered that this neutral point in the cycle was also responsible for much of the ancient sexual imagery associated with creation, for the ancients understood that the creative processing of consciousness was similar in principle to the procreation process. In brief, the ancients associated the positive and negative phases of a cycle with the gender opposites of male and female. The neutral point in the cycle was seen to correspond to the moment of sexual fusion, when the male and female opposites united in sexual intercourse and produced a child. In contrast to the mother and father, who represented the two opposite forces, the child was the embodiment of the third force. In the course of its development in the womb, the child itself became either male or female – i.e. one of two opposites – and so the cycle was repeated *ad infinitum*. But at the moment of conception, the child or *zygote* (the fertilized ovum) represented the 'divine spark' of creation produced by the union of opposites.

If we apply this symbolism to the Ouroboros, the snake's tail represents the phallus, its mouth the female vagina, and the two unite at the neutral point in the cycle. More importantly, this point in the cycle represents the 'organizing principle' – the synaptic pulse or spark – that drives the cycles and that is continually being ignited by the source-centre of creation.

The Grail and the Neutral Angels

In *Parzifal*, Wolfram von Eschenbach tells us that the Grail is a stone that was brought from heaven to Earth by 'neutral angels', so called because they refused to take sides when there was a war in heaven. Although they are also mentioned in Dante's *Inferno* (3:34-69), which was written in the fourteenth century, we could find no obvious source for Eschenbach's neutral angels. Instead, we discovered that the origin of the Grail goes back in time to the mysterious priesthood of gods and demigods known as 'the Shining Ones'.

The Egyptian gods of the pre-dynastic period were known as the N.tj.r – *Neter* or *Neteru* (plural) – which means 'god', 'spirit' or 'soul'. Some have translated Neter as 'neutral' or 'nature' and suggest that words like 'neither' and 'nether' (as in 'Netherworld') stem from it. The Neter gods included Osiris, Horus and Thoth. According to the Turin Papyrus, which lists the names of these gods and the later dynasties of the pharaohs, the long reign of the Neter was followed by that of a mysterious priesthood known as the *Shemsu Hor* (the 'Followers of Horus'), Horus having been the last Neter god. This priesthood was also known as the *Akhu*, which means 'the Shining Ones'. By all accounts, these gods and their priests or militant arm, who were known as the Watchers or Nephilim (the angels who were said to have come down from heaven), had been based in ancient Sumeria before moving to Heliopolis in Egypt. This mysterious race of beings has also been linked to the 'fish deities' who were said to have come from the sea. More specifically, they were said to have come from a 'submerged land', which inevitably evokes tales of the lost continent of Atlantis. The Shining Ones also settled in other places around the globe. In India they were known as the Nagas (Serpent Lords) (*see plate 2*). In Mesoamerica they were the 'feathered serpents' and in China they were known as the 'water beings'.

Our research into the Shining Ones suggests that they were an advanced shamanic-based culture. Although an account of their long and often deliberately distorted history lies outside the scope of the present book, we can learn something of their cosmology, spiritual knowledge and beliefs from the shamanic tradition, since both were based on an understanding of the neutral third force.

The underlying message conveyed by many of the myths and allegorical stories we studied is that this neutral force is the answer to the problems created by the apparent duality of human consciousness. The psychologist Carl Jung addressed the nature of these problems when he wrote:

Humanity, as never before, is split into two apparently irreconcilable halves. Psychological rule says that when an inner situation is not made conscious, it happens outside, as fate. That is to say, when the individual remains divided and does not become conscious of his inner opposite, the world must perforce act out the conflict and be torn into opposing halves.[8]

The mythologist C. Austin adds:

...while the dynamism of the world is held in duelling opposites, the healing and resolution of the world is found in the *tertium non datur*, the reconciling 'third' which arises as a synthesis of the opposites that, though in conflict, have been held in consciousness, in authenticity. This 'third' is the unforeseeable middle ground, which can express both sides, 'just as a waterfall visibly mediates between above and below'.[9]

How do the neutral point and the third force relate to the Grail? According to the mythologist Joseph Campbell, the Grail 'represents the spiritual path that is between pairs of opposites, between fear and desire, between good and evil'.[10] Writing about the Fisher King, whose one-sided wound has made him sexually impotent and caused a corresponding imbalance in the land he both governs and represents, C. Austin adds, 'It is fitting that the Grail King is restored by the hero Parzifal, whose own name means "straight down the middle"'.[11]

If we now re-examine Eschenbach's story about the neutral angels who carried the Grail between heaven and Earth, we can see that these 'angels' are the personification of the neutral third force. The third force is also represented by the Grail, which the angels bring from heaven to Earth – heaven and Earth being the two opposites – while the Grail that passes between them is both the dynamic beginning-end point (the Alpha-Omega) and the reconciling third force. As we will see, the Grail's ability to reconcile opposites holds the key to healing our divided consciousness.

In the next chapter we examine the techniques associated with the practical application of this third force, or middle state, which can be discerned by studying the way of the shaman.

CHAPTER TWO

The Mixing of Opposites

Shamanism has been described as a worldwide magico-spiritual system in which the tribal psychic or shaman – also known as the witchdoctor, medicine man, priest, magician, sorcerer, diviner and sage – enters an altered state of consciousness, or trance state, and travels to 'non-material' worlds by journeying *into himself*. There he gains knowledge of divination and healing through his interaction with what he believes to be the spirits of the dead and other supernatural creatures and intelligences. The tribal shamans were probably also the first storytellers, explaining the meaning of life and the cosmos to their fellow men through what we would now describe as mythical stories.

In the course of his inner journey the shaman travels through the higher realms. However, these can only be reached by first passing through the Underworld, the land of the dead, known to the ancient Sumerians as *Abzu*, to the ancient Egyptians as *Duat* and to the Greeks as *Hades*.

The most effective shamans are those who have the natural ability to enter the trance state at will. Most will have acquired this ability through some illness, crisis or trauma from which they re-emerge as if 'reborn'. This is their initiation into the mysteries. These first experiences are often terrifying, for the shaman may feel he is dying, being dismembered or torn apart – hence the Underworld's association with what we now call Hell. In effect, the initiate's consciousness is broken down and remade so that he can fulfil his new vocation as the mediator or medium between this world and the next. After his ordeal he is considered to be a new person with a new name, for like the archetypal resurrecting god he is born again with a profound wisdom concerning the mysteries of life and death.

In the same way that Jesus was guided by the Holy Spirit, Arthur was accompanied by the wise Merlin and the gods Osiris and Horus were instructed by Thoth, the new shaman-saviour will usually have an instructor, a 'spirit guardian', possibly a former shaman or ancestor. He will also be accompanied by the spirit of an animal from whom he derives great power – a 'power animal'.

Many of the Western anthropologists who studied indigenous cultures around the world at the beginning of the twentieth century believed that the symptoms associated with shamanic trance states were similar to those associated with schizophrenia and epilepsy. They therefore considered the shaman to be suffering from some kind of mental disorder rather than to be a spiritual mediator between this world and the next. These early observations may be more revealing in terms of the predominant left-brain perceptions of the anthropologists than of shamanism, however.

The shaman employs many techniques, all of which are intended to induce an altered state of consciousness that leads to higher states, which are often described as pleasurably ecstatic or even sexually orgasmic. This is also an appropriate description of the bright-light climax of the enlightenment experience – the biblical *Kardia* or Hindu *Kundalini awakening* – which has been compared to sexual orgasm, but is said to be a thousand times more intense. This experience of bright light, of the 'inner sun', gave rise to the term 'the Shining Ones'.

To facilitate his entry into these other states and worlds, the shaman will sometimes take hallucinogenic substances made from natural plants, after which he may be bound or tied up. Another technique involves a drum fashioned from the trunk of a tree, on which the shaman beats out various hypnotic rhythms to induce the trance state.

Stick and Drum

The shaman's stick and drum can be compared to the binary symbols '1' and 'O', which correspond to the male and female opposites we mentioned earlier and all similar opposites. This is no mere conjecture on our part, since African shamans describe the people of Western and other cultures that are left-brain dominant as 'the people of the line' and those of Eastern and right-brain dominant cultures as 'the people of the circle'. These ancient descriptions are clearly not referring to the modern binary symbols used in computer language. Instead, we suggest that the binary symbols were based 'coincidentally' on the ancient concept of the two opposites.

When the shaman beats his drum to enter the trance state, the two binary opposites are brought together with every beat of the drum and the male-stick and female-drum are momentarily fused together like the phallus and vagina, or sperm and ovum, during sexual intercourse. The moment of contact between the stick and drum corresponds to the neutral point at which the two opposites fuse together – the zero, transliminal point in a cycle. As the shaman beats his drum, the oscillating cycles of his own brainwaves attune themselves to the drum's hypnotic rhythm, causing his mind to zoom in on this neutral point and enter a hypnotic or hypnagogic trance also called the 'Transliminal State'.

The Fusion of Opposites

In alchemy, the union of opposites is represented by the Androgyne or Hermaphrodite – the perfect spiritual being – a composite figure depicted in art as possessing a body that is divided vertically into

Figure 3: Johann Mylius, Philosophia reformata, 1622

half-male and half-female, or as one body with both male and female heads (*see figure 3*).

In esoteric and occult lore, the physical world of appearances and the superficial surface of things are associated with the masculine principle, as symbolized by the full light of the sun. Conversely, the mental or psychical world and the underlying energy behind the physical appearance of matter are associated with the feminine principle, as symbolized by the reflected half-light of the moon. In alchemical texts we find many illustrations conveying these two opposite principles through the symbolism of the sun (associated with 'day') and moon (associated with 'night').

Because of male dominance in society, the correspondences associated with the masculine principle are traditionally seen as being predominantly *positive* – the male perceives all things objectively, in what he considers to be the true cold light of day – and the rational sciences, mathematical logic and physics stem from this male view of the world. On the other hand, the correspondences associated with the feminine principle are seen as being predominantly *negative*, at least according to the male point of view, which considers that when things are seen from a female perspective they are perceived as though by the half-light of the moon – i.e. in a vague, abstract or illusory way.

The association of the sun with the masculine principle and the

Figure 4: The Yin-Yang pictogram

moon with the feminine illustrates how the ancients applied their knowledge of the natural world to the processes of human consciousness. Similarly, the three phases of the cycle described in the preceding chapter correspond with the three phases of the moon – waxing (positive), waning (negative) and full moon (the alpha-omega point) – as well as the phases of the female menstrual cycle. These female cycles led to the concept of the Threefold Goddess. The fusion of opposites – sun and moon, masculine and feminine – was also observable in the natural world in the phenomenon of the solar eclipse. On the human scale, as already mentioned, this fusion of opposites was personified in the figure of the Androgyne, which also represented the fusion in consciousness that allowed the 'true self' or 'soul' of the individual to manifest.

The Chinese Yin-Yang pictogram, which is also known as the Tai Chi symbol, depicts the male-active and female-passive opposites as each containing their opposite within themselves (*see figure 4*).

Jungian theory expresses the same principle in that each person is said to possess both a male and female side – the *animus* and *anima*. Regardless of our predominant gender type, the 'true self' manifests in the transitory fusion and subsequent neutralization of the masculine and feminine aspects, especially during the shamanic-related 'enlightenment experience'.

In the course of our research into the beliefs of the past, we found that the positive-masculine and negative-feminine principles were once very much a part of the human perception of the world. Although our current beliefs may be very different, an understanding of these principles could help us to resolve some of the enigmas with which we are still struggling today. For those who might object that we are confusing 'gender' with 'polarity', we suggest that the ancients did not employ such dualistic terms, because, unlike us, they had no concept of 'division'. Furthermore, we are not promoting 'duality' or 'polarity'. Our references to the apparent duality or polarity of opposites are made in order to emphasize the existence of the mid-point or neutral point of balance between opposites. This occurs in all cycles and on all levels of existence, from the macrocosmic to the microcosmic. It is also a key to understanding part of the mystery surrounding the Grail.

In effect, the ancients saw the mid-point between opposites as representing the true non-dualistic nature of reality, whereas the apparent duality of opposites was regarded as an illusion – a false perception of reality. This particular understanding of reality was expressed through myths and symbols. For example, the half-male, half-female figure of the Androgyne was devised to illustrate the symbolic point in the cycle at which the opposites cross into each other and become momentarily united, fused and mixed together. It thus illustrates simultaneously the true and illusory facets of reality.

These illusory opposites also formed the basis for the ancient system of magical correspondences, i.e. the correspondence of the 'positive' phase of the cycle with the sun, the masculine principle and other 'positive' correspondences, and the 'negative' phase with the moon, the feminine principle and other 'negative' correspondences. By studying the cycles of these correspondences as they manifested in the natural world, the ancients acquired a profound understanding of the true nature of reality. It was for this reason that they also studied the heavens and the cyclical movements of the stars and planets. They wanted to know where and when the cycles would converge – for example, in an eclipse – since they believed that at such moments of celestial conjunction or superimposition a portal opened up to the Creator, the divine source-centre.

Moreover, as the expert astrologer the late Jeff Mayo points out, the symbols adopted by the ancients provide us with insights into the processes of human consciousness:

> Jung recognized the Sun's symbol as the classic symbol for the unity and divinity of the self… Jung sees the self as 'not only the mid-point, but also the circumference that encloses consciousness and the unconscious; it is the Centre of this psychic totality, as the ego is the Centre of consciousness.' The self is the very core of the psyche, and yet it represents the whole man. It is the function, which unites all the opposing elements in man and woman. It marks the last station on the way of individuation, which Jung calls *self-realization*. Only when this mid-point is found and integrated can one speak of a 'whole man'. We can see the close correlation between the traditional astrological symbolism for the Sun and this primordial archetypal process in man to achieve wholeness of being, self-integration, and conscious unity with his own true self and with his environment and fellow creatures.[1]

The ancient Egyptian symbol for the sun, a simple circle with a dot in the centre, to which Jeff Mayo refers, also represents the inner sun, the source-centre of consciousness. For the ancients both suns were intimately related.

The ancients conveyed a similar understanding in their concept of the birth of the 'sun god' (the 'son of the sun') between two mountain peaks. Since the Earth was believed to be the body or womb of the shamanic World Mother, these twin peaks represented her bent and open legs as she 'gave birth' to the rising sun.

On one level, the sun rising between two peaks illustrated the rising of the physical sun. In Egyptian cosmology, after journeying through the Underworld (the negative half of the cycle) the sun was believed to be 'reborn' every morning at the neutral point between night and day. The dividing line of the horizon was seen as yet another metaphor for the mid-point or middle ground between opposites, in this case the Earth and the sky. The reborn sun god was Horus, a Neter god who was also known as Horakhty, 'Horus in the Horizon', meaning that he personified the emergence of the sun from the neutral point on the horizon, the point where the sun is neither up nor down.

At another level, however, the rising of the physical sun was equated with the rising of the inner sun or true self. This symbolic linkage of outer and inner realities conveyed the esoteric teaching that the inner sun was also located at the neutral mid-point between opposites in the twilight zone of consciousness known as the hypnagogic state.

Ironically, the true self corresponds with the 'excluded middle' of Western, Aristotelian logic – a materialist view which does not recognize this neutral point in consciousness. In popular thought, this point is represented by the fence nobody is allowed to sit on and the vacuum which nature is said to abhor.

In relation to human consciousness, the true self corresponds to the source-centre of the mind or psyche, which is situated at the neutral point between the opposite states of 'conscious' and 'unconscious'. However, because our attention is focused either consciously on our external reality or subconsciously on the internal reality of our thoughts and feelings, we remain unaware of our source-centre. The solution lies in somehow becoming consciously aware of the opposite sides of our mind simultaneously, of becoming both 'observer' and 'observed', thus reintegrating the two.

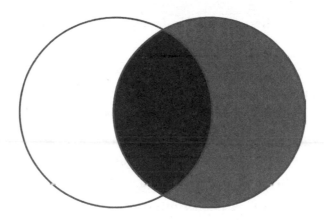

Figure 5: The creation of the vesica piscis

This reintegration of the mind can be accomplished through the shamanic trance state. Although the trance state is *not* enlightenment, we discovered that the two are closely related in that intensified practice of the trance state can initiate the enlightenment experience.

For the shaman, the reintegration of the divided mind was the gateway to the Underworld. We can illustrate this gateway with the hidden circles of the vesica piscis, which takes its name from the Latin *vesica*, meaning 'bladder', and *piscis*, the genitive of 'fish', because the central oval, known as the *mandorla*, resembles the shape of a fish's bladder (*see figure 5*). One circle can be related to the conscious self or left brain and the other to the subconscious or right brain. The central oval created by the superimposition and fusion of both circles represents the portal, or now open gateway, to the unconscious, the shamanic Underworld. It was believed that if this fusion were sustained, the portal would remain open, leading one back through many different levels of consciousness to the source of one's existence, the source of creation itself. It must be emphasized, however, that this portal is experienced as a psychic door and not as a physical door.

Having explored the meaning behind this symbol, we return to the shamanic concepts of the World Mother and the Underworld.

The World Mother and the Underworld

How did the concepts of the World Mother and the Underworld arise? The reasoning is that ancient man observed the fact that we are all born into this world through the female, which meant that the female (like the subconscious) was perceived as being closer to the source-centre. This in turn gave rise to the prehistoric concept of the Earth Goddess or World Mother. In other words, the female acts as the *intermediary* between humankind and God or, in the context of the enlightenment experience, between humankind and godhood. This explanation is supported by the intermediary role of the shamaness, who often accompanies the shaman on his journeys into the Underworld, the interior of the Earth, which the body of the shamaness actually represents.

Following on from this, it seems only natural that the female vagina would become a metaphor for the psychic portal or gateway between worlds, as also symbolized by the central oval of the vesica piscis. The 'other worlds' were therefore seen as existing inside the womb of the World Mother, a concept symbolized by the Pagan Celtic goddess Sheela-na-Gig, who herself is based on the Egyptian creation goddess Nun, whose name in Phoenician means 'fish'. Sheela-na-Gig figures were often placed above the doorways of Irish churches and castles, crudely displaying their open vagina as though it were a portal from one world to another.

The idea of entering *into* the Earth may also be connected with the Earth's underlying energy matrix. Our ancestors' understanding of this matrix is evident from the many Neolithic monuments that were erected over 'power points' in the Earth's energy field. It is therefore possible that the womb of World Mother, the Underworld, represented what some today would describe as the underlying 'morphogenetic template' of the physical world. That is to say, it contained the physical world *in embryo*, before it came into being. The shamanic journey into the Underworld was therefore a journey into the underlying energy matrix of physical existence. It was also a journey into the deepest recesses of consciousness and the psychic matrix of the mind.

As writer Gary A. David tells us, the Hopi word for the Underworld is *Tuuwanasavi*, while the word *tu'at* (also spelt *tuu'awta*) means 'hallucination' or 'mystical vision'. We noted with interest that 'Tuat' was the spelling employed by E. A. Wallis Budge, former Director of Antiquities at the British Museum, for the Egyptian Underworld, the Duat, 'that seemingly illusory realm of the afterlife'.[2] The word 'tuat' also forms part of the name of the mythical Celtic gods, the Tuatha dé Danaan, a race of 'Shining Ones' who are said to have arrived in Ireland before the present inhabitants. The pronunciation of 'Tuat-ha' is strikingly similar to the Hopi *tuu'awta* and provides further evidence for the early worldwide distribution of knowledge from a single source. The similarity between Egyptian and Hopi beliefs is also referred to by Gary A. David:

> When the Anasazi gazed into the heavens, they were not looking at an extension of the physical world as we perceive it today but were witnessing instead a manifestation of the spirit world. Much like the Egyptian Duat, the Hopi Underworld encompasses the skies as well as the region beneath the surface of the earth.[3]

As we saw earlier, the vesica piscis ('fish bladder') symbolized the portal between worlds as an oval. The ancient Egyptians named this isolated ovoid symbol the 'RU', which means 'birth passage' or 'gateway'. The same symbol appeared later on in Christian iconography as the oval aureole of light surrounding the body of Jesus. It was also an emblem of the Shining Ones, especially the so-called 'fish deities' who may have received their aquatic name from their ability to 'swim like a fish' in the astral amniotic womb waters inside the World Mother and in the inner experiences related to it. Some have interpreted these waters as referring to the vast 'sea' of space, thereby supporting the hypothesis that these fish deities were of extraterrestrial origin. However, as David Ovason says:

> The fish-man was one of the esoteric symbols of the initiate in that ancient culture [Babylon]. No doubt it was taught that the man or woman who had so developed themselves as to have free access to the Spiritual world could be regarded as being dual. Such people would be regarded as being equally content to walk on the Earthly plane or swim in the watery. Such initiates can live on the material plane, with the body of the flesh and blood, and they can also live in the Spiritual, in the aqueous world of the Astral for which the fish tail is an appropriate symbol, and where the physical body would be an encumbrance. The initiate's control over the two worlds is expressed in the mer-man form.[4]

The Three Cosmic Zones

Once he had passed through the inner gateway in his consciousness, the shaman experienced various 'otherworldly' states of consciousness. Over time he was able to discern an underlying logical order to these experiences, from which he began to devise a cosmology comprising three cosmic zones, planes or worlds. This is one of the primary concepts associated with the shamanic tradition and is found in a large number of cultures around the world. The Three Cosmic Zones are said to be connected by a central axis or pillar known variously as the World Pillar, World Mountain or World Tree. They are:

1. The lower plane or Underworld, which lies beneath the Earth, symbolized by the roots of the World Tree.
2. The middle plane, which is the Earth on which we live.
3. The heavenly plane, which, because of its symbolic association with the sky, is symbolized by the branches and leaves of the World Tree.

The symbolic imagery associated with these three planes had its parallels in the natural world, for the outspread roots of a tree (the Underworld) provided a mirror image of the outspread branches (the heavens). Also, when the branches of trees were reflected in water they took on the appearance of roots. Lakes, ponds and rivers were perceived as openings in the surface of the Earth (the middle plane) and were thus associated with the Underworld. There is evidence of the ancient Celts uprooting a tree and planting it upside down in a lake or other stretch of water as an offering to the ancestral heroes and gods whom they believed resided in the Underworld. These symbolic associations are one of the reasons why the shaman fashions his drum from the trunk of a tree. It was said that if the shaman reached the trunk of the World Tree while in the trance state and successfully climbed into its branches, he would reach the higher planes of consciousness and there undergo a powerful mystical experience. The tree – or rather a palm tree – also has a significant role to play in the story of the Phoenix, which we will look at later (*see page 55*).

We mentioned earlier the system of correspondences that the ancients applied to the masculine-positive and feminine-negative principles. The World Tree was part of a similar system of correspondences associated with the cosmic axis, or *axis mundi*. This symbolic axis not only expressed the interrelationship between different levels or worlds, but also symbolized the source-centre of all phenomena, from the visible to the invisible and from the cosmos to the atom. Its correspondences were essentially linear and vertical: the tree, the pillar or column, the staff, the spinal column, the male phallus, the binary symbol '1', etc.

A similar system of correspondences evolved around the phenomena that were both supported and sustained by this central axis. Since these were perceived as revolving around their axial source-centre, they were essentially ovoid or spherical in shape: the planet Earth, the human head, the egg-shaped aural sheath of the body, the female womb, the ovum, the binary symbol '0', etc.

The relationship between axis and sphere is illustrated in the shamanic journey in which the World Tree is the 'axis' of the shaman's 'sphere' of consciousness. The shaman's climb up the Tree is a metaphor for his expanding consciousness, which in its fully expanded state embraces both the lower and higher worlds. A similar expansion of consciousness is expressed through the shaman's journey into the womb of the World Mother, the Underworld. We suggest that the quest for the Grail expresses the same theme, although the proposition that the Grail corresponds with the sphere of consciousness may be difficult to accept if we adhere to the belief that the Grail is a chalice or cup.

Today, the realm of the Underworld is often linked with the unconscious mind or with the collective unconscious, but because of the subjective nature of these we would rather describe them as the 'subconscious', i.e. a realm that lies just beneath the surface of everyday consciousness. What we would call the 'collective unconscious' lies at the centre of the whole sphere of consciousness, being the 'source-centre' or 'life-force' of everything in existence. As such, it contains all the energy-information which is spread out and stored in both the subconscious and conscious levels of the human psyche.

CHAPTER THREE

The Mixing Bowl

According to Walter Skeat, the etymologist, the Old French *graal*, *greal* and *grasal* meant 'flat dish'. Skeat claimed that the word was a corruption of the Low Latin *cratella*, meaning a 'small bowl' or 'crater', from the Greek *krater*, which means 'mixing bowl'. If the Grail were indeed a mixing bowl of some sort, what was mixed in it?

When we discussed Eschenbach's 'neutral angels', we suggested that these angels were the personification of the third force and that this third force was also symbolized by the Grail which the angels were said to have carried from heaven to Earth. We have seen that this force manifests at the neutral point between opposites and this *mixing together* of opposites can be illustrated by the figure of the Androgyne. The Grail was the 'bowl' in which these opposites were mixed together. We will see later that this mixing of opposites also applied to the mixing of certain physical substances in a real bowl.

In the medieval period, the mixing of substances was an integral part of the work of the alchemist. The alchemists' 'mixture' was the same as that mixed in the Grail, producing the Elixir of Life and the alchemical Philosopher's Stone. The link between alchemy and the Grail can be seen in the thirteenth-century writings of Wolfram von Eschenbach. Furthermore, Eschenbach, the author of the Grail romance *Parzifal*, is known to have visited the Templars in Outremer (the Holy Land),[1] which suggests a direct link between the Grail myths and the Templars.

Indeed, it is beyond doubt that the Templars had a significant influence on the writing of the Grail myths.

Helinand, the most frequently quoted medieval author on the subject of the Grail, was greatly influenced by Bernard of Clairvaux (1090–1153), the same Bernard who had been personally responsible for obtaining the papal rule for the Knights Templar. There were also profound links between Bernard's monastic order, the Cistercians, and the Nasoreans, who fought and died for Jerusalem in AD 70.[2] The Cistercians wore white robes, as did the Nasoreans, and so too did the Knights Templar before adding their red cross. There was also another link between the medieval Cistercians and the Nasoreans which we will explain later (*see page 97*).

From the evidence we were accumulating, it was becoming increasingly clear that the Grail romances, through their association with the Templars, were based on earlier allegorical stories that alluded to an ancient system of knowledge.

It is widely believed that the name 'Templar' derives from the Temple of Solomon. This, however, is only the exoteric meaning of the name. Its esoteric meaning is connected with 'time'. A Templar was thus named *exoterically* because of his association with the temporal world and *esoterically* because of his knowledge of the worlds 'outside time', i.e. his shamanic knowledge of worlds where time ceases to exist: the Underworld, heaven and the esoteric Eternal Now.

The name 'Templar' is also associated with the human body, which has been described as the true 'Temple of God' or 'Temple of the Spirit'. The Temple of Solomon was based on the human body and, as Schwaller de Lubicz, the Egyptologist and esotericist, has demonstrated, so were many ancient Egyptian temples. The Holy of Holies, the inner sanctum of a temple, corresponds with the so-called 'third eye', which is itself associated with three organs found within the head or brain. They are the *pineal* and *pituitary* glands, which are said to correspond respectively to the masculine and feminine opposites, and the *thalamus* at the centre of the brain.

Towards the end of the previous chapter we suggested that the Grail corresponded with the expanded sphere of consciousness entered into by the shaman during the trance state journey. This sphere of consciousness has its physical counterparts or correspondences in the spherical shapes found in the natural world: the planet Earth, the womb, the head, the egg, the atom, etc. Moreover, it was believed to have up to seven concentric levels, just as we find in the atom, which has up to seven inner orbits, called electron shells.

Knowing that he could alter his own sphere of consciousness by journeying within it, the shaman believed that if he could penetrate to the very nucleus of the sphere of consciousness, he could also alter or transform these physical spheres. The belief that he could do this came from the awesome power he felt during the enlightenment experience, which is itself related to the pineal, the pituitary and the thalamus. We shall be returning to these three important organs later (*see page 83*).

The Grail and its Three Levels

At a particular stage in our research we felt it necessary to divide our perceptions of the Grail into three levels. These correspond to the Triad encountered in the teachings of the various esoteric mystery schools and in the trinities or triads of gods found in many of the world's religions. They also correspond to the Three Cosmic Zones of shamanic tradition, as well as the New Age triad of body, mind and spirit. By adopting the esoteric principle of the Triad and applying the Grail myth to it, we found that we were able to explain a great deal about history and about ourselves in terms of physiology and consciousness, as well as about the seemingly dual nature of reality.

We devised the accompanying diagram (*see figure 6*), which also

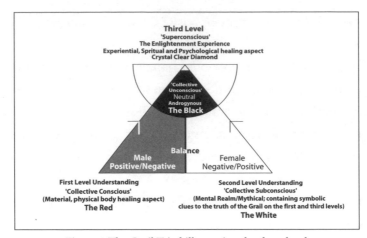

Figure 6: The Grail Triad illustrating the three levels
Illustration by Gary Osborn

incorporates the World Mountain and the World Pillar, to illustrate the three levels of the Grail. But before we look at these three levels, we shall give a brief explanation of the diagram.

All esoteric systems believe that the male *animus* and female *anima* (positive and negative opposites in the individual) should ascend together to the neutral point or Spirit (at the apex of the triangle), where they become *neutralized* and fused as one. Carl Jung, whose theories we will look at in a moment, was convinced, as many are today, that this union was the core principle behind the Great Work of alchemy, which is really *one's work upon oneself.*

The theme of the Red and White, which are the male and female divisions in our diagram, occurs frequently in esoteric literature and symbolism, sometimes with the non-colour Black, which here signifies the neutral point at the apex of the triangle. In the course of our research, we found the theme of the Red, White and Black was encoded in many of Nicolas Poussin's paintings. It is also present in the Christian Eucharist in the white communion bread or wafer and the red wine, which are combined in the chalice when the bread is dipped in the wine, thus symbolizing the union of opposites. These three colours correspond with the

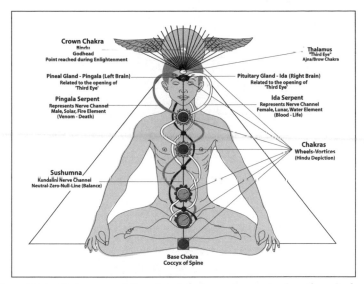

Figure 7: The Caduceus and the related chakra system centred on the spinal axis

Energy is said to move in a spiral fashion in and out and around the chakra vortices. The centres of these chakras are similar to the zero-nodes in a standing wave. Compare with the Grail Triad (*opposite*)

Illustration by Gary Osborn

three phases of the cycle we described earlier: Red (positive phase), White (negative phase) and Black (neutral point or zero-node).

The Red and White also correspond to the two etheric nerve channels or meridians (*nadis*) that are said to align the spine in the traditional Hindu physio-kundalini chakra system. These two channels are the *Pingala* (positive-male-red) and *Ida* (negative-female-white) and they cross each other several times along the central *Sushumna* nerve channel, which is zero, null or neutral, and therefore usually depicted as black. Situated along the spine are the seven vortices or chakras (*chakra* = 'wheel') (*see figure 7*). The centres of these chakras are where the two *nadi* channels cross, cancelling each other out like the nodes in a standing wave (*see figure 8*). These two nerve channels are symbolized by the two serpents that spiral around the Staff of Hermes, also known as the Caduceus, a powerful symbol that we examine in more depth later (*see page 79*).

The seven chakras correspond with the seven levels of reality often

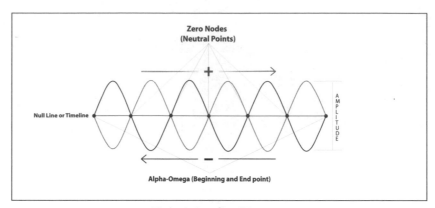

Figure 8: Standing Wave

A standing wave is a wave of energy-information that has become trapped between two points.
When the travelling wave hits a point 'where' and 'when' it can go no further, it turns back on itself,
becoming a 'two-way' wave of energy-information.

Illustration by Gary Osborn

referred to in esoteric literature and teachings, and with the seven concentric levels of the sphere of consciousness. These seven levels are also
echoed in the Seven Sacraments of the Christian Church, of which the
Eucharist is one. As we have just seen, this is itself based on the Triad.

The Red and the White represent the male and female opposites,
which are associated with the conscious and subconscious respectively.
Red signifies the fire element or heat of the sun in summer, associated
with the male. White signifies the cooling water element and the snow in
winter, associated with the female. However, these are interchangeable in
that each gender expresses both these colours. For example, the male produces white semen and the female red menstrual blood, which is why the
female is also associated with the rich-red lifeblood. We will find many
allusions to these two properties in the myths we will be looking at.

The Black is associated with the unconscious, or indeed the collective
unconscious, also the Void, where both opposites, as signified by the Red
and White – the outer and the inner – become one and are neutralized.

The significance of the crystal-clear aspect of this neutral point in
consciousness, as shown in our diagram, will become more apparent as
we go on. Suffice to say that both the Black and crystal-clear aspects of

the unconscious can be explained through the analogy of a piece of carbon or coal being compressed into a crystal-clear diamond – the esoteric 'Diamond Body' is a metaphor for becoming 'superconscious'. This analogy is clear when we remember that the physical body is mostly made up of carbon. A similar process can be seen in a heavy star, which at the end of its life will collapse in on itself, its mass being compressed down to a black hole and ultimately to a point of singularity.

Because our psyche is divided between two opposites, our normal perception is limited and can be likened to a darkened tunnel-like view of reality. This view can be transformed during the enlightenment experience into a crystal-clear point of illumined perception – the light at the end of the tunnel. The Black void of the unconscious becomes the sentient superconscious, in that its content – i.e. that which normally lies beyond our own 'unconsciousness' of this darkened and hidden part of our psyche – becomes empirically known and understood. It was believed that this experience could grant us the answers to everything. This transformation, which is the result of our piercing the 'veil of the unconscious' and taking a peek at the 'light' behind it, is the essence of the Grail, and a 'rebirth'.

Now we will take a closer look at the three levels of the Grail, both in how they are experienced and the meaning they convey.

The Practical First Level: The Elixir of Life

The first level of the Grail is *tangible*, *physical* and also *practical*, something which can be examined, measured and tested. As the Grail's 'positive' aspect, it is associated with the masculine principle and the physical body.

At this first level, the Grail is a physical mixing bowl, in which is mixed an elixir used to heal the physical body. Though one of the secrets of this elixir – the Elixir of Life – pertains to the fact that while the Grail is in itself neutral, it also expresses a duality: it has the power to both *cure* and *kill*.

Our research led us to discover that the original Elixir of Life was a combination of snake venom and blood. The blood used is either that of the snake or blood taken from a mammalian host (e.g. a horse, or a human being) that had been subjected to a series of snakebites or injections of venom. When the two elements were mixed together the unique properties of the blood not only rendered the venom harmless but also produced a powerful elixir. It was believed that if this was taken repeatedly it could boost the body's immune system, cure most diseases and even extend life. It is also possible that those who survived frequent snakebites would have built up an immunity against the venom and likewise maintained good health and immunity against disease and lived a prolonged life.

What makes snake venom so deadly and yet also gives it its unique capacity for healing is its high levels of protein. Western science is currently doing all it can to break down the elements of the venom and use them individually in the treatment of specific diseases. However, for the ancients, it may well be that it was the dilution of the venom with the blood which made it a virtual cure-all. Indeed, a Chinese herbalist told us that the blood of a snake is added to soup and other foods 'to extend a good life'.

We have already referred to the link between the Grail and the Templars. The activities of Templars were curtailed in 1307, and Jacques de Molay, the Grand Master of the Order, was burned at the stake in 1314. As the flames took hold, he is said to have cried out that his persecutors, Pope Clement and King Philippe of France, would join him within the year. Pope Clement was duly dead within the month, supposedly from a bout of dysentery, and King Philippe by the end of the year, from causes which remain unknown, although some say he was killed by a wild boar. The death of these two high-ranking figures was an example of the power of the Templars, for although they no longer existed in name, they continued to exist in number. And it was well known that they were proficient exponents of the art of poisoning, an age-old tradition that they had possibly discovered or rediscovered on their travels in the Holy Land – the land that had spawned, developed and ritualized the ancient secrets of the Grail.

We saw earlier how the shaman would use his stick and drum to send himself into a hypnotic trance, the stick and drum representing the duality of opposites and the beat from their contact the union of these opposites. We also mentioned that the trance state was sometimes initiated by or facilitated by certain psychoactive drugs or substances. Could the Elixir mixture have induced altered states of consciousness similar to the shamanic trance state?

This idea was not entirely implausible since the high levels of protein present in the snake venom would have provided a mental boost. We also discovered that in some instances the bowl in which the two ingredients were mixed was a human skull or skullcap. This led us to conclude that the mixing bowl or Grail itself symbolized the human skull. Furthermore, the mixing of snake venom and blood corresponded to the union of the two opposites – the conscious and the subconscious – thereby enabling the shaman to enter the Underworld, the body of the World Mother and the internal mixing bowl known as the Grail. This leads us onto the second level.

The Mythical Second Level: The Grail

This is the level at which we usually first encounter the Grail mystery. In fact, the mythical level is rather like the Grail itself since, like the mixing bowl, it contains the clues to both the first and third levels of our Grail Triad.

In relation to the Three Cosmic Zones of shamanic tradition, this mythical level is associated with the shaman's experiences in the Underworld or Lower World, the body of the World Mother. As an internal experience, this realm is the feminine-related subconscious. Through the union of opposites – the masculine-related conscious self and the feminine-related subconscious – the shaman initiates the trance state through which he is consciously able to penetrate the subconscious.

The second level is therefore highly subjective in that it conveys the mysteries of the Grail through myth, legend and fantasy. Here the Grail is like both the human mind and 'mind-stuff': it is *intangible*, a shadow of the real thing, and so it remains beyond the grasp of the materialist thinking mind, hidden away like the mythical cauldron which is said to reside in the Underworld.

It has been suggested by authors such as Roger S. Loomis in *The Grail: From Celtic Myth to Christian Symbol* that the Grail shares a common ancestry with the Celtic cauldron. We are told that the cauldron was a 'vessel of healing' and that there was both a 'cauldron of venom' and a 'cauldron of cure'. After his labours the archetypal hero would be plunged into both these vessels – not only to restore him to health, but also to toughen him up for future escapades and adventures.[3] The myths surrounding the Celtic cauldron are as mysterious as those about the Grail.

And yet this magical, imaginative element entices and seduces us. The mythical level of the Grail appeals to our imagination, our feminine side, while at the same time preserving the knowledge of the Grail, carrying its deeper significance like a child in the womb from generation to generation.

It must be said, we would not have to rely on the mythical level for clues if the first, practical level were not a secret. The same goes for the third, spiritual level (the apex of our diagram), which has also remained a secret to some extent in that it involves the experience of the Hindu Kundalini, which for many of us is totally unconnected with the Grail.

Moreover, these second-level clues are difficult to uncover because they are hidden in allegorical stories, many of which appear surreal, abstract or even absurd, yet at the same time deeply imbued with a seductive and alluring wisdom. Many of these stories emerged from the dreams and trance states of the ancient shamans. Shamanic trance, as already mentioned, is a non-ordinary state of consciousness which has many levels to it. It is accessed via the *hypnagogic state*. This is the mid-point or in-between state in the waking-sleeping cycle, where one is both 'awake' and 'asleep' at the same time – a superimposition or fusion of opposites, a 'third state'. While our consciousness is balanced like a tightrope walker in this third state, we transcend the normal duality of the mind.

We suggest that all non-ordinary states of consciousness are due to entering the hypnagogic state, also referred to as *lucid dreaming* – that is, dreaming *consciously*. As such the hypnagogic state is responsible for all kinds of paranormal, psychic and mystical phenomena, ranging from a flash of insight or a spontaneously received answer to a problem to creatively inspired dreams, synchronicities, ESP, remote viewing, out-of-body experiences (OBEs), mystical visions and enlightenment itself. The differentiation that exists in our interpretations of these experiences really depends on the degree to which we are able to focus our conscious attention in this neutral borderline state, or how successful we are at sustaining conscious awareness within it.

Meditation is really due to one trying to access the hypnagogic state. If done frequently, it can easily lead to one entering the hypnagogic state, whether one intends this to happen or not.

Earlier we looked at the vesica piscis, the central oval of which actually represents the hypnagogic state, being the union or fusion of the objective conscious (waking) and the subjective subconscious (sleeping). It also represents the perfect synchronization of the two sides of the brain by which one enters the hypnagogic state. This state of consciousness, if sustained, can trigger the orgasmic Kundalini enlightenment experience. Hypnagogia, then, is what the author and satirist Robert Anton Wilson termed the 'Cosmic Trigger'.

Whether the 'other realities' that are visited in the hypnagogic or lucid dreaming state are 'real places' in themselves or merely creations of the mind is another thing. (It could be argued that our everyday reality is a creation of the mind). Whatever the case may be, we would stress that access to such 'worlds' can only be achieved via a fusion of opposites within the psyche. Since in most of us the psyche remains divided, the extra energy that enables us to experience these things will not arise and we will understandably remain sceptical.[4]

The mixing together of the venom (death) and blood (life) of the snake corresponds to the superimposition of opposites that occurs in the mind during the hypnagogic state, i.e. being awake (conscious) and asleep (subconscious) at the same time and in equal measure. Furthermore, the high protein content of this potent elixir gave it hallucinogenic properties that could initiate a similarly hypnagogic state. The two ingredients also corresponded to the two serpentine energies of the Kundalini enlightenment experience, which unite in the centre of the head at the point of climax (*see Appendix II: The Quantum Grail and the Quantum Serpent*).

This reveals why it is required that the male unite with, or strike a balance with, his feminine half (his *anima*) and the female with her masculine half (her *animus*). This balance is important for many reasons, for without it one of the opposites – usually the male – will try to dominate the other.

In the not too distant past, the male of our species felt it necessary to constrain the female and suppress – or rather control – her energy, which he saw as potently powerful. As all human beings are born from the female, the male believed that she held the secrets of sex, life and death, which he wanted not only to understand but also to control. The rise to power of male-orientated religions was due in part to the desire to control humankind's feminine-related emotions. However, after years of being ruled by male-dominated religions, people felt they were becoming stifled by the dogmatic institutions they themselves had created. They began looking for answers to the fundamental questions about the nature of human existence outside religion, within the physical environment. This led to the so-called Age of Reason and the establishment of science.

Ironically, our observations of physical phenomena have revealed that these same gender-related opposites also manifest on both the macrocosmic and microcosmic levels of reality.

Not only is reality 'dual in nature', but we also have a dualistic perception of it. And as long as our mind is divided in two, we will never be able to comprehend the true nature of our existence – there will always be problems to overcome and paradoxes to solve. By uniting these two opposites, however, we attain the healing wisdom of the Grail and are reborn with a totally new perspective.

The feminine principle is the healing element here in that the feminine-related subconscious contains the meaning behind the seemingly random processes observed by the masculine related conscious mind. This is why the Grail is also associated with romance, chivalry and a moral code of conduct in which respect for the feminine principle is not only paramount, but is also essential for the initiate. The reintegration of the psyche is really only the first step in the Grail quest, however, since the goal of the quest is the *transcendence* of duality.

Ancient knowledge, especially that provided by Eastern scriptures, suggests that there was once a close working relationship between the male-related conscious and female-related subconscious parts of the mind, and that the male once worshipped the female and the feminine energy – hence the World Mother concepts and Goddess cults. It is this close working relationship that sets the shaman apart from the rest of the human race. Indeed, the evidence suggests that we were once all natural shamans, open to other levels of reality due to the unity between these two divisions of the mind and the two hemispheres of the brain.

As many theologians will know, inner wisdom and knowledge have often been associated with the female, the shamanic World Mother and Pagan Earth Goddess, as personified by the Gnostic Sophia, and Isis, the goddess of ancient Egypt. It is possible that the the hypnagogic state presents similar archetypes in the form of dreams and visual and auditory information. It is also possible that this information emanates from the domain of the collective unconscious – a theory first put forward and favoured by Carl Jung. Jung also studied alchemy and discovered that alchemical symbols contain many similar motifs – i.e. related images and patterns – which he called 'archetypes'. These archetypes, he observed, seemed to allude to a greater truth.

Jung would ask his patients to describe the contents of their dreams, and was amazed when they described events and situations featuring visual images similar to the symbols and illustrations found in many alchemical works. They also described the icons and symbols of the world's religious, mystical and esoteric traditions. What Jung termed the 'collective unconscious' can therefore be thought of as an underlying 'pool' of energy-information which contains the primordial *gestalts* or memories of our race in the form of recurring symbols or archetypes.

If Jung's concepts had been known during the time of ancient Egypt, his collective unconscious would have been compared to the Duat or Tuat – the Underworld or realm where the dead go to 'live' – which has many counterparts in cultures around the world.

In our view, however, 'collective unconscious' is a misnomer. Rather being the 'unconscious', this domain is the subconscious. The word 'unconscious' implies that we are totally oblivious to this underlying mental realm, which is not always true. We are subconsciously aware of the archetypes – in fact they constitute an enormous part of our inner psyche.

We are also subconsciously aware of the underlying stories, myths and legends that enthralled and mesmerized us when we were children. We will sometimes even apply them to our own life, for they often reflect our dreams, our hopes and desires. Even the image we like to have of ourselves seems to be mirrored at times by the gods, heroes and heroines we have heard or read about, or seen in films or on TV. But then the mythical level is also the realm of the imagination, a realm *where the impossible may become possible.* This is also why the second Grail level can be so frustrating to comprehend, for the information it contains is often conveyed in surreal dream-like events which contain all the enigmatic metaphors and symbols of the dreams or visions associated with the subconscious or sleeping half of the cycle.

The serpent (or snake) is indeed a major symbol – it appears all over the world in one form or another. Although often presented as an image of evil to be conquered by an initiate or hero, it also symbolizes the life-force itself. This is the main reason why the symbol of the serpent is universal, and an important archetypal clue to the knowledge pertaining to both the first and third levels of the Grail.

The Transcendent Third Level: The Philosopher's Stone

This level, which is represented by the apex in our diagram of the Grail Triad, is in itself neutral since it is here that the positive (first level) and negative (second level) are united and neutralized. At this level, the Grail represents knowledge both of the underlying forces of reality and how these forces are linked with our own consciousness.

This level is associated with the final stage of the alchemist's work: the Philosopher's Stone. It also corresponds to the sky or Higher World of the Three Cosmic Zones – later called the 'kingdom of heaven' by Christians. It is also the source-centre of the concentric sphere, the centre of the Earth and the centre of the womb or ovum of the World

Mother – the centre of the mixing bowl known as the Grail.

It is the goal of the Yogi to achieve enlightenment through following the mystical path to this source-centre. The shaman, however, does not always have this as his goal. The shaman is a sorcerer, a magician, and so he takes the magical path – a short cut – and seeks to use the inner realms of consciousness for his own and others' purposes. He brings back knowledge from them, through which he and others can learn. However, we would stress that the wisdom of Yoga has its origin in the knowledge gathered by ancient shamans.

The shaman is able to enter the Underworld – the 'land of the dead' – and return to the land of the living by feigning death. This is achieved through the reintegration of the mind and the ego, which is also said to happen at the point of dying – as in the 'Bardo experience' described in the *Tibetan Book of the Dead*. The word *bardo*, formed from *bar* ('interval') and *do* ('two'), means 'gap' or 'between two', so we are again talking about an in-between state – not only between life and death, or this world and the next, but also between the opposites of male and female, conscious and subconscious.

The *bardo* can be equated with the synaptic gap in the lattice structure of reality. The latter is said to be made up of waves, whose positive and negative lines of force meet and converge, thus cancelling each other out and creating a void or gap (a 'synapse') in the space-time continuum. This synaptic gap, or zero-point-node – the *bardo* – in the cycles of reality is said to be located at every point in space and time, and reflects the same synapse or 'unconscious gap' in the oscillations of our own consciousness. It is this 'unconscious gap' in human consciousness which the shaman pierces consciously in order to reach the 'other worlds' within.

This connection with the *bardo* suggests that the shaman's experience of the Underworld is comparable to what we now call the 'near-death experience'. The shaman's ability to enter the 'realm of the dead' and return from it, bringing back knowledge, has earned him the nickname of 'trickster', for he can 'cheat death'. The same name is also associated with the female, including the archetypal shamaness who is said to accompany the shaman on his otherworldly journeys. Like Eve who offered the 'apple of knowledge' to Adam, the female – i.e. the Underworld/World Mother and the female domain of the subconscious – is believed to trick the male by seducing him into entering her, or becoming one with her, so that he can gain knowledge through this experience.

In effect, each time the shaman comes back from the realm of the dead he is 'reborn' in that he possesses a new perception of reality due to the knowledge he has accessed. The method by which he accomplishes this feat provides him with insights into the cyclical process of the birth-death-rebirth cycle, known to us today as 'reincarnation'. Our research suggests that the avatars and spiritual teachers who have appeared throughout the course of human history have had a similar understanding of these processes, which they have chosen to communicate in their own way. However, their words have usually fallen on deaf ears, or been distorted and exploited, and have therefore lost their original meaning.

CHAPTER FOUR

The Seed at the Centre

One of the most popular Grail romances is the Middle High German epic poem *Parzifal*, composed by the Bavarian poet Wolfram von Eschenbach sometime between 1200 and 1216. Although, as he himself admitted, Eschenbach did not invent the story, he gave a deeper spiritual meaning to it. His profound insight into the Grail is evident from the following quote, which we will analyse in some depth.

> Well I know that many brave knights dwell with the Grail at Munsalvaesche. Always when they ride out, as they often do, it is to seek adventure. They do so for their sins, these Templars, whether their reward be defeat or victory.
>
> A valiant host lives there, and I will tell you how they are sustained.
>
> They live from a stone of purest kind. If you do not know it, it shall here be named to you. It is called *lapsit exillis*. By the power of that stone the phoenix burns to ashes, but the ashes give him life again. Thus does the phoenix molt and change its plumage, which afterward is bright and shining and as lovely as before.[1]

The *lapsit exillis* in Eschenbach's text has been translated in many ways. It has been suggested that it is a corruption of *lapis ex caelis* ('the stone from heaven') or *lapsit ex caelis* ('it fell from heaven'), but the most common translation is as *lapis elixir*, meaning 'the Philosopher's Stone'.

The latter tends to have more backing due to the large number of other alchemical inferences within Eschenbach's work – for instance, his reference to the Phoenix in the above passage. As for the qualities of the stone,

> There never was a human so ill that, he one day sees that stone, he cannot die within the week that follows. And in looks he will not fade. His appearance will stay the same, be it maid or man, as on the day he saw the stone, the same as when the best years of his life began, and though he should see the stone for two hundred years, it will never change, save that his hair might perhaps turn gray. Such power does the stone give to a man that flesh and bones are at once made young again. The stone is called the Grail.[2]

Although not overtly apparent, there is a substantial amount of information hidden within these few lines. First, we found that the 'stone' referred to by Eschenbach was a metaphor for something that had so far gone unrecognized by Grail researchers. In esoteric terms, the Grail 'stone', which is also the Philosopher's Stone, is simply the stone we find at the core or centre of a piece of fruit – for example, a cherry or peach, or even the pips in an apple or orange.[3] This may sound a little odd, but we should note that the stone at the centre of the fruit contains the seed or germ from which another tree that bears that fruit can grow. To understand the further significance of this analogy, we need to take a closer look at what the alchemists understood and what they were really trying to achieve.

> A serious difficulty which confronted the apprentice to alchemy at the outset was that he did not know what raw material to work on. Many of the masters of the art would only say that the 'subject' of the work, the material to be worked on, was something which is found everywhere and universally regarded as valueless. Some

adepts maintained that the subject of the work was the same as the apparatus in which it was carried on, the philosopher's egg or egg-shaped vessel from which the Stone would be hatched like a chick.[4]

The 'philosopher's egg or egg-shaped vessel' was the crucible which contained the 'seed' – the seed being likened to the nucleus of an egg.

As some readers will already know, there are two aspects to the Great Work of the alchemists:

1. *The transformation of matter,* by which a base element such as lead was transformed into a higher element such as gold.
2. *The work upon oneself,* by which the alchemist sought to induce the life- and consciousness-changing experience of enlightenment. This is the reason why we encounter so many alchemical illustrations of a male and female conjoined in one body. The emphasis here is on one's access of the internal 'soul body' – the spiritual 'astral vehicle' – which was seen as androgynous and neutral, hence Eschenbach's reference to 'neutral angels'.

As Richard Cavendish points out, the two aspects of the work are very closely related:

> From a spiritual point of view, it seems clear that the subject of the work was the alchemist himself. *Ars totum requirit hominem,* 'the art requires the whole man'. The alchemist was both the vessel of the work and the material within it. The valueless thing found everywhere is matter, which in man means the body and the animal nature that is closely linked with it. In matter there is concealed the spirit or divine spark, the moon spittle or star semen or star-mucus which is something fallen from heaven, or the vitriol found in the interior of one's own being.[5]

'Something fallen from heaven' – surely Richard Cavendish is here talking about the *lapsit exillis*, which, as mentioned earlier, may be a corruption of *lapis ex caelis* ('the stone from heaven') or *lapsit ex caelis* ('it fell from heaven'). If so, then this stone is also found within us – 'in the interior of one's own being' as Cavendish says. In other words, within one's own *consciousness*.

For the alchemist, the transformation of matter mirrored a similar transformation process occurring within himself, and it was said that he could not achieve either of these works without achieving the other. The two are complementary in that the alchemist of the past knew that matter was connected to the mind, and that both mind and matter were essentially one and the same energy. He also knew that the 'matter' around him – i.e. that which lay within his own immediate sphere or 'bubble' of reality – was his own energy, energy that had become distanced from the centre of his own consciousness. If he were able to find the centre – the 'spirit' or 'soul' – of a piece of matter, then he would also have found his own centre, his true self, and the source of All. This same centre or seed also existed within inanimate matter in that it was the germ essence, the spirit – the 'vitriol' – which also contained within it the blueprint of all the elements, much like the DNA molecule or genetic code of biological systems.

As with the dilution process practised in homoeopathy, it was believed that by continually diluting a piece of matter, purifying it and reducing it down to its very essence, one could access its 'seed-point' or 'source-centre', which could then be used to transform the elements in matter. From this came the belief that it was possible to transform matter from one state to another, as exemplified by the transformation of lead to gold.

But what if this were just a metaphor for an even greater truth? What if we could find this source-centre within ourselves? Wouldn't we, to a greater or lesser extent, be able to transform the overall pattern of our own reality? Such a transformation would indeed be a *rebirth* in that it would represent a fundamental change in our consciousness. It was also believed that through this process one became 'immortal', for by becoming aware of the immortal source-centre within ourselves we become aware of our own immortality. At the same time, we become aware that we are all reborn from this same source-centre or 'stone' – like the serpent Ouroboros swallowing its own tail. As Eschenbach says, this stone is 'called the Grail'.

But how can we look upon something that is within ourselves? Clearly, we are not meant to take this literally. Rather, we look within the mind. As Petrus Bonus, the fourteenth-century writer of the alchemical treatise *The True Pearl of Great Price*, says, 'The ferment may be invisible to the eye but it can be seen by the mind.'[6]

The Stone and the Phoenix

The rebirth or transformation in consciousness described above is allegorized in the myth of the Phoenix. In some versions of the myth, the Phoenix is reborn after it has been consumed in a fire caused either by it flying too close to the sun, or by the sun's rays igniting its nest. However, since this is an allegory of an inner experience, it is not the physical sun at the centre of our solar system that is being referred to here. Rather, it is the inner sun at the centre of every one of us, the source-centre of consciousness itself, the divine spark that grants us our very existence and sustains us, just as the physical sun sustains life on Earth.

So the *lapsit exillis*, the 'stone' that has the power to burn the Phoenix to ashes, which Eschenbach mentions in the passage from *Parzifal* that opened this chapter, is nothing substantial or solid at all. In fact it is the opposite: it is the zero-point, the Void or vacuum, the spiritual source-centre, the Absolute. This is why alchemists and mystics describe it as 'a stone that is not a stone'. References to the physical stone we find at the centre of a piece of fruit, and from which another tree is seeded and grows to bear the same fruit, are a clever 'occult blind', which was itself seen as a metaphor for the source-centre of creation. But more importantly, it was believed that this same source-centre – this 'proto-atom' – existed at the centre of every atom or subatomic body, and within every one of us *as the centre of our own consciousness*. The 'fruit' is merely a metaphor for what surrounds this central 'stone': the individual physical body and its experience of reality.

> [Jesus said] 'The kingdom of heaven is like to a grain of mustard seed, which a man took, and sowed in his field: which indeed is the least of all seeds: but when it is grown, it is the greatest among herbs, and becometh a tree, so that the birds of the air come and lodge in the branches thereof.'[7]

The metaphors at the heart of this well-known parable tell us that the trance state is the 'gateway' or 'portal' into the kingdom of heaven, which is itself the 'seed' or 'stone'. In this regard, we noted with interest that the ancient Mayan word for 'stone' was *tua*, which is similar to the word *tuat* or *duat*, the Egyptian name for the Underworld, as well as *tu-hua*, the Chinese for 'self-created'. From our own perspective, the expression 'smaller than a mustard seed' can be taken to mean that the 'heavenly kingdom' – the zero-centre – resides at the centre of every atom or sub-atomic particle. (Interestingly, some modern physicists are working on the theory that 'mini black holes' exist at the centre of all elementary particles.) On the subject of the 'seed', the New Testament teachings of Jesus are similar to those of the older Hindu Vedas, as is evident from the following passage taken from the *Chandogya Upanishad*:

> There is a spirit that is mind and life, light and truth and vast spaces. He contains all works and desires and all perfumes and

tastes. He enfolds the whole universe, and in silence is loving to all. This is the Spirit that is in my heart, smaller than a grain of rice, or a grain of barley, or a grain of mustard seed or a grain of canary seed. This is the Spirit that is in my heart, greater than the earth, greater than the sky, greater than heaven itself, greater than all these worlds.[8]

The shaman, like the alchemist who came after him, sought to access this source-centre and by doing so believed his consciousness would take its rightful place at the centre of the Earth, the solar system, the universe and all creation. This, in essence, is the true meaning of the enigmatic term Philosopher's Stone, which for centuries has led people to search for a solid material stone. Eschenbach's 'stone that heals' is the reintegration of mind and body in the 'spirit' via the enlightenment experience referred to in the Bible by the Greek word *Kardia* and known to the Hindus as *Kundalini*.

Also known as the 'Serpent Fire', this third-level healing corresponds closely with the first level of the Grail and its practical application in the healing of the physical body. The latter used real substances – the venom and blood of the snake – that were physically mixed together while the bright-light climax of the enlightenment experience mixes the male and female opposites in the centre of the head. The male-related venom and the female-related blood were correspondingly mixed in the centre of a bowl or skull.

The Stone of Life and Death

Although we believed that we had now discovered the identity of the Philosopher's Stone, it had become clear that almost every detail of the Grail code contained multiple layers of meaning. Often we would find several themes being conveyed at once, so the *lapsit exillis* of

Eschenbach's text could still provide us with a few clues. For example, it was also said to be the 'stone of death',⁹ which reminded us of its 'kill-and-cure' duality of purpose. There was also the notion that it could be the green 'emerald jewel' that fell from the crown of Lucifer as he was cast out of heaven. Could this be a reference to some kind of forbidden dispersion of knowledge relating to the Shining Ones of Sumeria and Egypt and other places around the world, who were also known as the 'Serpents of Wisdom'?

Lucifer, the 'angel of light', is another alchemical inference. In Old French, *luce* means 'fish', as does the Latin word *locus*. These meanings reminded us of both the description of the Grail as a 'dish for fish' and the 'Fisher King' element of the Arthurian cycle – and as we shall see, the ancient use of the word 'fish' is linked very strongly with the serpent. For many people, however, the fish is associated with Christ, the Ichthus (Greek for 'fish'), and there are claims that he is the Fisher King, or at least his distant grandfather. The Roman god Bacchus was also known as Ichthus, 'the fish'.

We also noted that the word for 'fish' in the Judaic Talmud is *dagh*, and that the name of the Celtic 'god of gods' was Dagda or Dagda Mor, from which we derive the words 'dad', 'dadda' or 'daddy'. Dagda owned a cauldron that contained limitless sustenance of which it could never be emptied, a metaphor for the limitless energy of the transcendental Void of the Hindu mystic, or indeed the vacuum in physics, of which the ancient shaman seemed to have some knowledge.

Similarly, the 'Solar Fish being' of the Philistines, and later the Phoenicians, was called Dagon. Otherwise known as Odakon, On and Oannes, he was also Iannes, a 'serpent deity' linked with healing.

As we were to discover, these Middle Eastern fish and serpent deities were derived from the ancient fish deities of Sumeria and Mesopotamia, who were also the 'serpent beings' known as the Shining Ones. Moreover, On, the name given to Oannes, the 'fish being' of ancient

Mesopotamia, was also the Hebrew name for the city of Heliopolis, the city in ancient Egypt where the newly reborn Phoenix first came to rest.

Each nation and culture has its own version of the Phoenix myth, which suggests that they derive from a common source. However, apart from acknowledging that the Phoenix is related to the concept of immortality – as in the cycle of death-birth-rebirth, referred to by some as the 'law of reincarnation' – the real significance of the Phoenix remains a mystery for most of us.

The Phoenix derives from the ancient Egyptian concept of the *ba*, which is depicted as a human-headed bird representing the soul of the sun god Re or Ra and the later Atum, both syncretized as Atum-Ra or Re-Atum. For the ancient Egyptians, the 'divine bird' – the bennu bird or heron – thus personified the source-centre of creation. Atum's soul naturally resided in his son, the resurrecting god, who died and was reborn around the Spring Equinox. With the rebirth on Earth of this resurrecting god or Shining One, the soul of Atum-Ra came into the world.

The Phoenix has its symbolic counterpart in the dove of Christianity and the Grail legends. In the same way that the Phoenix arrived at the pillar in Heliopolis, the dove arrives at the Grail Castle every Good Friday, a day that heralds the death and resurrection of Christ and falls on or around the Spring Equinox – the beginning-and-end point in the yearly cycle. However, the calendar of Christian festivals is such that Easter can now fall anywhere between 21 March and 25 April, being celebrated on the Sunday following the first full moon after the Spring Equinox. This was arranged so that it would coincide with the Jewish Passover, the date of which was fixed by the first full moon of spring.[10] The full moon at this time of year represents the ovulation of the World Mother, while the traditional Easter eggs are derived from the Pagan symbol for the rebirth of the resurrecting god.

In terms of wave phenomena, the Grail or 'seed-stone' symbolizes the node in the cycle that keeps the wave moving, the pulse that keeps the wheels (cycles) of time turning. How this node or pulse does this can be explained through the analogy of a pendulum. A fixed pendulum will only start swinging if we give it a gentle push and it will only keep swinging if we keep tapping it at regular intervals. In this analogy, the Grail symbolizes the moments in the cycle when we tap the pendulum. Similarly, we could say that everything in the universe, from the microcosm of subatomic particles to the macrocosm of swirling galaxies, is 'tapped' by the source-centre at regular intervals to keep it oscillating, vibrating, moving, revolving, active and in existence. These pulses of energy are the nodes in wave phenomena and all oscillating and periodic systems, and are what actually drives these waves and cycles onward and keeps them in motion.

The ancients' understanding of these pulses of energy, which was derived from their observation of cyclical phenomena, came to be symbolized in later times by the cauldron and its esoteric counterpart the Grail, whose limitless nourishment symbolized the pulse of infinite energy that kept everything going. This crucial 'pulse-point' in each and every cycle was also symbolized in various cultures by the resurrection or rebirth of a 'slain god' or 'vegetation god' (e.g. the Green Man) at the precise moment 'where' and 'when' it was believed that a pulse of energy was delivered by the source-centre of creation to replenish the Earth.

The positive and negative opposites were seen as the two halves in the yearly cycle: summer (positive-male-sun) and winter (negative-female-moon). The Spring Equinox is the zero or neutral point that begins the positive half of the cycle, while the Autumnal Equinox marks the same neutral point from which the negative half of the cycle begins. The solstices, which were also celebrated, are those moments 'where' and 'when' the positive and negative halves of the cycle reach their peak – i.e. their extremes.

But what we are really being told here is that we are usually 'unconscious' *of* and *at* these neutral points in the cycle, and this extends to the higher-frequency rapid wave-oscillations of the brain, the mind and consciousness, whose patterns are recurring and repeating many times a second. Because we are unconscious of the neutral point or third force we are unconsciously perceiving the world in terms of division and duality. We thus remain trapped in a series of repeating patterns that we ourselves have created.

To the divided ego, the zero-point in the cycle represents death, chaos and annihilation, for the ego fears that it will lose its separate identity by being swallowed up in the unknown Oneness of existence. This fear was reflected in the rituals of the Maya and later the Aztecs.

For the Maya, the Spring Equinox not only marked the beginning-and-end point of their Haab cycle, but also the point at which time itself came to a momentary end and might even end altogether. At this and certain other times of the year, they would sacrifice a hapless victim who personified the 'god of death'. In essence they were killing death itself – the zero-point in the cycle – so as to keep the sun moving and the wheels of time turning.

This Mayan ritual parallels the Egyptian sacrifice of the 'evil' serpent, Apophis or Apep, so that the sun god Atum-Ra or Re-Atum (who personified the sun) could travel unhindered through the Underworld every night and rise again in the morning, thus perpetuating the cycle. The sacrifice of this serpent god or serpent being was the ego's way of keeping the zero-point (the unconscious) at bay, and this is one of the reasons why in the past the zero, the vacuum or infinity, has been rejected wherever it has appeared or reared its unwelcome head.

The powerful image of the Grail was a means both of diffusing this limited view and of healing the divided ego. It was only natural that this 'icon of plenty' brought to Earth by 'neutral angels' appeared at the zero-point in the cycle, as did the divine bird and the resurrecting god, to remind us of our divided or 'fallen' condition and perhaps awaken us to the truth that *in Nothing is Everything*. For many, this awakening would be the enlightenment experience through which one comes face to face with the Grail and the 'Shining One', the 'God' or 'Light' within.

We believe that this ancient understanding of the crucial neutral point in all cycles has been overlooked for far too long – not always intentionally, but because we are generally unaware of it. Many of us tend to trip over the truth, pick ourselves up and dust ourselves down only to carry on as before. Our mind unconsciously 'skips' over that point in the cycle, like Jack who jumps over the 'Light' of the candlestick.

We believe that this concept provides the answers to many of the mysteries that surround the Grail, especially the complex mythical ideas that confuse many of us. For instance, it explains why the vegetation god is resurrected during the Spring Equinox and why, like the Horn of Plenty, the Grail is said to provide a limitless supply of food and drink, which appears 'suddenly' inside a cup or on a platter or dish. These are archetypes to remind us of, or awaken us to, deeper truths.

Now that we have explored the deeper meaning of the Grail, the Elixir of Life and the Philosopher's Stone, we will look at the evidence supporting our theory within the second level of our Grail Triad – the allegorical myths, legends and stories from around the world – and apply to them what we have learned.

PART TWO

History, Myth and Legend

CHAPTER FIVE

The Hidden Wisdom in Arthur's Grail

The legendary tales of King Arthur and the Grail are now so well known that they have been extensively researched and commented upon by hundreds of other authors. Yet many people are totally unaware, as we were, that the meaning and origin of these tales are still hotly debated. Indeed, it seems increasingly likely that the Arthurian cycle was accumulated from many different sources and influenced by a number of different cultures, both near and far. As we were to discover, however, these influences all point back to the same source as that of the Grail myth. Moreover, these sources, no matter where they came from, seemed to originate in one great secret that had been divided in two parts – one physical, the other spiritual.

It seemed that we were alone in making these discoveries, and so we decided to look more closely at the various elements of the Grail myth to see if we could uncover the Grail's practical application in terms of healing and the prolongation of life. We also wanted to see what correspondence there was between the Grail and the enlightenment experience through which one *knows* one is immortal. Our research enabled us to identify the hidden elements that conveyed this knowledge, but had been buried beneath layers of confusing ambiguity and misinterpretation.

The Cauldron of the Head of Hades

Our modern understanding of the Grail has been shaped by a late medieval addition to the Arthurian legend. However, if we accept that the Grail is actually much more than just a chalice of Christian origin, then we can find all manner of clues pointing to its earlier existence. For instance, in the Celtic sources that are the assumed origin of the Arthurian legends, we are told that the Grail is a cauldron, a symbol both of fertility and immortality. The cauldron was a powerful religious icon of its day. As mentioned earlier, it brought forth marvellous and magical feasts, revitalizing and resurrecting great and powerful armies.

> The Cauldron of Rebirth is a recurring theme in Celtic tales. In the Welsh story-cycle, the *Mabinogi*, warriors slain in battle are put into it and emerge alive. In old Welsh Arthurian material, Arthur goes to the Underworld, Annwfn, to retrieve the same magic cauldron – this is probably the origin of the Grail Quest, since the cauldron of Annwfn is also an inexhaustible source of food, as is the Grail.[1]

Like the Grail romances, the Arthurian legends were based on earlier Celtic Pagan myths which were themselves of ancient shamanic origin. So Arthur, like many heroes before him, was an updated version of the hero-god-king *par excellence* who sought the Grail, but who in doing so was really *seeking himself*.

Arthur's journey into the Underworld is the metaphorical expression of an internal experience. In this, he is just like the shaman who re-enacts the roles of gods such as Ra and Osiris or saviours such as Horus and Jesus, and many other mythological characters. This in turn not only identifies Arthur with the ancient myth of the resurrecting god, but also means he is shaman-like in origin.

Since the shaman could find nothing on Earth that related to the other worlds he visited during his journey through the Underworld (i.e. the internal realm of the subconscious), he believed that his journey took place inside the body of the World Mother or Earth Goddess. This is one reason why the ancients also referred to this 'heavenly gateway' as the 'watery abyss', and why rivers, lakes and wells were seen as portals to this other realm. Water, linked symbolically with the moon, was associated with the feminine principle.

Many writers and researchers suggest that the Celtic cauldron of rebirth represents the Underworld or land of the dead as well as the womb of the World Mother – a suggestion that fits the shamanic concept of the Earth as the body of the archetypal female. The cauldron seems to have represented the Earth on a collective level too. Indeed, the Earth could itself be described as a huge vessel or cauldron whose mixed contents represent the many labyrinthine sub-worlds and creatures that were believed to exist within the interior realm of the Earth known as Hades, which the Church renamed 'Hell'.

In the Arthurian legend, we are told that Arthur went into the Underworld in search of the 'cauldron of rebirth'. This confusing detail indicates that the Underworld and the cauldron were also seen to be two entirely different things. It could be, however, that the Underworld (the large cauldron) contained within it another cauldron – possibly the vessel known as the Grail. As Arthur's descent into the Underworld is an allegory for an internal experience, we would suggest that the particular 'cauldron' sought by Arthur refers, in psychological terms, to something deeper than the subconscious. In other words, if the Underworld symbolizes both the collective subconscious and the physical interior of the World Mother, this means that, where the individual is concerned, the cauldron or Grail is to be found *within oneself.*

However, the more deeply we dug into these myths, the more confusing things seemed to get. It was only later that we discovered that the cauldron or Grail was also associated with the human head, and in particular the male head. This raised the inevitable question: why would the male head be located at the centre of the Earth when that was believed to be the body of the archetypal World Mother? The correlation between these two elements – the centre of the Earth and the centre of the body – was surely leading us towards something very profound, and both elements were associated with the head.

In Celtic mythology we find an item called the 'Cauldron of the Head of Hades', which was to be found at Caer Pedryvan, the 'four-cornered castle' or 'fire castle'. This castle was a special and magical place where the people were said to drink sparkling wine. Now, Pedryvan or Pedraven means 'newt'. In Cornish, a newt – or in more precise etymology 'an ewte' – was a lizard, serpent or dragon. *Ewte* means 'resplendent mind' and the 'tails of newts' were illustrated by the Hebrew letter-symbol *Yod*, the first letter of the god Yahweh or Jehovah. Jehovah was originally a god of volcanoes and is therefore associated with the Roman Vulcan. As such, he was the fiery ejaculation from the top of the World Mountain – and an active volcano is a metaphor for the internal Kundalini enlightenment experience, during which the pranic energy ascends from the base of the spine towards the brain and the top of the head.

This has further interesting connotations, because the Celtic word *caer* means 'hill' or 'sacred mound', a reference to the primordial mound, and an ancient shamanic concept associated with the vortex of creation. In other words, Caer Pedryvan (the 'four-cornered fire castle') represents both the primordial mound and the matrix of creation itself. It is also home to the Cauldron of the Head of Hades – i.e. the head of the god of the Underworld or the Afterlife.

We have already referred to the shaman's use of the hypnagogic trance state to unite the two aspects of the divided mind. But we now found that the subconscious (the Underworld) contained within it something else – the cauldron of rebirth. This suggested that the trance state was only an initiatory experience, a state of consciousness which led to a kind of 'rebirth' and 'resurrection'. In other words, the hypnagogic trance state was an experience that could trigger another experience, namely the enlightenment experience. From this we concluded that both the cauldron and the head of the archetypal resurrecting god symbolized the process of enlightenment through which one became transformed – reborn.

So is this what Arthur was seeking? If he were seeking enlightenment, then he entered the castle Caer Pedryvan to access the Underworld within himself. This archetypal castle must therefore represent the gateway both to the Underworld and to the body of the World Mother. Since these myths are describing an internal experience, the 'castle' would seem to represent a physical gateway that can facilitate access to the mental gateway within oneself. This may signify a sacred temple or construction of some kind that marks a specific location on the Earth, perhaps a neutral point or zero-node on the Earth's surface, or a co-ordination point in the Earth's energy matrix of ley lines and positive and negative lines of force. This is outside the scope of the present book, and something we will follow up in subsequent works. But, as we will see, the clues we are given in these myths and allegorical fables are pointing to this conclusion.

Arthur's journey into the Underworld to find the cauldron of rebirth would therefore seem to be connected with the Latin alchemical phrase *Visita Interiora Terrae Rectificando Invenies Occultum Lapidem*. The phrase translates as 'Visit the interior of the Earth and by purifying, you will find the secret stone, the true medicine' and its initial letters produce the word 'vitriol'.

The only conclusion that seemed to make sense of this was that saying that one's head was at the centre of the Earth was another way of saying that the centre of the Earth was in one's head. That is, the two centres could be superimposed to become one.

If we take the story of Arthur to be one of many Celtic versions of a more ancient story, then we need to look towards Egypt for its origin, since everything tends to lead us back to Egypt or Mesopotamia. If the origins of the Arthur story do indeed lie in Egypt, then it could be that the head that Arthur is searching for is also the head of the ancient Egyptian god Osiris, the archetypal shaman-god-king – a resurrecting god associated with rebirth. As mentioned earlier, the hypnagogic trance state which is accessed via the synchronization of the left and right hemispheres of the brain takes place at the centre of the head. This would seem to explain the importance of the head in this ancient story. The fact that this illuminative experience occurs at the centre of the head would also explain why the shaman was known as the 'Shining One' and why 'All things are lights' was a popular Cathar saying.

Incidentally, in Italian the word 'lizard' means 'shining lights' and it is similar in English etymology to 'wizard'. The lizard also features on the breast of the wise Minerva, the snake-healing goddess of Rome, since wisdom is one of the attributes of the serpent. The words 'lizard' and 'wizard' translate in Latin as *opher*, which is associated with the snake and serpent. It is also associated with the Ophites (*see page 97*) and is part of the word 'philos-opher', meaning 'a person of wisdom'. We should add that the term 'philosopher' is also an appellation given to alchemists.

Popular Christian tradition has it that the lizard conceived through the ear and brought forth 'the Word' through the mouth. Indeed, Pope Felix III (483–92) believed that the Virgin Mary conceived through her ear, and in Seville Cathedral and many other cathedrals across Europe the figure of a lizard appears above a doorway as an indication of this belief.

From our previous research, we knew that there was a strong mythological, folkloric and historical tradition associated with heads and head worship. The head (or heads) of the vanquished were considered to be a great prize and it was even said that the head – or the right kind of head

– would give extended life. Along with the heart, the head was regarded as one of the principal members of the body. It was the 'great seat' of the life-force, the 'carrier of the soul'.

Heads of horses were also believed to contain the all-important vital force as well as the ever-present and necessary element of fertility. It is said that the Merovingian kings were sometimes buried with a horse's head – for example King Childeric I.[2]

Horses' heads were also carried on ritualistic occasions. The Pagan hobbyhorse, for instance, which is really a shamanic accoutrement, symbolizes the shaman's trusty steed which carries him to the Underworld. In a myth associated with the Norse god Odin, the horse actually carries Odin into the Underworld, and in many myths the shaman deity is set to return on a horse. The powerful horse that one rode therefore symbolized the trance state vehicle – known today as the 'astral body' – which enabled one to travel internally to other worlds. Today we would possibly use the modern automobile as a symbol for this and, like the white horses of our ancestors, it would no doubt become a symbolic device scrawled upon the landscape, with each tribe having its own particular style (*see plate 4*)

According to one tale, Arthur dug up the head of Bran the Blessed, which was said to have been buried underneath a tower on a 'white hill' to protect England. (Some say this is Tower Hill in London.) This head was known as *Uther Ben*, or 'wonderful head', and so we could say that Arthur had found his cauldron of rebirth and that it was also the head of the Celtic god Bran – the Shining One – who is the Celtic version of the Egyptian vegetation and resurrecting god Osiris. It seems that everything leads back to Osiris, as if he is the archetypal Shining One who personifies these internal experiences.

Arthur's finding of the 'head' of this god is of course symbolic, and suggests the rebirth of both Arthur and the god-king, the ancestral father or figurehead of his people. In other words, the myth is telling us that the person who, via his own internal experience, finds this special head becomes empowered and takes on the persona of the archetypal shaman god. But to have found the 'head', or to have become aware of it, meant that Arthur had to have had the same enlightening experience as the archetypal god-king whose head resided at the centre of the Underworld, or rather at the centre of creation itself. And why would he have had the same experience? Because the archetypal hero, on whom Arthur was modelled, was believed to be the reincarnation on Earth of that first god. As we will see, Arthur's father was named Uther, and so it is possible that Arthur had found the head of his father. If so, then Arthur is the Celtic version of Horus, the reincarnated Osiris, and so both are the same soul being reincarnated over and over again.

In brief, these confusing stories are telling us that the shaman is consciously aware of the processes behind the life-death-rebirth cycle – processes that apply to all cyclical phenomena. The shaman therefore knows he is immortal. Most of us, however, are unconscious of our immortal aspect and therefore reincarnate unconsciously, repeating the same old patterns.

We now had some idea as to why the head was deemed sacred, and as we moved forward on our journey we found the idea of the sacred or 'wonderful' head cropping up again and again. We also found that the cult of the head or skull had confused many researchers. Many still believe that the importance of the head lies in the ancient custom whereby a warrior beheaded his victim and, by owning his head, absorbed the energy of his vanquished foe.

In fact we discovered that many ancient societies actually practised the ritual decapitation of a snake. Why would they do this, if not as a symbolic representation of partaking of its energy? Especially when we consider that the mythological enlightened serpent was said to have a jewel in the head. The head of the snake is also where the venom is held and, as we have seen, when mixed with its blood, that would enable the shaman to attain the trance state and experience immortality.

Stories of the hero who enters the Underworld in search of the cauldron or some other treasure, such as the head of god, symbolize the hero's own enlightenment experience. He is then empowered by this experience and therefore becomes the newly resurrected god-king on Earth. This experience is open to any of us, and so the stories are also symbolic devices to enable a teacher to pass on to an initiate the secrets of how to obtain the venom and blood, or indeed enlightenment, and connect with the gods.

If this is correct, then we can understand why the shaman would have been given the name of 'serpent' or been described as a 'serpent being', for the serpent is synonymous with wisdom. This may be because the ancients observed that the eyes of the snake never blinked and were wide open at all times and therefore believed that the snake could see everything and knew everything. This observable phenomenon was also applied to the Shining Ones, the shamanic-led race of 'serpent beings', also known as 'the Watchers', who were depicted with distinctive large round eyes, as evident in a group of marble statuettes from Tel Asmar in Sumeria (c.2700-2600 BC). The eyes in some of these figures are also black and hollow, and we can see the same distinctive feature in the Wondjina rock art of the Australasian aboriginals.

Were these strange shamanic people – the Watchers of Sumerian and biblical legend – responsible for the origin of the Grail? It now seemed obvious to us that they were, and everything we have looked at – including things that couldn't be incorporated in this book – indeed supports and confirms this theory. We are also aware that the many ancient sacred sites, circles and monuments are perhaps a legacy of these people and form part of a code they left behind. That said, we again turn our attention to the archetypal castle or castles.

The Grail Castle

In the Grail legends there is a castle known as the 'Grail Castle', which Eschenbach names as Munsalvaesche, meaning 'Mountain of Salvation'. This is possibly a reference to the primordial mound or shamanic World Mountain – the *axis mundi* ('World Axis'). Esoterically, this recalls the 'temple of the body' and the spinal axis associated with the Kundalini enlightenment experience. But could this castle have also been a real monument or temple? If so, was it used as a gateway to the Underworld – i.e. an initiation centre for the enlightenment experience?

We realized that the existence of just one such temple would be unrealistic. Perhaps there were many of them dotted around the world at special sacred locations, at neutral points or ley-line convergence points where the Earth's positive and negative lines of force cross and cancel each other out at zero. We decided to look again at the Celtic castle.

As we have already mentioned, the word for 'newt' was *Pedraven*. *Pear* means 'four', 'fire' or 'father'. *Pedravan* is also spelt *Pendryvan*. *Pen* means 'head', and Pendryvan sounds remarkably like 'Pendragon', meaning 'head of the dragon' or 'serpent's head'. Pendryvan could also mean 'father of Evan', the Welsh equivalent of the Roman god Bacchus and the Greek god Dionysus. Bacchus/Dionysus was the serpent god of wine and the inhabitants of Caer Pendryvan were said to have drunk 'sparkling wine'. This link could well have some foundation, since wine – like blood – symbolizes the universal energy, the 'creative force' or 'lifeblood' that one experiences through enlightenment. Bacchus/ Dionysus can also be equated with the ancient Egyptian god Osiris, and the true father of Osiris is the god Atum-Ra.

According to the legend, the magical cauldron was kept at Caer Pedryvan, i.e. the place of Evan/Bacchus/ Dionysus/Osiris, whose head is the 'serpent's head'. But why would the cauldron or Grail be kept there? The answer is that the structure of Caer Pedryvan itself represents the serpent's head. In other words, this castle or temple, this magical place where sparkling wine is taken, represents either the human head or something important within the head. We suggest this is the activation of the 'third-eye' trance state and the enlightenment experience.

Lastly, Caer Pedryvan – the *ewte* or 'resplendent mind', which is also a 'newt' and therefore linked to the lizard and serpent – was also called Caer Sidi, the 'revolving castle'.[3] Some researchers believe that the revolving castle is a metaphor for the precessional circle traced in the sky by the tilted Earth's axis. This may be true, and there are good reasons for accepting this hypothesis. However, we are dealing with multiple meanings here, and with information that seems to be arranged on several levels. Each level becomes more meaningful the closer we get to the truth. Like climbing the sacred mountain, we ascend until we reach the apex.

According to some, the revolving castle is also another name for Stonehenge, which was used to chart the revolving sky and the positions of the sun, moon and stars.[4] This would mean that the Grail or an element of the Grail was used and kept at Stonehenge, because if Caer Sidi represents the head, or something within it, then so does Stonehenge. It is therefore the 'serpent's head'. Caer Sidi was also known as the 'temple of the Shining Ones' and Sidi is similar to *Sidhis*, the Sanskrit term for 'mystical' or for the paranormal abilities associated with the Kundalini enlightenment experience, and thus brings to mind the psychic skills attributed to the shaman.

We decided it was time to take a look at Stonehenge and other similar temples and related earthworks.

Serpent Temples

Stonehenge is a fascinating ancient monument located in Wiltshire, England, yet no one can be absolutely sure of its original purpose. For many, the monument's solar, lunar and astral alignments indicate a ritual basis connected with the heavens. Even experts at NASA in the United States believe that Stonehenge was either a planetarium or an astronomical model of the planets.[5] What is relatively certain is that Stonehenge was built over three major periods between 3500 and 1100 BC. Another certainty is the existence of a considerable body of folklore surrounding Stonehenge. Strangely, much of this folklore bears no relationship to the astrological significance attributed to Stonehenge in modern times.

Recently it has been theorized that Stonehenge was associated with death, since it was the gateway or portal to the Underworld, the realm of the dead.[6] This would agree with what we have said concerning the trance techniques of the shamans, who probably used such sacred places to go into trance and contact the dead. In addition, archaeologist Michael Pitts says that nearby Woodhenge (a series of post-holes in which pillars of wood would have been erected, said to be a 'cousin' of Stonehenge) represents 'birth' and that the dead were transported along a path that connects the two henges. So it could be said that the two henges represented the 'portals of birth and death'.

Legends also attribute to Stonehenge a peculiar and profound healing ability. It was said to be able to cure any ailment in a number of ways, from crushing and powdering the stone and then mixing it in water to just touching the stones. To us, this healing element seems to relate to our first level of the Grail and the use of the snake. This, together with the belief expressed by the antiquarian and scholar Dr William Stukeley (1687–1765) that Stonehenge was a serpent temple, provides us with a clear link to the ancient story of the Serpent Grail.

According to anthropologist Lionel Sims, Stonehenge was associated with the union or fusion of opposites and was built to demonstrate this fusion by 'capturing' the setting sun and the setting moon. Sims says that the setting sun (masculine principle) and the setting moon (feminine principle) were captured through adjacent windows created by the central sarsen trilithon, one of five large stone structures that stood in the centre of the temple in a horseshoe arrangement.

Stukeley believed that Avebury, a Neolithic monument close to Stonehenge, was also a serpent temple. The close proximity of Hackpen Hill ('Snake's Head Hill') confirms that he may have been right. Stukeley also believed that an ancient serpent-worshipping race was responsible for many of the ancient structures found across Britain, which he called Dracontia. The problem with Stukeley is that he also believed that the Druids both worshipped at and built on these ancient locations, whereas modern history places the Druids as entering Britain sometime around 400 BC. However, this popular modern belief is based upon little evidence, which is mainly archaeological and minor at that.

The fact that the Druids worshipped the snake is connected with their original title of 'Adders', from the adder snake. The Druids can also be shown to be related to various sects or religious leaders across the globe, including the Brahmin of India and possibly therefore also the Naga, the name given to the serpent people or Shining Ones.

It is obvious that Stonehenge and Avebury were once linked. The closeness of the two temples and the fact that Stonehenge is precisely south of Avebury cannot be coincidental. It is also no surprise to find that these places of serpent worship are related astronomically to the constellations and to solar and lunar worship, just as other serpent temples across the world. Whether Stonehenge and Avebury were actually constructed by the Druids or not, it is possible that the Druids were the descendants of the shamanic priesthood who built these serpent temples.

It has been suggested that the Serpent Mound of Ohio in North America is related to Stonehenge in that it is the 'Dragon Guardian' of the East to Stonehenge's Secret of the West. (Whatever this means is of course left to the imagination, as there is no further explanation).

Indeed, it is thought that the two ancient structures share the same timeframe and may very well relate to each other, if ancient man did share the same beliefs and travel extensively, as is the growing belief of many scholars.

The Greek historian Diodorus Siculus (90–21 BC) called Stonehenge the 'Temple of Apollo'. This led us to investigate possible connections between Apollo and our theory of the serpent elixir. We found that Apollo – the Greek version of Horus, the Egyptian sun god – was the god of healing and the father of Aesculapius, the archetypal god of medicine who was taught the healing arts by the centaur Chiron. Apollo wielded the famous Caduceus, a staff with two serpents entwined about it, while Aesculapius possessed a one-serpent staff, known as the Rod of Aesculapius. It is imperative that we now examine these two symbols and note their differences.

The Rod of Aesculapius and the Caduceus

A very ancient symbol, the Caduceus is found the world over and different stylizations appear in the ancient cultures of Mesopotamia, Egypt, India, Europe and Mesoamerica. Many of us know it as the winged staff with two entwined serpents held by the Greek god Hermes or the Roman Mercury, a god based on the ancient Egyptian god Thoth, who instructed Horus (Apollo). The 'Staff of Hermes' was often carried by Greek messengers and ambassadors, and later became a Roman symbol for truce, neutrality and non-combatant status.[9]

The Caduceus is now used as the emblem of the medical and allied professions. However, the staff symbol first used by the medical profession in the eighteenth century was often a simple roughly-hewn knotted tree branch or wooden staff with only one serpent entwined around it – the Rod of Aesculapius.[10]

The Rod of Aesculapius

The staff entwined with a solitary snake was originally the symbol of Aesculapius and is often wrongly named the Caduceus. Often shown with Aesculapius leaning on it, it is mostly used to signify the medical profession. Of course, there are variations. In some emblems or corporate logos, it is lit at the top like a torch, symbolizing the divine Light of wisdom.

This particular staff corresponds to the healing properties of the snake associated with the first level of the Grail and the Elixir of Life. It was known to a few, who kept it secret, that for healing purposes one snake provided the real and original Elixir of Life, i.e. the venom associated with death and the masculine principle and the blood associated with life and the feminine principle. The snake therefore symbolized wisdom and immortality.

The Caduceus

Whereas the Rod of Aesculapius has one serpent, the Caduceus – also known as the Arcadian Rod and the Staff of Brahma (the Hindu supreme god) – features two serpents, symbolizing the opposites of male and female. The name 'Caduceus' comes from the Latin word *kerykeion* and in Greek *kerykeion skeptron* means 'herald's wand'.

As with the Rod of Aesculapius, the rod or staff symbolizes the spinal column and exemplifies the straight and upright spine, demonstrating confidence, good health and longevity. But on a higher level this particular staff also reveals the dynamic processes associated with the Gnostic enlightenment experience, especially the seven-levelled chakra-gland-related system known as Kundalini.

As already mentioned, Apollo is the Greek version of the ancient Egyptian god Horus, which is interesting as the Caduceus was additionally held by Thoth, the wisest of the ancient Egyptian gods and the

Egyptian version of the Greek god Hermes. Like Thoth, Horus the sun god (a title associated with the spiritual inner sun) was also the embodiment of wisdom. Apparently, Hermes was given the Caduceus by Apollo in return for his lyre, a stringed musical instrument not unlike the Celtic harp. In esoteric terms, musical instruments – such as the flute, syrinx, and lyre – symbolize the seven major notes of the musical scale, which in turn correspond to the seven primary colours of the electromagnetic spectrum and the seven levels of consciousness reflected in the seven chakras that align the spine.

Other versions of the myth tell us that the Caduceus was created when the Greek god Hermes struck two warring snakes apart with a staff – a metaphor for bringing harmony and balance to the opposites and uniting or neutralizing them.

This ancient symbol is thus evidence that our ancestors knew about the three 'forces of consciousness': the positive, negative and neutral. It has always been a symbol of immortality.

The Caduceus also represents the idea that good health and intelligence arise from a well-balanced attitude to life. We should strive to be *centred*, like the central staff of the Caduceus, and not be sent off balance by focusing on the opposites or the cycle of opposites represented by the two snakes entwined around the staff. It is a maxim of all esoteric mystery schools that we should try to maintain a neutral, non-judgemental, indifferent or detached stance as we interact with our environment.

The two energy channels represented by the snakes on the Caduceus – one male (Red-solar, the *Pingala*) and one female (White-lunar, the *Ida*) – imply that the snakes symbolize the division, imbalance and disease associated with the positive and negative opposites. Like the two properties of the one snake encountered on the first level of our Grail Triad, the two should be brought together and united (crossed) on the central staff – the *Sushumna* – which symbolizes neutrality.

Our theory is that the *Pingala* and *Ida* channels of the Caduceus correspond respectively to the venom and blood of the solitary snake of the one-snake Rod of Aesculapius. This theory finds support in the words of Ram Kumar Rai, a contemporary author on the Hindu religion, who states that the poison or 'excessively heating venom flows full through the Pingala and goes to the right nostril, and the Moon-fluid of immortality goes to the left'.[11] We discovered that this 'Moon Fluid' was menstrual blood and therefore it was the feminine-related 'blood' element which was reflected in the dark-red colour of the moon during the lunar eclipse. The venom and *Pingala* link speaks for itself, but the identification of the moon-fluid confirms that there is a definite link between the *Ida* channel on the spiritual level and the blood of the snake on the practical level of the Grail Triad.

As we know, the snake is associated with healing, health and longevity, and these qualities are symbolized by the neutral points – the centres of the chakra vortices – where the two opposing energies cross each other on the central staff and are united, fused and balanced. The wings surmounting the Caduceus staff belong to the Phoenix of resurrection and rebirth, while the orb at their centre is the egg of the Phoenix as well as the Stone of the Grail legends, otherwise known as the Philosopher's Stone. It is associated with the 'soul essence' or spirit, which was believed to leave the body as an orb of light – an astral vehicle. This winged orb is depicted in the art of many ancient cultures (*see plate 10*). As regards the physical body, the orb symbolizes the human head or skull, or more specifically the thalamus, whose appearance has been described as egg-like, and which is therefore represented by the Cosmic Egg and the Stone of esoteric tradition.

And on this point we will leave the reader to make their own connections with everything we have said so far and return to Stonehenge:

Omphalos: Navel and Axis of the Universe

Caer Sidi has been related etymologically to the 'revolving castle', with arrows of poison shooting from many holes. This is a clear allusion to the poisonous venom of the snake and reveals that Stonehenge too could very well contain, or even be, a real rendition of the 'serpent's head'. But what profound truth lies behind this strange metaphor?

Like many other places around the world, Stonehenge was called the Omphalos, suggesting *Om Phallus*,[12] the ever-enkindling (immortal) Light, the Zodiac, Axis or Elixir, and the spores of the mighty Hueel (*hu* = 'light', *eel* = 'snake'). So Stonehenge, the mythical Temple of Apollo, is not only linked with serpents via mythology, but also linked with 'poison' and is an 'elixir' in etymology. And, as we have just seen, it is etymologically, astronomically and architecturally linked with the snake or serpent in that it was referred to as the 'serpent's head'.

If we consider this one example together with the evidence we have just presented regarding the mythology of Stonehenge and its link with the Arthurian legend, we now have many of those 'scholastic markers' that are required to prove a historical case. The case we have presented so far is for a link between the Grail and the symbology of the serpent and snake. Of course, Stonehenge also had a practical purpose associated with astronomy, but it was built by people who perhaps understood the traditional holistic knowledge of the ancient Shining Ones and so it is no surprise to find that it encompasses all the information we have looked at.

The mainly Celtic origins of the wonderful Arthurian tales also tell us that the snake was deeply associated with healing and water. For instance the Gallic goddess Sirona (meaning 'star') was a healing goddess with snakes entwined about her arm. She had healing shrines associated with Grannos, another name for Apollo, and was also associated with regeneration and resurrection – i.e. immortality.

Ireland is reputed to have been an important centre for healing and here again we find similar snake-related healing gods, even though the country actually has no snakes. One example is Dian Cecht, a god of healing who killed Meich, the son of Morrigan, who was said to have three hearts, each of which contained a serpent. Dian Cecht was also fabled to have dipped the mythical Tuatha dé Danaan (the people of the goddess Danaan) into a 'cauldron of regeneration' to save them from death. Irish mythology also tells us that three sons brought three healers from Sirona, the snake goddess. Yet more allusions, more encoded clues.

Those familiar with esoteric wisdom and both Western and Eastern mysticism and metaphysics will understand what is being alluded to straight away. The 'three healers' make up the Triad of positive, negative and neutral energies, while the 'three serpents' are surely an allusion to the Hindu Kundalini serpents – the *Pingala*, *Ida* and *Sushumna* triad, which are respectively associated with the pineal and pituitary glands and the thalamus. Once we begin to cross-reference all this mythical material, we discover certain pieces of information that are consistent in that they all point to the same processes – the processes of human consciousness. This realization can lead us back to the very source of existence itself.

This is not to say that this prehistoric archetypal material has not been exploited, twisted, manipulated, suppressed and utilized in many different ways, often for purposes of power and control. Such manipulations of the mythical data have led to confusion. Take, for example, the manifold expressions of one particular hero or deity. The gods Horus, Apollo, Thoth and Hermes, for instance, could all be the same individual because they all possess the magical accessory of the Caduceus – apart from Horus, that is. But since Horus is the Egyptian equivalent of the Greek Apollo, and Apollo is associated with the Caduceus, Horus must be associated with it too – and Horus is the son and heir and reincarnation of Osiris.

The only way we can make sense of all this is to realize that the emblem of the Caduceus reveals a process by which we can attain enlightenment and immortality, or at least the realization of it. It is this factor which all these deities (and more besides) have in common and which brings them together as one. This individual, being a composite of all these gods and heroes, is the archetypal shaman god *par excellence*. This is the god of the Shining Ones, a shamanic 'supreme being' who expresses all their principles. If we take the Heliopolitan-Egyptian pantheon as an example, sometimes this god is Thoth, while at other times he is Osiris or Horus or Atum-Ra.

Once we realize this, we can make sense of the other mythical motifs which consistently turn up in all manner of abstract ways. A prime example is the World Mountain (the 'mountain of salvation' or 'Grail Castle' of the Grail romances) which, as the *axis mundi* or World Tree, also symbolizes the spinal column. This is brought together with the snake or serpent in the Caduceus staff, and a similar motif appears in the story of adam and Eve (*see plate 11*).

Even though we may be familiar with symbols like the Caduceus, however, and understand how the serpent is associated with the enlightenment experience, the question still remains: what does the snake or serpent really have to do with healing and the Elixir of Life? The Shining Ones knew. After all, it was they who had experienced the very mechanism that had produced the Elixir of Life in the first place, and they who had encoded their knowledge in the myths and legends that featured the universal god or hero. In some instances, the myths referred to an élite race with special powers, similar to those of the Tuatha dé Danaan of Celtic legend. Sometimes the gods or heroes were themselves the personification of those who could attain self-illumination and who possessed the knowledge, abilities and benefits that came with it.

From our research into Hermetic philosophy, we discovered that the ancients believed that a defect existed within human consciousness. As a result, they believed human beings were trapped within the cycles of the material world through their reliance on one half of the cycle (the material aspect) to the detriment of the other (the spiritual aspect). This dualistic theme was crucial to the beliefs of the Gnostics and Cathars. However, the universal hero was able to transcend the world of matter, the 'trapped mind', and all cyclical phenomena through having experienced the mid-point (neutral or zero-node) between these two divisions, thereby resolving his dualistic human nature.

It was also believed that such an individual would have become familiar with the 'serpent' within and around him. That is, he would have observed the wave phenomena and cycles in the natural world. He would thus have been able to control the serpent that had others mortally trapped within its spirals, waves and cycles of divided energy. He had healed the division of energy within himself and was therefore an 'immortal', a 'god'. And, having transcended the physical laws of reality, he had some control and influence over the collective, or so it was believed.

The Greek historian Plutarch once said, 'The men of old time associated the serpent most of all beasts with heroes.' In fact, it seems that all heroes in one form or another have serpents among their symbols. For example, as Carl Jung said, there is a series of medieval pictures in which the communion cup contains a dragon, a snake, or some sort of small animal. Jung pointed out that a relief in Hereford Cathedral clearly depicted a chalice with a dragon rising from it. There are actually images across the Christian world of this dragon or serpent rising from the 'poisoned chalice' held by St John the Evangelist, another archetype for the 'shamanic serpent being' or 'Shining One', as we shall discover in the next chapter (*see plate 12*).

Finally, there is the remarkable story of the Arthurian knight Sir Lancelot, who in a vision saw a man surrounded by stars and various other wondrous things. He afterwards learned that it had some meaning in respect of his lineage.

It seems that 42 years after the Passion of Christ, Joseph of Arimathea left Jerusalem[13] and came to Sarras, a fabled island city like Atlantis, where he helped a certain Evelac. (Could this be 'Eve-Lake', where 'Eve', from the Hebrew *Havvah*, actually means 'female snake'?) Evelac was baptized (i.e. anointed or initiated), together with her brother-in-law Seraphe (meaning 'snake' or 'shine'). It is said that Seraphe then took the name Nasciens (meaning 'serpent') and became a pillar of the faith. The secrets of the Grail were opened up to Evelac after Joseph, the bearer of the Grail, had turned Seraphe/Nasciens into a serpent follower. Evelac then had a dream in which Nasciens issued forth a great lake, whence eventually came Lancelot. The secret that Lancelot learned concerning his lineage was that he was a member of the bloodline who were the protectors of the 'secret of the serpent'.

We will end this chapter with an excerpt from Wolfram von Eschenbach's *Parzifal*, which also holds many clues to the identity of the Grail on the first level pertaining to the Elixir.

And sore was the King we sorrowed – Then a magic herb we found, (Men say, from the blood of a dragon it springeth from out of the ground,) With the stars, and the wind, and the heaven, close-bound, doth it win circling hour, And the moon draweth near to her changing, The herb might our grief have aided – Yet its magic we sought in vain.[14]

But we felt we were not searching in vain. All these clues pointed to the enlightenment experience on the third level of our Grail Triad, but they had a double meaning in that they also alluded to the neutralizing property of the snake or serpent elixir on the first level.

The next question that faced us was, why was the head symbolized by a cauldron or cup?

CHAPTER SIX

The Cauldron of the Head of the Underworld

O ur research had revealed that, on one level of understanding, the cauldron symbolized the Underworld, a magical realm to which many cultures believe we go when we die. The universal hero or arche-typal shaman is able to visit this realm and then come back again, bringing information, knowledge and profound wisdom. On another level of understanding, we had concluded that the cauldron also sym-bolized the head, the place of enlightenment. This was relevant to certain key aspects of the Arthurian story. For instance, Arthur was the son of Uther Pendragon, a name that contains the word *pen*, which means 'head'. But were there any further clues in these ancient plays on words?

Uther (meaning 'wonderful') is similar to Aither, the father of the Pagan god Pan (meaning 'all'), and may be equated etymologically with 'ether', otherwise known as the *aether*, the superfine all-permeating atmosphere or underlying energy of the universe which the ancient Greeks attributed to their principal god, Zeus. So Uther-Zeus was the father of Arthur, who, like Osiris, Horus, Pan and Jesus, was deemed to be a 'son of God'. Uther was also known as Uther-Ben, and *ben* is a Hebrew word meaning 'first', 'original' and even 'head'. It was customary for the Jews to name their first or favourite son Benjamin. So, the name 'Ben' can be associated with the first point of creation and with the head. This name is also related to the ancient Egyptian word *ben-ben* and to the *bennu* bird (the heron), the Egyptian Phoenix. The ben-ben was the pyramidion or capstone that was placed at the top of sacred pillars and pyramids, constructions that represented the shamanic World Pillar and World Mountain. Pillars or obelisks also symbolized the upright human spinal column, which is why the pyramidion capstone would have represented the head – or rather, something within the head.

In the fifth century BC, the Greek playwright Euripides wrote, 'Seest thou the immense Aether on high and the earth around held in its moist embrace? Revere Zeus and obey god.'[1] And in the first century BC, the Roman poet Virgil said, 'Thus the Omnipotent Father, great Aether with fecund showers, descends into the bosom of his rejoicing wife, and, united in love with her great body, nourishes all her offspring.' From this we are led to believe that we are all the offspring of this source or 'well-spring', the centre of our very being.

Arthur is said to have had a stronghold at Tintagel in Cornwall, which was alternatively known as Dundagel (dun-d-ag-el), meaning 'Stronghold of the Resplendent Mighty God (or Shining One)'.[2] The word *dun* in 'Dundagel' means 'hill' or 'mound', recalling the primordial mound, the underlying energy matrix of creation.

The title 'Pendragon' was understood to mean 'King of Kings', and not just by the Britons, but also by the Chinese Manchu dynasty and the Phoenicians. As *pen* means 'head', Pendragon can also be translated as the 'head of the dragon'. In mythology, the dragon is interchangeable with the serpent and snake. It is also the 'fish', as in the Mesopotamian fish being known as Dagon, a name that reminded us of the African tribe the Dogon, who say their ancestors were visited by 'fish beings', as well as of the Celtic god Dagda. These names are also related with the word 'dog', and dogs are often guardians of the Underworld – for example, the Greek Cerberus and the Egyptian Anubis. Even Thoth was depicted with a dog's head. The word *dagel* in Dundagel is similar to both Dagon and Dagda. Although confusing on the surface, we can now see the deeper meanings behind these etymological connections.

The dragon emblazoned the standard of, among others, the West Saxons, the Welsh, the Phoenicians and the Chinese Manchu dynasty. A point worth noting is that the Welsh dragon, which is red in colour, is set on a white background. We have already touched on the deeper significance of these colours and so it came as no surprise to find battles between red and white dragons in the Arthurian tales. These battles convey the continual struggle between opposites to reach a level of harmony and equilibrium – or, better still, to be neutralized altogether so as to manifest or reveal the source of both. They not only symbolize the Kundalini serpents relating to the third level of the Grail Triad, but also the practical use of the venom and blood of the snake on the first level.

There was also another thread to follow here. The link between Uther and Zeus led us to the ideas put forward in a fascinating book, *Arthur: The Dragon King*, by Howard Reid, who claims that much of the Arthurian cycle can be traced to the Scythians. These people were initially brought to Britain from the Russian steppes by the Romans as a mercenary horseback-fighting force. The employment of mercenaries was not an uncommon practice in antiquity: the Assyrians, for example, had employed the cavalry skills of the Cimmerians, who were themselves closely related to the Scythians. Many alliances were thus formed and then broken. And all along, as these warriors were thrashing out the great political power battles of the day, there was a subtle transference of folklore, myths, legends and other traditions, not to mention religion and mystical insight. It was in this way that the Scythians brought their beliefs with them from Siberia to Britain.

Like the Celts, the Scythians were a shamanic-based culture. The Scythians and Celts shared a peculiar ritual in which the blood-soaked blade of a sword was thrust into the ground and then drawn slowly out. This ritual has its parallel in Arthurian legend in the drawing of the 'sword from the stone', and thus provides a link between the Arthurian story and the shamanic Scythians. The sword being thrust into the ground is an obvious allusion to the Underworld, which was believed to exist both 'underground' and 'inside the Earth'.

As we have already mentioned, the ancient Egyptians would observe the sun going down in the evening in the belief that it was going into the Earth, into the Underworld, the Duat, or the land of the dead. This night-time phase of the daily cycle was seen as the negative and dark half of the cycle and was associated with death, whereas the daytime phase was seen as the positive half and was associated with light and life. Here again, the emphasis is on cycles, and especially on the crucial point – the neutral or zero-node – which was seen as the gateway to these earthly cycles as well as to the abode of the gods.

To return to the connection between Uther and Zeus, Zeus was a god of the Scythians as well as the Greeks, and is said to have taken the form of a serpent and visited Olympias, wife of Phillip II of Macedon, who subsequently gave birth to Alexander the Great. The similarities between Uther and Zeus are an obvious attempt to link Arthur with Alexander and the royal serpent lineage as well as with the powers of the ancient shaman, as evidenced in the shapeshifting ability attributed to Uther.[3]

It is also interesting to note that many of the archetypal deities who became legendary figures were in fact solar deities from ancient times. Alexander was himself associated with Apollo, as his son, and Arthur was similarly the son of Zeus (aka Uther), another solar deity. But this only became apparent in the Arthurian stories when Geoffrey of Monmouth, the Welsh-Breton cleric, introduced it, probably for political purposes, in about 1136. We must note, though, that the original story of Zeus required the god to take the form of a snake in order to create a powerful, fertile and vibrant warrior. The Arthurian tale is too similar to the Alexandrian legend to be mere coincidence, for Uther is said to have shapeshifted in order to visit Igraine, wife of the Duke of Tintagel, who subsequently gave birth to Arthur, who, just like Alexander, was a great warrior leader. In this way, Arthur, like Alexander and many other legendary leaders and avatars from around the world, is portrayed as being of 'serpent' descent.

The Scythians had a practice of attaching to their saddles the severed heads of those they had defeated in battle, as if to scare off potential combatants. All the heads of the warriors killed in the battle were taken to the king, who would pay a dividend of the booty. Of particular interest in our quest for the Grail was the fact that they would also cut off the top of the skull, clean it out, gild it and turn this macabre object into a mystical drinking vessel. This practice was extremely widespread and by no means just the preserve of the Scythians. Golden heads have been found far and wide, and it was not always the heads of adversaries that were used. Nobody is sure where this practice originated, but through the Scythians the Arthurian tales are linked to a people who revered heads, drank human blood and worshipped both the snake and Zeus, the god who was able to shapeshift into a serpent, via the limitless creative energy of the *aether*.

The cup or chalice is a relatively late addition to the Arthurian canon, a Christianized version of an older Celtic and Scythian tradition. In part in a desire to suppress shamanic and Pagan practices and in part to assuage the sensitivities of Christians, a tangible cup or chalice replaced the mysterious, sometimes macabre, vessel that was associated literally and metaphorically with the human head. The Christianized Grail, the cup or chalice that was said to have caught the blood of the crucified Christ, now took on the mystical qualities previously associated with the head and became a symbol of regeneration, resurrection and immortality.

Despite attempts to hide these ancient shamanic or Pagan concepts, we believe the evidence we have presented so far is sufficient to establish a link between the original Grail and the human head. It explains why the head was revered, and why cups and chalices were used as symbols for the head and the important glands and organs within it. It also explains why skulls were collected and why the tops were then cut off and used as bowls or cups to contain the elixir associated with the practical first-level usage of the snake and its two opposing properties. This in turn corresponded to the third-level enlightenment experience in which the two energies of the psyche were fused together at the centre of the head.

Having revealed the clues that point to the third-level aspect of our Grail Triad, we shall now look at the clues that point to the first level.

The Tale of Gaileach

In the Arthurian myths we are taken on a special quest to search out a maiden, save a land from devastation or indeed discover the Grail. The stories often feature symbolic elements, such as a grove of trees, a ford, a bridge or a gateway, that introduce an ancient and universal initiation ritual into the story. There we find a maiden or holy lady, who is always a semi-divine being, almost a deity or spirit, and her colour is always white. In Celtic or other ancient Pagan legends, these women are always associated with snakes or serpents. In the Tale of Gaileach this is quite blatant, for a particular snake is transformed into a beautiful maiden.

In most stories the maiden is either a prisoner in some great tower, or an enchantress, like Eve with the apple. Either way, she is a seductress and draws a knight-errant to her cause. She is accompanied by a champion and protector, usually in the form of a black knight. The newcomer – the knight errant – must be victorious in his battle with the black knight in order to gain his prize, which is often a night with the magical snake maiden. The black knight symbolizes our 'unconsciousness of the source', which must be overcome before we, as the hero or newcomer in the story, can claim our prize – the wisdom and knowledge deep within ourselves, which is personified as the maiden or World Mother. The important element, however, is the blood of the vanquished, and this brings us back to the role of the head or skull.

Like the mammalian host whose blood acts as an antidote to the poison of the snake (*see page 279*), the blood of the black knight is said to have the power to heal and bestow eternal life. Significantly, the most powerful blood is spewed forth from the head of the knight. Could this be relevant to the story of John the Baptist? Was it symbolically significant that his head was offered up on a plate or indeed Grail? John baptized with water, which as we have already mentioned is closely associated with the serpent – and the prize Salome desired most was his head. We shall look into this matter in more detail later.

To return to the Arthurian myth, in *Perlesvaus*, King Arthur is sent off on a voyage by his wife, Guinevere, who is identified as the 'snake queen' or 'crowned serpent' by the symbolic 'crown and snake' of the Royal Sarassins, an ancient legendary and serpentine race of Britain. Eventually Arthur comes to a magical clearing where he finds a maiden seated at the foot of a tree. The maiden shows Arthur to the chapel he is seeking, and there a black knight suddenly appears and hurls a 'lance of fire' into Arthur's arm. Fortunately, the flames are extinguished by 'Pendragon' blood of Arthur, who goes on to kill the knight. Twenty other knights then appear and finish the job by hacking the corpse to pieces. Arthur takes the knight's head to the maiden, who anoints his arm with the blood of the head and he is miraculously healed. The maiden then tells him how she can now use the head of the black knight to restore her fortunes.

Many explanations have been given for the recurring motifs that appear in this story, but the story makers encoded their secrets well. To decode the story we need to look elsewhere and at a subject which, on the surface, seems to have little connection with it.

The *red* dragon of Arthur Pendragon, the serpent king, is sent off by the *white* serpent queen to rescue one of their kind – the maiden seated at the foot of the Tree of Life and Knowledge, who is herself a symbol of wisdom – and restore her fortune. The dark knight is a simple replacement of the dragon guardian of other popular worldwide myths. The lance of fire hurled at Arthur – the lance and the oval spearhead have the form of a snake – symbolizes the attacking bite of the snake and the fiery pain of its venom. Only by taking the blood of the serpent can Arthur create the antidote, thereby enabling his own blood to extinguish the flames of pain. The head of the serpent contains both the healing blood and the poisonous venom – the *red* and the *white*. The blood from its head therefore becomes the 'all-healer', the 'resurrecting power' and 'life eternal'.

Significantly, the head is also the centre of enlightenment, which links the story to the Kundalini enlightenment experience. The chapel in the story can be understood as a metaphor for the chakra at the base of the spine where the serpent energy is said to lie like a sleeping serpent or coiled snake at the base of a tree. As well as symbolizing the dormant serpent energy, the sleeping serpent represents our own ignorance or unconsciousness of the Source. Guinevere, the serpent queen who sends Arthur on the errand, and the maiden seated at the base of the tree by the chapel represent respectively the serpent energy awakening us to its presence and the release of the energy from its dormant state. Arthur's struggle with the black knight depicts our own inner process whereby the awakening of the serpent energy leads to the healing of our divided mind and our enlightenment.

The enlightenment connection seems obvious to us now. But could we also have here the first-level secret relating to the head and the serpent myths? Moreover, could there be a literal truth hidden within these medieval stories? In one way these ancient storytellers were not telling literal truths – well, not openly anyway. Rather, in relating stories that encoded ancient beliefs and medicinal practices they were passing on symbolic truths and at the same time producing popular propaganda.

It was becoming increasingly clear that the head of the serpent was the most important element for these ancient storytellers. First, in regard to the third-level enlightenment experience, the head is where the climax of the experience takes place. Second, in regard to the first-level practical application of the venom and the blood, the decapitated head symbolizes the sacrifice of the host – the serpent being or Shining One – whose blood is used to heal.

It is now well known that the Knights Templar and Cathars were said to have worshipped severed heads in one form or another. It is also well known that they were supposed to hold the secret of the Grail. Did the secret die with these mysterious people? What really made the Templars so rich? Why is there such a strong link between the Templars and the weaving of the tapestry that became the Arthurian legend? The answer lies in both the medicinal secret and the propaganda.

The Knights Templar are a fascinating historical group: warrior monks destined for greatness and yet also for a great fall. There are literally billions of words dedicated to their history and yet we seem to be no closer to the real truth underlying their remarkable rise to power and to the secrets they are said to have held. It is claimed that they were an order of Christian knights of the twelfth and thirteenth centuries. Yet many of their traditions and writings show a clear Gnostic belief which was at that time more attuned to Mandean than Christian thinking. The Mandeans, or 'Disciples of John', still exist in Syria, Palestine and Iraq, sometimes under the title of Druzes.

The Mandeans or Druzes

The Druze were originally a mixture of Cuthites, Mardi Arabs and possibly also the remnants of Christian crusaders. According to *Mackey's Encyclopaedia*, they 'are supposed to be the descendants of those Hivites ['Ophites' according to Deane] among whom the Hebrews dwelt in the time of Joshua; and afterward on Mount Lebanon'. The Cuthites and Hivites were serpent worshippers, especially the Cuthites, who are said by some to have emerged from Ethiopia (Cush). Following the idea that they also mixed with the Crusaders, it is possible that the Templars (amongst others) received some of their knowledge from these peoples.

The name 'Druze' is said to come from their founder Ad-Darazi, who died around AD 1019. Later on, the famous Assassins emerged from the Druze via Nizari (named after Nizar, the son of Caliph al-Mustansir). Several authors have pointed to a link between the Assassins and the Knights Templar through agreements which were expedient for both sides, such as the one made when the Templars wished to take Damascus.

The Assassins secured loyalty with the use of the drug hashish, hence the term *hashashin*. The use of hashish, an hallucinogen, is interesting in light of the shamanic trance state techniques used to access the Underworld. The name 'Nizar' is also interesting, as we note that the Hindustani term *nazar*, which is very similar, is the Yogic term for the so-called esoteric third eye, the *Agnya* or *Ajna* chakra, which is 'opened' (i.e. activated) through meditation and the hypnagogic trance state. Moreover, John the Baptist was known as the 'Great Nazar'.[5] The Gnostic term 'Nazarean', which is used in the title 'Jesus the Nazarean' and often mistakenly interpreted as referring to the town of Nazareth, means 'to envision' or 'behold' and is also linked with the snake.

Following a period of expansion which was stopped by the Mongols, the Assassins rested in India, and are said to have 'grafted on to their own beliefs a primitive form of nature-worship and of Sabeism', which the scholar John Bathurst Deane points out is just another version of serpent worship. However, the fact remains that the 'grafting on' of this nature-worship was just a reinvigoration of the ancient beliefs.

The Druze are thought to have influenced Freemasonry, probably via the Templars, and this influence can be seen in the degrees of Masonic initiation and ritual. As the author C. W. King points out:

Of their present creed, preserved in inviolate secrecy, nothing authentic has ever come to light; popular belief amongst their neighbors makes them adorers of an idol in the form of a calf, and... their nocturnal assemblies [which the Templars were also said to hold] orgies like those laid to charge of the Ophites in Roman, Templars in Medieval, and... Freemasons in modern times. Their notion of their Head residing in Scotland has an odd resemblance to the German appellation of 'Scottish brethren' given to our Masons.[6]

The last sentence relates to the idea that the secret of the ancient 'serpent cult' resides in Rosslyn, Scotland, where it is said that the 'Head of God' is kept underneath a pillar. The idea of calf worship has parallels in Hathor, the Egyptian cow goddess (who was also a serpent), and Moses, the wielder of the Brazen Serpent, who was implicated in the worship of a golden calf. However, as Horus was seen as the Golden Calf, the worship of the Son of God is implied here.

Incidentally, the Druze say that John the Baptist was El Khidr, the 'Green Man'. In their earliest forms, both El Khidr and St George the Dragon Slayer derive from the ancient vegetation god Osiris, the Egyptian equivalent of the Sumerian/Akkadian vegetation god Tammuz, who, as we shall discover, is implicated in the ancient cult of the serpent. The cult of St George was spread abroad by none other than the Templars.

All these groups have one common origin: the so-called 'heresies' of the Nazareans (Nasoreans) or Ophites. It was from this group that the Templars acquired their beliefs and the white robes that were also worn by the Cistercians.

The snake symbolism of the Ophites goes back right through Greek, Egyptian and Phrygian cultures, encompassing such ideas as conquest over death, immortality and wisdom, and opens out into a group of ancient snake cults such as the Ophite-Cainites, Ophite-Sethians and Ophite-Nachaites. Out of these groups evolved the Gnostic tradition of the Ouroboros, the universal symbol for the cycle of birth-death-rebirth and immortality.

The Mandeans have no belief in Jesus as the 'only Son of God', or in the scriptures associated with him. Instead they place their faith in St John and Sophia (Wisdom). The head of John the Baptist, the Great Nazar, was offered up on a sacred plate to Salome as King Herod's payment for her 'dance of the seven veils'. The story is an allegory for the Kundalini enlightenment experience, with the seven veils representing the seven chakras or energy vortices aligned along the spinal column.

By tradition John was an Ophite, one of those who worshipped the snake, while the name Sophia (S'Ophia) is the name of this very cult. The serpent or snake has symbolized Sophia or Wisdom since ancient times. The Latin word *ophts* means both 'serpent' and 'stone' (*lithos*). This double meaning reminded us of Wolfram von Eschenbach's notion of the Grail as a stone, a linguistic ploy created to hide the snake while pointing yet again to the link between the Grail and the Philosopher's Stone. The implication here is that the Philosopher's Stone is indeed related to the snake. But this is not too difficult an idea to assimilate since the serpent represents the life-force of the universe, which is itself symbolized by the stone, the seed of creation, or the Cosmic Egg. These divine archetypes are brought together in the symbol of the Orphic Egg, a snake wrapped around an egg.

Baphomet

It is known that the Templars worshipped John the Baptist. They also preferred St John's Gospel to the other three, and so it is possible that they also worshipped St John the Divine or the Evangelist, who was often depicted as clean-shaven and effeminate looking.

Figure 9: Johann Mylius, Philosophia reformata, 1622

Images of heads (both male and female) abound in Templar literature and art. When King Philippe IV of France and Pope Clement
decided to disband them, the Templars were accused of worshipping an
'evil' image of a human head – a carved head reliquary – which they
called Baphomet. This head has been described as having two faces back
to back, or perhaps three heads or faces – two faces back to back with a
third placed centrally. Some say that Baphomet had the face of a man or
a woman or both. But if it had two faces, then in our view it was most
probably a head with a male and a female face back to back, in which case
it is more than likely that it was modelled on the two-faced Roman god
Janus, the god of new beginnings and/or endings, of spiritual portals
and gateways, of change, transition or transformation from one condition or 'world' to another. The two-faced image symbolized the three
forces in consciousness – positive, negative and neutral – whether the
mid-point, or Alpha-Omega, was clearly indicated by a third face or not.

Our reasoning here is based on alchemical symbolism and the
Androgyne, the union of male and female opposites. An example of this
can be seen in the sculpted figure of a young woman representing
Prudence, one of four statues guarding the tomb of François II in Nantes
Cathedral, France. The most striking feature of this sculpture is the face
of a full-bearded wise old sage who looks out from the back of the girl's

head (*see plates 21 and 22*). This compound image suggests the total wedlock of opposites – male and female – which recalls the androgynous being, the final stage in the alchemical process, whereby the division in human consciousness is healed. Baphomet, which some say represented the 'Head of God', also symbolized this non-divided condition. Perhaps it was for this reason that the Templars were charged with ascribing Grail-like powers to this peculiar head.

As for the curious name 'Baphomet', it has no known origin in any mythology, tradition or religion. Having said that, it is possibly a compound of the words *baphe* (baptism) and *metis* (wisdom). If so, then it is more than likely that the Baphomet head was a composite of the two Johns of the Christian Gospels: John the Baptist (*bathe* or 'baptism') and John the Evangelist (*metis* or 'wisdom'). The former, who is portrayed as bearded, possibly represents the masculine principle, while the latter, depicted as clean-shaven and effeminate, represents the feminine principle. Like the archetypal goddesses – e.g. Inanna, Ceridwen, Brigid and Mary Magdalene – who hold a vessel or cup, the Evangelist is often shown holding the 'poisoned chalice' (which some associate with the Grail) with a serpent or winged-dragon signifying wisdom emerging from it (*see plate 12*).

All the above suggests, as some researchers and writers have recently been saying, that the rather ambiguous male figure of John the Evangelist was really Mary Magdalene. It is said that Leonardo da Vinci alluded to this secret in his paintings, especially *The Last Supper*, painted between 1497 and 1498. For some, this would also mean that the Gospel of John could be attributed to Mary Magdalene. However, although this would make sense to a lot of people, who see in it a hidden relationship between Jesus and the Magdalene, the characters of John the Baptist and Mary Magdalene are really based on the opposites of the Janus image and what it conveys. In other words, if these people existed at all, then they were later moulded into the symbolism associated with the internal processes of the human psyche. John and Mary can therefore be equated with the ancient Egyptian Osiris and Isis, and Jesus with Horus. All three members of this Triad symbolize the three forces of consciousness known as the 'Secret Combination' in Masonic lore. The triadic aspect of the Janus image is commented on by writer Alice Ouzounian:

> The symbolic image of Janus/Jana is androgynous, since the mas-
> culine and feminine energies and qualities are in complete balance
> and harmony and their respective attributes make the head of
> Janus/Jana crowned. This shows us that their dual nature unites at
> the mind level and becomes one complete new being.
>
> The crown that harmonizes and unites them after their "mys-
> tical wedding" gives rise to the third face, which remains invisible
> and represents the crowning of the great work, the androgynous
> level of consciousness where God incarnates in the seeker. Thus,
> the seeker knows in all humility that he is a Son of God. For this
> reason, the crown is a solar symbol and, therefore, the two streams
> of the moon within the seeker blend, and from a level of duality,
> they unite with the Sun symbol of the Father and God. The

Figure 10: Rosarium philosophorum manuscript, sixteenth century,
balanced by all the elements of the serpent

alchemical symbol of the rebis reminds us of the same principle hidden behind the cartouche of Janus/Jana.

Whenever the symbolism of Janus relates to time, between the past (which is no longer) and the future (which is not yet), the true Face of Janus – that which looks at the present and is supposed to face us – is not shown; it is neither one nor the other of the two we can see. This third face is, in fact, invisible because the present in its temporal manifestation is but an intangible and imperceptible instant.[7]

The Goat of Mendes

Eliphas Levi, a great exponent of magical rites, translated 'Baphomet' as a reversed composition of three abbreviations – Tem. Oph. Ab. – which stand for *Templi omnium hominum pacis abhas* (The God of the Temple of Peace Among All Men). Levi believed this to be a reference to the Temple of Solomon.

According to author Michael Howard, Levi's portrayal of Baphomet was based on a gargoyle that appeared on the Commandry of Saint Bris le Vineux, which was owned by the Templars. This gargoyle is described as a bearded horned figure with female breasts and cloven feet, sitting cross-legged with a Caduceus poking up from between its legs like a phallus. This is obviously a symbolic device in which the beard represents great wisdom – a serpent trait – and, as any Templar historian will know, a beard was a required part of the Templar image. The horns could represent a number of things, but usually symbolize duality of opposites. They are closely linked with serpent symbolism, because the venomous serpent is often referred to as the 'horned serpent', a symbol of the illumination aspect. The breasts of the gargoyle, which are symbols of fertility, fecundity and immortality, are also serpent symbols (*see Chapter 8,*

Lactating Goddesses). As for the cloven feet, this could mean stamping down the 'base' man (i.e. the unconscious 'lower self'), or to 'split into two', or indeed 'forked tongue', all of which are allusions to the division in consciousness and the point at which the two opposites are One.

It was from this image, now called the 'Sigil of Baphomet' or 'Goat of Mendes', and others that the pentagram, the five-pointed star, emerged in the modern era as a symbol of power widely used in the rituals of secret societies. Mendes is a place in the Egyptian Nile Delta, and we discovered that Mendes was also a ram-headed god as well as the dwelling-place of the Ba where Re and Osiris met, uniting in their *ba* or soul. This is obviously related to the internal experience of enlightenment. The association with the Ram, the first sign of the Zodiac means that Mendes is also associated with the head, which brings us back to the significance of the skull, and the *ba*, the soul that resides in the head or skull.

Taking the word 'Baphomet' backwards, which seems to be a common practice, we get Tem, Oph (ohp), Ab. 'Tem' could come from the root word for 'time', or it could mean 'to proclaim'. 'Ohp' or 'Oph' is the 'winged serpent' or dragon of the Ophites. 'Ab' means 'father', 'the Creator' or 'Great One'. It also means 'wisdom', 'intelligence' or 'will' and is a root word for 'snake' or 'serpent'. If we turn 'Ab' back, we get 'Ba', the soul of Atum-Ra, the creator god. We also find the word 'Ab' in 'Abzu', the Sumerian name for the Underworld, from which we possibly derive the word 'absolute', the source-centre of creation, and in 'abaton', meaning *mundus* or 'Earth womb'. Other 'Ab' words and names to be noted are 'abode', 'abyss', 'above' and 'aboriginal' (meaning 'first'). With the name 'Abel' (as in Cain and Abel), *Ab* means 'wisdom' and 'serpent', and *el* means 'god' or 'shining', giving us 'wise serpent god'. We also have 'Abraham', 'abstract', 'ability', 'abbot' and 'abbey', all of which are associated with wisdom and the serpent.

Our conclusion is that 'Baphomet' means 'to proclaim the wisdom of the serpent' and provides further evidence of how far back in time the

secrets of the Templars extend. But we are not alone in reaching this conclusion. Dr Hugh Schonfield, a world-renowned scholar of the Dead Sea
Scrolls and the author of *The Essene Odyssey*, retranslated the word
'Baphomet' using the Atbash cipher, a Hebrew device applied to secret
texts in order to hide the words from prying enemies. Very simply, you
substitute the first letter in the alphabet with the last letter in the alphabet, the next letter with the second to last letter and so on – i.e. 'A'
becomes 'Z', 'B' becomes 'Y', etc. 'Baphomet' in Hebrew reads *Bet Pe Vav
Mem Taf*. Using the Atbash cipher, this becomes *Shin Vav Pe Yud Alef*,
which in English reads as 'Sophia', a word with both 'serpent' and
'wisdom' connotations. The Tanaim (Hebrew scribes) actually used this
method when writing and called it 'ploughing the field' because of the
zig-zag effect across the page. It was also called the 'Serpent Way'. We thus
have the very secret of the serpent name hidden by the Serpent Way.

We mentioned earlier that the Sigil of Baphomet was the modern
pentagram. Today the pentagram is often shown with a goat's head
drawn inside, enclosed by two circles with the Hebrew letters *Lamed,
Vau, Yod, Tau* and *Nun* located between the two circles at each point of
the pentagram. Together these letters spell the word LVYThN or
Leviathan,[8] the aquatic dragon/serpent named for its twisting and
coiling around the Earth and therefore around its axis – an image that
recalls the serpent energy associated with the enlightenment experience,
which is said to lie dormant, coiled at the base of the human spinal axis.

The Hebrew root word of Leviathan means 'to cleave' or 'to divide',
which suggests that the cloven feet of the Sigil of Baphomet are an allusion to the division in consciousness, which is itself seen as the root of
human ignorance, and therefore of 'evil'. But in these sigils or designs we
are also given some clues as to the nature of the processes that provide a
solution to the problem of duality. What these clues tell us is that our
lack of awareness of the life-force which is both within us and around
the Earth is what divides our consciousness in two. This division in

human consciousness is the real reason for all the problems and ills of the world, for the external wars and conflicts are a reflection of a similar conflict going on within us. If we become conscious of the neutral life-force (the serpent energy) and its source, our divided consciousness will be 'healed' – i.e. united, or 'made whole' – and in the process we will realize that we are all immortal. This is one of the meanings behind the healing element of the Grail.

For many of us, our deep primal fear of snakes is really a subconscious memory – a recall – of the awesome power within us. But it is also a reflection of the ego's fear of physical death, which we may perceive to be a black hole about to swallow us up. However, the 'black void' of 'nothing' and 'non-existence' is a mere reflection of the 'black void' of our own unconscious, our unconsciousness of the very Source, the hidden 'Light' of existence itself, that lies within us.

Caput LVIII M

In the fourteenth century, a great head of gilded silver was discovered at the Paris Preceptory of the Templars. It was a woman's head with a hinged top, which, according to the authors Baigent, Leigh and Lincoln, symbolized the zodiac constellation and astrological sign of Virgo, the Virgin. This explanation arose from the label bearing the legend 'CAPUT LVIII M' that was found inside the head. The French word *caput* means 'head', and so the inscription reads 'Head 58M'. The label was attached to a red cloth, which was wrapped around another cloth – a piece of white linen. Inside these red and white wrappings were two bones that belonged to the skull of a woman. Once again we have the alchemical colours of red and white, both placed at the centre of a head.

Looking at this strange inscription, we felt that the number 5 was tied in with the pentagram or five-pointed star, as utilized in the Sigil of Baphomet, and which means simply 'perfect life'. The number 8 is both the symbol of eternity and the number of the serpent. The letter 'M' has always been seen as symbolizing the eternal aspect of the serpent, but it is also said to be the glyph ♍ of Virgo, the shamanic World Mother and mother of the Shining One, the archetypal shaman, the serpent being. From this we concluded that '58M' stood for the perfect eternal aspect of the serpent in the form of the Baphomet head image. The Templars therefore worshipped the Grail of the serpent, which they understood to be connected to the Gnostic enlightenment experience.

According to Von Hammer, the formula written on the side of a chalice that had belonged to the Templars was 'Let METE be exalted who causes all things to bud and blossom, it is our root; it is one and seven; it is octinimous, the eight-fold name.'[9] The numbers 5 and 8 are also associated with the Rosicrucians, the self-proclaimed inheritors of the wisdom of the snake.

Everywhere we looked, we seemed to see the serpent. But we wanted to be careful not to pull out every serpent connection just for the sake of it. The situation was a little like when we buy a car and we suddenly see that same make of car everywhere because our perceptions have been opened up to it. We did not want to be taken in by our own perceptions. We have therefore left out many of the references we discovered relating to the serpent, deciding instead to include only those that were both relevant and valid. However, as the reader may by now be aware, there was no shortage of relevant material.

To return to the story of King Arthur, it was now obvious to us that the serpent was not merely a part of the story, it was the whole story. Yet there were certain elements that at first sight did not appear relevant or valid. It was only by using the tools at hand, such as etymology, that we were able to see deeply into these stories and discover what they really meant. For instance, the three queens who appear many times in Arthurian legends may be equated with the Threefold Goddess, i.e. the Three Fates, Three Muses or Three Graces of Greek mythology, and the three maidens seated at the root of Yggdrasil, the World Ash Tree, as featured in Nordic mythology.

These three maidens were also the builders of another sacred castle, Camelot, and were said to have come out of a sacred mountain cleft towards the sunrise. The symbol for the mountain was 'M', and the sunrise cleft between the twin mountain peaks is highly symbolic in all Grail lore. It also recalls the '58M' inscribed on the label found inside the Templar head. It is said that the Pharaoh Akhenaton built his city of Armana close to a mountain range where the sun could be seen to rise between two mountain peaks. These two peaks are symbolized by the letter 'M', being the two open legs of the World Mother giving birth to the head of the sun god who is reborn every morning with the rising of the sun.

Furthermore, in Egyptian iconography the image of the sun disk rising between the twin peaks is also placed between the two lions of the Egyptian god Aker, the guardian of the gateway to the Underworld. These two lions sit back to back and face in opposite directions – one looking west and the other looking east. One lion represents yesterday, the other tomorrow. The sun disk rising in the middle represents the present moment or the eternal now. The ancient Egyptian two-headed god Aker is therefore the equivalent of the Roman god Janus, and the two lions of Aker flank the birthplace of Horus of the Horizon, the sun god and reincarnation of Osiris, who is also linked with John the Baptist.

These clues led us back to the five-pointed star, the Sigil of Baphomet, which is said to represent the body of the World Mother and the Underworld. This interpretation is supported by the fact that the five-pointed star inside a circle is the ancient Egyptian symbol for the Duat, the Underworld. It is therefore possible that the pentagram at the centre of the design symbolizes the womb of the World Mother. We also have the 'M' linked to Virgo, the Virgin, and representing the open legs of the World Mother who gives birth to the head of the sun god Horus, on whom the figure of Jesus is said to be based.

In the Dorian alphabet, the letter 'M' was called *san*, as in *san graal*. *San* actually means 'Light of the One', and its secondary meaning is 'Holy', as in 'Saint', *San*, *Santa* and *Sanctus*. According to H. Bayley, this 'Light of the One' is symbolized by IO, the universal etymological god.[10] 'IO' appears on the Vase of Light (a Grail image) in conjunction with the lemniscate (∞) or symbol for infinity, which is also a symbol for the snake. The point in the centre of the lemniscate symbolizes infinity, and is also the crucial point in all cycles – the zero-node – which is crossed over twice during one complete revolution of the cycle. It is also the Source from which we are reborn. The same point exists in between the twin peaks (M) where the sun rises.

In many of these legends we also find that the serpent is associated with water, and water is subsequently associated with healing, baptism and resurrection.[11] Is it possible that water symbolically had this healing ability due to the snake or serpent being at home there? If so, it opens up a whole new meaning to the ritual of baptism.

In regard to the first level of our Grail Triad, we have seen how the ancient Celtic peoples venerated the healing power of the snake, often symbolizing it with a cauldron. We recall how the archetypal hero was immersed in two cauldrons, the 'cauldron of venom' and the 'cauldron of cure', from which he emerged reborn and healed of his wounds. We have seen that the cauldron in which the two opposites were mixed was an actual physical vessel that became known as the Grail. We have also seen an association between the Grail and the human head, for it is here that the two opposing aspects of human consciousness are 'mixed' together in the Kundalini enlightenment experience, healing our divided consciousness.

We are now going to follow the winding serpent through many of the different cultures in history and note any supporting evidence for everything we have seen so far.

CHAPTER SEVEN

The Serpent in Classical Myth

From the bewildering imagery of the Arthurian tales, our research took us into the world of classical mythology. In this chapter we have grouped the myths of Greece, Rome, Egypt and other classical civilizations together for the simple reason that these civilizations took on the earlier shamanic beliefs associated with the Shining Ones and fostered them, adding their own unique elements. Western mythologies then took these classical structures and built upon them, yet the former prevalence of the serpent culture is evident in the names of various places and deities of antiquity.

According to Eusebius of Cæsarea (first century AD), the Father of Church history, the Zoroastrians named their expansive heaven after the serpent. Since many historians claim true Zoroastrianism to be 10,000 years old, this provides us with a substantial historical starting-point. In Chaldea, that most ancient of places, the city of Opis on the River Tigris was named after the serpent and it was said that the people there were addicted to serpent worship. Serpent worship spread far and wide and returned to Egypt, one of its places of origin, where the deity was known initially as Canoph, Caneph and C'neph, and later became Ob or Oub, the Royal Serpent or Basilisk.

One of the principal Egyptian deities was Ptah, whom the Greeks associated with Hephaistos. In turn, Hephaistos became the Roman god Vulcan, whom the Roman statesman and philosopher Cicero styled as

Opas, another serpent term. Under his name of Ptah Seker Osiris, Ptah's identity merges with that of Osiris, the ancient Egyptian god of the sun and the Earth, who is also seen in serpentine aspect on many occasions and has been linked to the Hebrew Jehovah or Yahweh. Osiris was also known as Ob-El ('Shining Serpent'), or Pytho Sol ('Serpent Sun'). Great pillars of stone were dedicated to his worship and in Grecian times these were called Obelos or Obeliscus. They are now known as Obelisk pillars and related to the Basilisk (*see plate 23*). These pillars were obvious allusions to the *axis mundi* or World Axis and symbolized both the Earth's polar axis and the human spinal column, as also evidenced in the Djed column, the Egyptian symbol for stability, which was also associated with Osiris and referred to as his 'spine' or 'backbone'.

Even place names show a link with the most ancient serpent worship: Opis, Ophis, Opionia, Ophiusa, Obotha, Obona, Opici and many more originated from the widespread serpent cult. The name 'Ethiopia' may come from Thoth and Athoth or a mistaken translation of Ath-Ophion, a sacred title for followers of the serpent deity. Or it could be that 'Ethiopia' or 'Athiopia' came directly from the terms Athe-Ope and Ath-Opis ('worshippers of the snake'), an obvious link with the Egyptian serpent Apophis or Apep.

Even the original name for the island of Rhodes shows the remarkable divergence of the snake cults. The Cuthites or Heliadae, also known as the Hivites or Ophites ('followers of the snake') settled on this beautiful island, which became known as Ophiusa. According to oral tradition, Rhodes once swarmed with snakes. It was in fact swarming with *snake followers*. The modern name for Rhodes may itself derive from *rhad*, the Syraic term for 'serpent'. Similar etymological origins apply to many other places, including Cyprus, which was once called Ophiusa or Opiodes after the proliferation of serpents said to have been found there.

From the mysteries of Osiris, Isis and Horus to Attis and Cybele, from

Ceres and Proserpine to Bona Dea and Priapus, we discovered a remarkable association of the serpent deity with creation and regeneration. The serpent people who spread these myths were also disseminating a great secret – a secret that spread across continents and then embedded itself in the local culture, changing slowly with time into the myths we know today. We became increasingly convinced that these ancient serpent cults had spread throughout the known world, naming places as they went and building megaliths and monoliths. At the same time, they carried with them sacred stories of 'serpent-bred' kings and queens that were to foster new and profoundly complex 'messianic' tales. This suggests that our modern world evolved from a single source. There is thus more to the serpent than meets the eye. Its coils lie at the very foundation of the Western world.

Throughout the course of our research we were always aware that there must have been a time when the ideas surrounding the power of the snake were first fermented. What we discovered was that the widespread snake cult established a link between the concept of the Grail and ancient Sumeria, for it was here that that the Shining Ones – the 'fish deities' led by Oannes or Dagon – were said to have first emerged from the sea and educated the people of the area. The origins of the Grail could therefore be traced back to over 5,000 or even 8,000 years ago. Many centuries later, however, following the establishment of the Christian Church, those in power sought to erase all traces of the serpent. But Christian symbolism itself could not avoid being infected with the serpent symbolism associated with the 'anointed' or 'Christed ones' who preceded the Christ of Christianity. We have already seen evidence of this in the 'lizard' that enters the Virgin Mary's ear and exits through her mouth, an obvious allusion to the serpent shaman who enters the World Mother and is reborn through her mouth as the archetypal Logos or Word. The oval shape of the mouth is a metaphor for the RU gateway revealed in the symbol of the vesica piscis, and an allusion to the fact that this journey of spiritual rebirth really takes place inside the centre of the head.

Although the Church authorities sought to do away with the serpent connection, they also wanted to use the serpent peoples' archetypal 'solar god-king' without revealing his shamanic 'serpent-being' origins. The serpent and its associate, the dragon, were thus demonized. But we believe the main reason why the people in power in the Church wanted to get rid of the serpent was because of its link with the enlightenment experience, the very experience encoded within so many ancient myths and stories, even those contained in the biblical Old and New Testaments. In their ignorance of this aspect of the human experience, the people would have to rely on the Church as a mediator to the godhead that naturally resides within all of us. A god-like figurehead was needed, but one that gave no indication of the enlightenment process by which he reached godhood, a state that we all have the potential to attain for ourselves. This exclusion of the enlightenment experience from religious teaching has created a void in our knowledge of our own true nature, a void that has been filled by various philosophical concepts which have always fallen short of the original knowledge of the Shining Ones.

In the period before Sumerian serpent myths evolved, gigantic snakes were depicted on vases winding over the entire universe, sun, moon and stars. We also discovered the snake growing out of plants, chalices and wells. From this it seemed evident that it had been seen by ancient races as a symbol of the life-force energy, or quite simply 'health'. It also symbolized the resurrection or immortality they so desperately desired, and which was embodied in the 'serpent people'.

Spirals, Mazes and Labyrinths

One of the most widespread symbols of the snake was the spiral, which was also a symbol of the Mother Goddess or shamanic World Mother.

On early Middle Eastern coins there are images of spirals around the heads of gods, which underlines the significance of the head for the ancient world. This imagery also provides archaeological evidence for the widespread belief in the power of the snake and connects the spiral directly with the serpent gods.

The spiral is said to be the initiator of the labyrinth, which is also thought to symbolize the snake's path. To follow the coiling path of the serpent is to follow symbolically the way to immortal life. The labyrinth symbolizes the path to both the centre of the Earth and the centre of the head, the folding and spiralling path being reminiscent of the folds of grey matter within the brain. Here we are brought back to the significance of the head or skull, and the power it was seen to contain, which is why the labyrinth and the maze are also intrinsically linked with the Gnostic brotherhoods and are to be found all over the Christian and Muslim world.

The distinction between the labyrinth and the maze has to do with initiation. The labyrinth has one path whereas the maze has many paths, and many dead ends. A maze is about confusion and the possibility of being lost. It illustrates the esoteric maxim 'Know thyself' in that most of us can get lost and come to certain dead ends or 'resting-places of the mind' that we create ourselves, a situation created by the ego through its limited understanding of the Self and nature. On the other hand, the spiral labyrinth symbolizes the 'way of the serpent', that is, the way of the wise and enlightened one who takes the 'middle path' to the centre so that they can attain the superconscious knowledge that allows escape from the cycles of life, death and rebirth. This is an inner path that unfolds within one's own consciousness and culminates in enlightenment.

Going back to the pre-classical period, we discovered the earliest dragon probably appeared in Sumerian legends. The Sumerian word for 'dragon' was *ushum* and its origin can be traced back to 5000 BC in the story of Zu – 'Zu' meaning 'he who knows' or the 'Wise One'. However, the Chinese also claim that their dragons can be traced back to 5000 BC. We will quickly run through a few of the oldest legends in which we found links with our theory to show just how old some of the legends from the classical period are. As we shall see, these legends emerged largely from Africa, probably fermenting in the growing evolutionary power struggles that accompanied the increase in population and the emergence of different civilizations.

The Dogon people of central Africa, who say they descend from the ancient pre-dynastic Egyptians, have a sacred serpent called Lebe, who is the first or head-member of the 'living dead', that neutral 'alive-dead' state which exists between the opposites of life and death and is related to the positive and negative halves of a cycle (*see Appendix II*). It is this 'serpent' that first had the power to overcome actual death. This belief goes back to the origins of the Dogon and has been passed down by oral tradition. As a means of transmission, this is sometimes more reliable than written texts, since many ancient texts have been altered and manipulated by those in power.

In Benin, the Dahomey or Fon people have a great serpent that is seen as a rainbow named Danh, a name that is similar to that of the Celtic god Dana, which spawned the names 'Danube' and 'Denmark'. This serpent symbolizes the life-force and encircles the world as the Ouroboros.

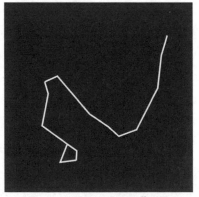

Figure 11: Draco Constellation
Image by Philip Gardiner

These and other serpent gods of Africa share attributes relating to creation, the formation of the universe, the stars, the heavens and the mountains. The serpent is itself in the stars, as the constellation Draco. But another element kept cropping up in our research into the early imagery of the snake – the 'Tree'.

Axis Mundi

In Sumerian and Akkadian artefacts we find images of trees or poles symbolizing the *axis mundi* or World Axis. This is the Tree of Knowledge and/or Life, and is the same tree as that found in Genesis and in many other traditions around the world. Invariably, a snake is either spiralling or twining up the tree or lying coiled at its base. Sometimes this snake is personified as the archetypal Goddess, as in the Tale of Gaileach from the Arthurian cycle (*see page 92*). In the Greek myth of the Golden Fleece, the fleece is draped across the top of a magical tree guarded by a dragon or serpent. In myths such as these, the serpent is the guardian and protector of the secret knowledge of eternal life. But, as we had discovered, the secret of immortality also lies within the snake itself.

According to author Adolf Erman, the Egyptians believed that 'if the soul comes to Nut or to the Serpent which guards the Sun, either of them greets him as her son. She has pity on him and offers him her breast that he may suck, and thus he lives and is once more made a child.'[1] This is a perfect example of how the serpent god or goddess was believed to be able to give 'new life' to whoever asked for it. It also indicates that the ancient Egyptians knew about the Elixir of Life.

We find a similar idea expressed in the myth of Osiris, who it was said entered the tail of the great serpent, was drawn through its body and came out through the mouth, as if born anew. The tail of the serpent represents the end of the old life and its head the beginning of the new life – an image relating to the Ouroboros. The Osiris myth is also related to the '12 hours of the Duat', the 12 hours of the evening or night-time, the 'dark' and therefore 'negative' half of the 24-hour daily cycle, during which time it was believed that the sun journeyed through the Underworld or Duat.

Another important figure in the Egyptian pantheon is the goddess Isis. Sacred snakes with oracular powers were said to have lived in her temples and it was believed that horrendous disasters would befall Egypt if the snakes ever decided to leave. Isis was given power over the poison of both the serpent and the scorpion. In one text she lays her hands on a poisoned child and casts out the poison. In several places Isis is seen as Isis-Meri, suckling the young Horus in images extremely similar to those of Mary and Jesus – a point to remember later on when we consider the symbolic serpent origins of Jesus.

We should not forget that the *axis mundi* was symbolized by the Caduceus, the emblem of the modern medical profession. Health was also intimately associated with the serpent in ancient Egypt, as is shown by the crown formed of the Asp or sacred Thermuthis, a particular attribute of Isis, goddess of life and healing. According to Hargrave Jennings, author of *Ophiolatreia*, this was 'no doubt intended to symbolize eternal life'. It was also Isis, the serpent 'Queen of Heaven', who, like the dog or wolf (sheepdog), guided souls through the 'twists of the Amenti' or the 'Halls of Amenti', another name for the labyrinthine Underworld. This is yet another image of the serpent as the guardian or protector of sacred treasure or knowledge. Isis and Nephthys, deities respectively of the opposites of life and death, became the dual-serpent – an association that recalls the *Pingala* and *Ida* serpent energies associated with the Kundalini enlightenment experience. The rising of these two serpents in and around the chakras aligning the human spinal cord is echoed in an Egyptian legend in which the 'serpent mother' weaves the red thread of life together with the black and white threads of day and night, thus ensuring immortality.

Egypt's mother of creation, Per-Uatchet, or Wadjet, was also a serpent, and the hieroglyphic of the snake stood for 'goddess' and eventually for 'Uraeus' the Sacred Asp, which later became one of the secret names for 'God' in medieval alchemy – a subtle allusion to God being both male and female, i.e. androgynous. The Egyptian Wadjet, Uraeus or Asp was a guardian goddess of the delta region and a pre-dynastic cobra goddess of Lower Egypt around 4000 BC. In the Pyramid Texts found at Saqqara, she is strongly linked with nature and growth. Uraeus, the Egyptian cobra, is the snake seen on the foreheads of pharaohs and was said to be the snake Cleopatra chose to use when committing suicide. This is not surprising since Cleopatra worshipped Isis, who was known as Wadjet-Isis in the city of Dep (otherwise known as Buto), and it was the 'fiery' venomous bite of the Sacred Asp that would lead her to eternal life. Cleopatra's 'death' was not the wasteful suicide we understand it to be today. It was a stealing of her soul from those who would oppress her by delivering herself up to life immortal and into the afterlife via the enlightenment experience. Cleopatra, or those who created the legend, saw immortality as being delivered by the snake, and the snake is the important part of this tale, not the suicide or the loss of Cleopatra's union with her lover, the Roman Consul Mark Antony.

The Egyptians believed that the Book of Thoth, now regarded as an important alchemical text, was guarded by snakes. Thoth himself is said to have incarnated 'as a serpent', and Sanchoniathon, a historian and writer thought to have lived around the thirteenth or fourteenth century BC, describes him as the founder of serpent worship in Egypt because of his ability to become the 'serpent of wisdom'.

And then there is Apep or Apophis, the great primordial serpent of death and chaos who was said to live in the Nile and who represented the black Void. Apep was worshipped by the Israelites as the Golden Calf and is etymologically closely related to Pope/Papa. He appears in another form as Typhon, the dragon.

One particular Egyptian god is now known to the Western world as

Satan. This is the ancient Egyptian god Set, whose name 'Set-hen' or 'Sa-tha-ten' (words possibly connected with the 'seven', 'suffering' and 'severing') became 'Satan' when the Israelites emigrated during the XIX dynasty. Set's serpent attributes led to Satan being identified with the snake. The snake's 'evil' connotation is related to our ignorance of the serpent energy, which is neutral and transcends the opposites of 'good' and 'evil'. Set or Satan is also associated with the planet Saturn, the ancient 'seventh' planet from the sun, the centre of our universe. An important god, Set or Sata was able to glide over the ground silently observing human life. He embodied immortality and was the 'son of the Earth' reborn each day from the womb of the Great Mother. He was the consort of the goddess Setet (Sati), who is said to have eventually evolved into the biblical temptress Eve. Sata later appeared in Russian folklore as Koshchei the 'Deathless' before moving on to become the dragon that must be slain to obtain immortal life.

Probably the most famous of all Egyptian gods was the sun god, Ra or Atum-Ra, the Greek Zeus. As the serpent, he is associated in male form with the sun and in female form with the moon. Ra tamed the serpent and, according to Egyptian magical texts translated by F. Chabas, a nineteenth-century Egyptologist and historian, he put the serpent 'in chains', which means he personified those Shining Ones who were seen to control the primordial energy of the cosmos embodied in the serpent. Ra also produced a special liquid that bestowed eternal youth. Said to be the most secret liquid, it was held in a sacred vase or urn.

This Egyptian myth alone indicates a link between the serpent or snake and the Elixir of Life mixed in the Grail. But the evidence of one ancient myth is not enough. However, the knowledge of the ancient Shining Ones passed over into the Hellenized period of Egyptian history, and from there to Greece. The Greeks not only took on the mythology and terminology of the snake, they also fostered it, cared for it and made it even greater than before.

The Greeks had many terms for snakes – *aspis, drakon, echnida, herpeton* and *Ophisi* – the latter being the name of an Essene cult and later the name of an early Christian sect. The Kraken is also a powerful Greek serpent, this time of the sea. The first two letters ('kr') are the same as the Sanskrit root *kr*, meaning 'to do', 'to make' and 'Creator',[2] thus providing an etymological link between the various cultures of the ancient world and also linking the serpent to creation. We also noted that another name for the Caduceus symbol is *Kerukeion* and this etymological link with creation suggests that the bodily process symbolized by the serpent Caduceus could be the process by which one 'creates' the cycles of reality.

Akeraken, another related term meaning 'great fire/light' or 'great one', is associated with the twin-lion or twin-jackal god Aker, who is said to 'keep ward over the wicked'. The same root gives us Cerberus, the three-headed serpent dog that guards Hades, the Greek Underworld, while Aker is sometimes depicted as two jackals. In early images, Aker is shown as two lions with either a human or lion's head, facing both east and west. Between his two lion bodies we find either the sun disk between two mountains or a Neter-god or Akhu (usually Sokar-Osiris) complete with serpents. The two lions of Aker face towards yesterday and tomorrow, yet another allusion to the opposites in the cycles of time, and the serpents between them symbolize the infinity or eternity implied by the name 'Aker' through its link with *Akh*, meaning 'spiritual source' or 'shining'. As an 'earth god' of Egypt, Aker was formalized as the Sphinx that we now see in Giza, which suggests that maybe there were once two sphinxes on the Giza plateau.

The Greek Iacchus or Bacchus is claimed by most etymologists to be the same as Ichthus, the secret name of Jesus. As Longfield Beatty points out in *The Garden of the Golden Flower*, 'Bacchus bore the same mystery name as Jesus – i.e. "Ichthus, the Fish".'[3] The name 'Bacchus' is part of the code that reveals 'the *aether* is in the serpent's head', for he was the son of Zeus (Aether), as Arthur was the son of Uther Pendragon and Osiris of

Atum-Ra. Known to the Greeks as Dionysus, who was born as a serpent, Bacchus is represented as a bearded man crowned with vines and ivy, two plants associated with the serpent. He is essentially a serpent god, and the sign of the serpent was Ichthus, which became a fish when taken up by the followers of Jesus. Bacchus is also the 'guardian spirit' of Islam.[4]

According to King Midas of Phrygia, Dionysus possessed the Philosopher's Stone. That is, he could 'turn water into wine' or give 'new life', and indeed it was Dionysus – a serpent deity – who gave Midas the 'golden touch', a gift both wonderful and deadly, like the snake. Gold was the symbol of immortality and as such was revered by the alchemists, who claimed to be able to transmute base metals to gold. Here the story of King Midas contains a subtle lesson. Not only was his golden touch both wonderful and deadly, it had to be used sparingly. The same applies to the gift of immortality: it is a gift that should be bestowed carefully. The ancients who held the knowledge of the serpent elixir would have felt the same, and so the story of Midas could very easily be the archetypal memory of a king who was let loose with the elixir and brought down the crown in the process.

The association between gold and immortality also brought to mind the Christian story of the Magi, who brought gold as one of their three gifts to the new king. Could this be an indication that Jesus was seen as a serpent god? Were the Magi themselves part of the serpent cult? Possible links between Christianity and the Shining Ones, the original serpent people, were taking on a whole new light.

Dionysus provided further links. His bride Ariadne, was made immortal, just as the Gnostic 'bride' of Christ is said to have become immortal. The symbol of Dionysus was 'IHS', sometimes 'IES', which derived from *In Hoc Signo*, the ritual cry of Iacchus, Bacchus or Dionysus. In *Antiquity Unveiled*, J. M. Roberts tells us that IES is 'the Phoenician name of the god Bacchus or the sun personified; the etymological meaning of that title being, "I" the one and "es" the fire or light;

or taken as one word "ies" the one light'.[5] Here we have the union of the duality in the 'one light' or the 'shining'. Roberts continues, 'The same letters IHS, which are in the Greek text, are read by the Christians "Jes" and the Roman Christian priesthood added the terminus "us".'[6] IHS is now a Christian symbol, assimilated from a shamanic and Pagan tale that had originated with the serpent people or Shining Ones. It became a symbol for Christ, who was himself endowed with the regenerative powers of an earlier god of the shamanic serpent people.

In *The Story of Christian Origins*, Martin A. Larson tells us that 'Dionysus became the universal saviour-god of the ancient world. And there has never been another like unto him: the first to whom his attributes were accredited, we call Osiris; with the death of paganism, his central characteristics were assumed by Jesus Christ.'[7]

The rituals of the followers of Dionysus confirm the crossover of the Greek element of serpent worship into Christianity, for the mysteries of Dionysus were celebrated by 'ingesting the god' through a magical meal of his body and blood, symbolized by bread and wine. As Roberts says, 'Like Christ, and like Adonis, Attis, Osiris and Dionysus also suffer and rise again... They are all alike in that their mysteries give immortality.'[8]

But there is yet more in the Greek mystery plays and traditions of interest to us. The Thyrsos, a staff similar to the Caduceus, is entwined with a vine or ivy, which we know to be symbolic of immortality and the serpent. It is surmounted with a pine cone, which signifies immortality and, some say, the pineal gland which, as its name implies, is indeed shaped like a pine cone. If this is indeed so, then the Thyrsos staff represents the human spine and its vine or ivy the life-force energies symbolized by the Kundalini serpents. The ivy is chiefly associated with Bacchus and Dionysus, but is also found in Egypt, Phoenicia and among the Hebrews.

We had found links between all the 'messianic' deities in myths and legends, and now here was a symbolic link. All the saviours from classical and Hebraic literature bring us 'eternal life', and their tool is the serpent, which is associated with enlightenment and with the knowledge, wisdom and 'powers' that come as a result. In the case of Attis, for example, we have a god associated strongly with the serpent. It was also said that the shedding of his blood through sacrifice brought back fertility to the land, just as the Grail brings fertility back to the land in the Grail legends. The ritual and celebration of Attis's death and resurrection involved fastening his image to the trunk of the pine tree, which is related to the pine cone of immortality that surmounts the Thyrsos. The pine tree associates Attis with Osiris, and the two are basically the same deity. It is said that Osiris was born through the mouth of the serpent, or that he was fashioned from the trunk of the pine tree, a symbol for both the Tree of Life and the human spine. This links in with the stories of the Phoenix, which is perched at the top of this tree as a symbol of the soul's connection with eternity. It also links Osiris with the serpent of the Garden of Eden, who represents his brother Set or Seth.

Attis was born of a virgin, as was the Greek Adonis. In his voluminous book *The Golden Bough*, Sir James George Frazer refers to Adonis, saying that 'The true name of the deity was Tammuz: the appellation of Adonis is merely the Semitic Adon, "lord".'[9] Now Adon, meaning 'Lord', can be applied to both Ea/Enki and his brother Enlil, the Mesopotamian god, who equate with the Egyptian gods Osiris and Set. This is not surprising since we are dealing with the same archetypal gods: the 'fish deities' of Mesopotamia, who were also seen as the 'serpent beings' known as the Shining Ones.

We had to ask ourselves, could it be that the idea of 'virgin birth' was an allusion to the erroneous idea that the snake was self-creating, sexless and androgynous? The idea was obviously symbolic in that the snake or serpent was seen as the androgynous life-force – the Spirit that was delivered throughout the body via the head and spine. This was confirmed when we looked further into the Gnostic mysteries, for we discovered that the belief was widespread. The various 'saviours' associated with the world's religions embodied the life-giving immortality and healing benefits manifested in the serpent or snake. It was also a Gnostic and alchemical ideal to return to this serpentine, androgynous state related to the fusion of opposites – in modern terms, the quantum state. Indeed, the evidence suggested that, at their very core, the world's religions were all the same. It was just the outward cultural dressing which differed. And at the root of them all was the snake – the giver of immortality.

The asp or sacred 'horned serpent' of the ancients was alternatively known as the *cerastes* in Latin, and *karastes* in Greek. The word *ceras* is the equivalent of 'cross', and in Greek the word *keras* means 'horn'. This may have some association with the horn of the Unicorn (*see page 132*), which protrudes from its brow and symbolizes the 'third eye' chakra vortex. The Greek word *Keras* is obviously connected with the Egyptian *Karast*, from which we get the name 'Christ', meaning 'anoint' (i.e. 'caress' with oil), as well as the Chaldean word *Chris*, meaning 'sun'. The figure of Jesus therefore has much in common with the sacred horned serpent, which is sacrificed on the cross and associated with both 'anointment' and the sun, meaning the inner sun of Eastern mysticism, the sol or soul. In Hebrew, *cerastes* might be rendered as 'Great Beloved', like Jesus. The word also recalls Ceres, the Earth goddess linked with Isis.

In Greek mythology the hero Cadmus was worshipped as a serpent and said to have created an army by sowing dragon's teeth in the ground. He is also said to have pierced the head of a serpent with his lance and pinned it to a tree. As already mentioned, the tree symbolizes the *axis mundi* or spinal column, while the lance represents the fiery, venomous, red-hot male energy associated with the Kundalini *Pingala* serpent. In Hindu mythology, the primordial waters were stirred with a lance or spear in an event known as the Churning of the Milky Ocean in order to make the elixir. This is similar to the creation story of Atum-Ra, in which the male-related 'lance' is his phallus, which is said to have arisen from the primordial mound and the primordial waters of Nun. On occasion, the Holy Grail is described as a lance. It could also be that the lance or spear was developed as a symbolic replacement of the poison-tipped teeth of the snake, the administrators of both death and life.

One of Cadmus's daughters was Semele, the mother of Dionysus (Bacchus), the 'serpent god' of wine. Dionysus rescued her from death but soon afterwards was captured by pirates. He stopped the ship, twined (i.e. spiralled) himself up the mast like a Caduceus and turned the oars into serpents that swam off. He then went to Tartarus (Hades, or the Underworld) where he rescued his mother. It is said that 'grape flames' ran through his veins, giving him matchless radiance (i.e. shining).

Ino, another daughter of Cadmus, had a white veil that conferred immortality against drowning. She was renamed Leucotha, meaning 'white goddess', and was seen as a sea serpent. She floated Odysseus across to Drypane and to safety. She also created a sacred lake of 'prophetic waters'. Some see her as the Lady of the Lake. It is possible therefore that the Lady of the Lake derives originally from the Egyptian creation goddess Nun, while the lake derives from the 'primordial waters' that were stirred to create the vortex or matrix of reality.

This brings to mind the many hundreds of water nymphs and goddesses found across Pagan Europe, all of whom seem to be personifications of the creation goddess Nun, a World Mother associated with the vortex of creation. How many of these nymphs and goddesses were linked with the serpent in this way we shall never know, but it seems that there were sufficient numbers to draw the conclusion that the serpent, the water goddess and healing are all intrinsically linked.

Ariadne, the wife of Dionysus, is the Greek equivalent of Ishtar or Astarte, who became identified with serpents. As a goddess of fertility, she represents the sacred force of the 'power of life' and is depicted wrapped in snakes. Links between Ariadne and Dionysus go back as far as 5250 BC. As the wife of Dionysus, Ariadne is the female consort to the male serpent – the moon to the sun – or, in alchemical language, Luna to Sol.

Another benevolent mother goddess or World Mother, Medea, was associated with dragons. She was also mistress of magical herbs and could bestow youth and invulnerability as she flew overhead with her winged dragons.

We have so far looked at various characters and stories in the great pantheon of gods from the ancient world and, as we have noted, there are some remarkable associations between the serpent or snake and healing. We now come to the most significant god to be associated with serpents and healing. He is to be found throughout the ancient world and even today he is found in medical establishments across the globe. We have already met him. He is Aesculapius, the son of Apollo.

Aesculapius – Imhotep

Although he is primarily associated with Greek mythology, Aesculapius or Asclepius is the archetypal 'medicine man' and the most obvious of the snake gods. As a man, he is strongly associated with the Egyptian I-Em-Hetep ('he who comes in peace'). This is Imhotep, the pyramid architect and builder of the twenty-seventh century BC, who was attached to the priesthood of Atum-Ra, the sun god. It is said that he became chief minister of the Third-Dynasty Pharaoh Djoser (Zoser), for whom he also became chief architect, showing profound excellence in building skills.

This part of the Aesculapius story seems to be data 'encoded' by those who have encoded clues associated with the Grail in many prominent events of history. Are we intended to understand this as being literally true? Or is the story of Aesculapius more in the nature of symbolic truth, conveying a more holistic knowledge that can only be deciphered when we recognize similar symbolic motifs, all of which seem to have been placed, deliberately or otherwise, around the world? We suggest that this 'holistic knowledge' is conveyed via the symbol of the serpent.

Imhotep is said to have been a scribe, poet, astrologer, doctor and physician-priest. He was so revered for his scientific knowledge that even the Greeks held him in high esteem, giving him the Greek version of his name, Asklejion, some 2,500 years after his death. Today, people across the globe know Aesculapius as the man-god who knew how to revive the dying and recently dead using the blood or venom of a snake.

The fact that Imhotep is equated with Aesculapius reveals certain links. However, some of these are exclusive to one or the other of the two gods, so need to be compounded together as if the two were one person so as to communicate important data. We would remind the reader that Aesculapius was the son of Apollo and Apollo is equated with Horus, which would make Imhotep the son of Horus. But perhaps this is all part of a clever code meaning that Imhotep was not really the son of Horus but rather that he was in receipt of the knowledge of the Shining Ones.

Figure 12: Horus Djed

It is said that Aesculapius' wisdom came from his spirit guide Cabir Teleshoros and the serpent of Epidaurus. According to myth, this son of Apollo discovered medicine when, after he had killed a snake, he watched another snake slither into the room, bringing a herb in its mouth which was used to bring the dead snake back to life. Aesculapius snatched up a little of the herb and thus gained the ability to restore life. This incident with the snake led to Aesculapius using as his symbol the staff with the one twining snake: the Rod of Aesculapius. Obviously, this was not the first appearance of this staff: the Staff of Aaron, the Uraeus staff of the Egyptian priests and the Rod of Moses are all similar but are less associated with healing. Aesculapius then became the god of medicine across the known world superseding the Hindu Nagas and the various other snake-related healing mythologies as Grecian ideas and philosophies were disseminated by the great military campaigns of Rome, Greece and Egypt.

Over time, the Greek god Ophiuchus came to represent Aesculapius. Ophiucus was believed to have been an ancestor of Hippocrates (460 BC), the great physician of Cos, from whom we derive the 'Hippocratic Oath' and whose symbol of healing was the serpent. He held the serpent with the venom which could both kill and cure. Like Ra, who had placed the serpent in chains, he had conquered it and could control it. The constellation of Ophiuchus was said to represent the serpent charmers, or Psylli, of Libya, who were noted for their skill in curing the bites of poisonous serpents.

The name 'Ophiuchus' comes from *ophis* ('serpent') and *cheiro-o* ('to handle'), so Ophiuchus means 'snake handler'. *Cheiro-o* sounds remarkably like the name given to the *Chi-Ro* monogram attributed to Jesus, which implies that Jesus too was a 'snake handler'. This is something we would expect if he was one of the long line of 'anointed Messiahs', each of whom represented the resurrecting god of the shamanic serpent people who could control the serpent energy associated with life and death.

Figure 13: Bronze coin, AD 200, from Pelopennesus Hygieia

A group of physicians called the Aesclepiadae established themselves in Greece, and temples to Aesculapius were built throughout the land, especially near healing springs, mirroring the older Egyptian cults of Imhotep. It was said that Aesculapius was taught the healing arts by the centaur Chiron, whose name is similar to the *Chi-Ro* mentioned above, and that Athena gave him the blood that had flowed through the veins of the snake-headed Gorgon. The blood from the left-hand side spread fatal poison whilst the blood from the right-hand side could be used to bring people back to life. These dual properties recall both the snake's power to kill or cure and the two serpent energies associated with the Kundalini enlightenment experience. They also remind us of the left- and right-hand paths of the old Pagan Wicca religion, which correspond to the traits of the left and right hemispheres of the brain.

We described earlier how Aesculapius had been initiated into the healing arts when, having just killed a snake, he saw another bring it back to life with a herb. Some say this herb was mistletoe, and mistletoe was said to be an 'all-healer', a remedy against all poisons. The story thus alludes to the practical usage associated with the first level of our Grail Triad.

Whichever way we look at them, the mythical stories about Aesculapius' healing skills indicate that the substance he utilized came

Figure 14: Bronze coin, AD 200, from Pergamum in Mysia, with healing serpent

from the snake. Whether it was the Gorgon's blood or the all-healing herb, it was the snake or serpent that brought eternal life – the Elixir of Life.

The teachings surrounding Aesculapius spread, and he was seen not just in association with, but actually *as* Apollo, Hermes, Thoth and Mercury, who all held the Caduceus-styled staff (the Rod of Arcadia), the symbol of the Shining Ones. These gods, either individually or combined into one unique god, were later to become the greatest of Gnostic gods, the god Thoth, the initiator of wisdom, writing, art and, greatest of all, healing, who in later centuries became known as Hermes Trismegistus.

But what about Zeus, the greatest of Greek gods? Surely there would be some indication to show that he was related to the ancient truths associated with the serpent? Although Zeus, the universal Aether and father of the Greek pantheon, is never depicted with serpents, as the Olympian Zeus Meilichios he takes on the form of a serpent to attend the spring rites of the Mother Goddess, Earth. This shapeshifting ability – an ability attributed to the shaman – would be only natural if he personified those able to control the serpent energy of the cosmos. As we further discovered, Zeus took the form of the serpent Ophion to avoid the ravages of his father, Chronos, the god of time, from whom we derive the word 'chronology'. (In Rome, Chronos is equated with Saturn.) Zeus thus avoided the two things we all fear the most: time catching up with us, and death itself. But even Zeus, the greatest of all Greek gods, needed to take on the form of the serpent in order to gain immortal life.

Zeus also had his own angels, the invisible beings known in Greek as *daemons*, which have become our Westernized 'demons'. They appeared as handsome youths or wise serpents, and Zeus assigned them as guardian spirits to guide and give wise counsel.

Although in today's age we know that Zeus did not really exist, the myths and legends about him were either created or adapted from older myths in order to teach us how to live and how to relate to our fellow beings. As such, they are part of what many call the 'wisdom literature' of the ancients. We cannot therefore ignore what these stories are telling us. We need to see that hidden somewhere within them are ancient universal truths, one of which is the utilization of the snake as an instrument of healing.

If we subscribe to the widely accepted belief that Western democracy came about because of the influence of the ancient Greek philosophers, then surely we can accept that other influences must have been at play as well. If democracy crept into our world through art and literature, and by means of war and invasion, then it is equally possible that the encoded influence of the serpent has permeated our wisdom literature and religious beliefs.

At the heart of our theory is the proposition that both the Holy Grail and the Elixir of Life were originally linked to the serpent and the snake. At some point in history, the knowledge of the mysterious powers associated with the first and third levels of our Grail Triad were encoded in the myths and legends of the second level which tell of resurrection, rebirth and immortality. On the first level, the snake is the source of the Elixir of Life in the form of a practical cure-all substance. On the third level, the serpent is the source the Elixir of Life in the form of enlightenment and wisdom. On both levels, the Grail is the mixing bowl in which the Elixir is created from pairs of opposites. On the first level the Grail is a physical bowl, sometimes made from a human skull, in which blood and venom are mixed together. On the third level, the Grail is the human head within which the two sides of our consciousness are united and the twin serpent energies of the Kundalini become as one in the enlightenment experience.

It remains a paradox that such a dangerous creature as the snake should have come to be seen as the saviour of humankind and personified in the resurrecting gods of the world's religions. Because the knowledge associated with the snake was carefully concealed to prevent it being abused by those who sought to have power over others, misunderstandings arose over the motives of the 'serpent worshippers' – the enlightened Shining Ones – and their enemies turned the snake/serpent into a symbol of evil. As a direct result of this sleight of hand, people have for centuries searched in vain for the Elixir of Life and the Philosopher's Stone, while the quest for the Grail has become a search for a fragment of some long-lost chalice.

Although we believed we had sufficient evidence to support our theory, there was one point that could have destroyed our entire argument: what if other poisonous creatures shared the healing powers of the snake? When we read the myth of how Orion swore he would kill all the animals on Earth and Gaia, the Earth Goddess, sent a scorpion to dispatch the god, our hearts began to flutter a little. Could the scorpion, equally as deadly as the snake, also be a healer? However, when Scorpius, the scorpion god, stung Orion, who fell mortally wounded, his victory did not last long. Just as Scorpius was gloating in the heavens over his triumph, Ophiuchus, the serpent god, stood above him and trampled him to death. The very act of his 'standing above' reveals his greater power, and this power comes from the healing element of the snake or serpent. Ophiuchus then gave Orion a 'sip' of his snake or serpent elixir, which restored him to life. This incident is similar to Horus bringing

Osiris back to life (Osiris is equated with Orion) and Jesus restoring life to Lazarus. It is the serpent elixir (or serpent knowledge) and not the venomous sting of the scorpion that brings the god back to life. Indeed, the myth reveals that the snake is much more powerful than the scorpion. We found no instances in which the story was told the other way around, and, search as we might, we could discover no other animal or insect that had the power of death and life, either in symbolic or real terms, in the same way as the snake.

Unicorn (One Horn)

Although we could find no actual creature that equated with the snake in literature, history or mythology, we did find a fabled animal with similar properties: the Unicorn. Nobody is really certain why this horse-like beast has a twisting snake-like horn protruding from its forehead, though some say that it relates to the 'horns of Moses'. When Moses came down from the mountain having received the wisdom of God on tablets of stone, it is said that 'rays of light' emerged from his head as a sign that he had just absorbed the wisdom of the great Shining One. The words for 'rays of light' and 'horn' are the same and thus horns are utilized in Gnostic and Christian imagery to show the god-like 'shining' nature of Moses.

There is another possible explanation, however. It could be that the Unicorn originally had the symbol of the Caduceus emerging from its head, a reference to the third eye, or sixth chakra. Why would those who created the myth have invested the Unicorn with such a device: a medicine staff, protruding from the forehead of a horse, entwined like the one snake on the Staff of Aesculapius, or possibly like the two snakes of the Caduceus? Perhaps the answer lies in the fact that the horn of the Unicorn is said to be an antidote to poison. But it is not only the horn that has healing properties – the blood of the Unicorn is said to bestow eternal life.

The Unicorn is first mentioned by Ctesias, an early historian on the subject of India who lived around 400 BC, in his *Indica* ('Book on India'). Ctesias claimed that it was similar to a horse with a white body (symbolizing purity), a purple head (royal protection) and a long single horn protruding from its forehead. It was said that one way of catching this fabled beast was to stand in front of a tree and taunt the animal. At the last moment you would step aside and, as the horn impaled itself in the tree, you would cut off the beast's head.

There is more to this little tip than meets the eye. The serpent is often portrayed as the protector of the Tree of Life, and so the impaling of the tree with the horn and the ensuing decapitation represent the twin themes of union and sacrifice. The decapitation ritual also recalls the Baphomet head of the Templars. Also, as we had previously discovered, the saviour is always pinned to the Tree of Life in sacrifice, and is always linked with the serpent.

The monarchs of Europe esteemed the horn of the Unicorn due to its legendary efficaciousness against poison. It was deemed 'chivalrous' to protect the beast, almost as if this were a hidden message to protect the Grail. The Unicorn became associated with the Virgin Mary and, as author John Baldock reminded us, there is a legend that it can only be tamed by a virgin in whose lap it lies down to rest.

However, Aelian, a Greek military writer of the second century AD, claimed that people had actually got things wrong and were being duped. They were being sold the horns of the narwhal or rhinoceros which, he said, had straight horns. The Unicorn, on the other hand, had a twisted horn, like the 'entwined snakes of the Caduceus'. So we were not the first people to link the horn of the Unicorn with the Caduceus after all, although we would say that its horn resembles more the Staff of Aesculapius, which has the one entwined snake associated with the first level of our Grail Triad, rather than the Caduceus, which has the two entwined serpents associated with the third level. According to Aelian, the home of the Unicorn was Tibet and India, the very places that were once the homes of the Nagas, the most powerful of the world's mystical serpent deities and India's Shining Ones.

In Africa, however, the Unicorn was known as the *a'nasa*, a word that brings to mind the etymological origins of the Nazareans (Nasareans or Nasoreans) as the 'followers of the snake'. The word 'nag', an alternative name for the horse (*hacka* in Spanish) also sounds remarkably similar to *naga* (cobra). There was also a goddess by the name of Hippa (possibly linked to the Egyptian hippopotamus goddess of childbirth, Taurt), who was sometimes represented with the head of a horse. She is said to have been the nursemaid of Bacchus, who has been equated with John the Baptist, Osiris and Jesus/Horus. So we have a horse goddess as nursemaid to a future head of messianic serpent worship and etymology, thus linking the Unicorn or horse with the snake gods. Author John Baldock informs us that the French still use the word *hippique*, which derives from the Greek *hippos* (horse), in connection with horse-related activities.

The Japanese Unicorn, known as *Ki-Rin*, which was borrowed directly from Chinese sources, is said to be covered in scales like a serpent. Could it be that the Chinese took the idea of the Unicorn from their western frontier across to Japan, leaving with it some resemblance of the snake in its appearance? The Chinese say that this Unicorn is holy and, like the messiah, is expected to come as a saviour. Is this another archetypal memory or a direct link with the role of the snake as the bringer of life? We found that the Unicorn (also known as the *reem*) was the crest of the ancient Kings of Israel.[10] As is well known, Jesus had to be of royal lineage to become the Messiah. Were the Kings of Israel a royal protectorate with the hidden image of the healing serpent?

Greek mythology also relates the story of Pegasus, the winged horse, who is said to have sprung from the blood of the decapitated Medusa, the Gorgon sister with a head full of twisting serpents. Pegasus later went on to carry the hero Perseus on his exploits. Why would a horse with wings, which indicate that is a spiritual or heavenly being, spring from the blood of a serpent? As mentioned earlier, the horse is symbolic of the 'astral vehicle' that carries the shaman into the 'other worlds' associated with the trance state. With regard to the first level of our Grail Triad, does it mean that something good, something *eternal*, can come from the head, or the blood of a snake or serpent? Are we to decapitate the snake and take its blood in some form or other? After all, it was Perseus who chopped off Medusa's head, so it was the victor who benefited. It was also said that Medusa's look could turn anyone to stone. Is this another link between the serpent and the Philosopher's Stone? Possibly. But if the serpent bites you, you may become paralyzed, rigid, like stone, or you may develop the elixir or serum that saves lives. However, the body also becomes paralyzed as one goes through the enlightenment experience.

Today, horses are injected with snake venom to produce anti-venom. Pegasus was a horse with wings greater than a horse, but nonetheless a 'horse eternal'. We were now under the impression that the Unicorn was nothing other than a symbol of the 'healing snake'. The hidden power of the snake had been turned into a legend, then a myth, and then forgotten. The legend twisted and turned like the serpent on the horn of the Unicorn until eventually the words and imagery took on a greater significance than the original truth, because the truth had been lost. The words, the etymology, remained, but the reasons were now mythical. For some reason the snake was the healer, for some reason the Unicorn represented the snake... for some reason...

Suddenly it dawned on us that, once lost, the truth of the serpent became instead a Gnostic truth, a hidden truth, a truth nobody quite understood anymore, a truth attributed to the Self, the great 'I am' as the 'Son of God'. And the snake/serpent became a symbol of wisdom in its feminine aspect, a wisdom for which there is no more powerful image than Sophia.

The serpent is Ophis; so too is Sophia (Wisdom), as in S-ophis, another name for Isis and the star Sirius. In most of the world's mythical, folkloric and religious traditions the snake/serpent is equated with wisdom, even in the Bible.

In the pre-Christian period, the rose was identified with Sophia. In the Biblical Song of Solomon, the bride is described as the 'rose of Sharon', and is the keeper of the vineyards, the vine being a symbol of serpent worship. Wisdom is equated with the rose in Ecclesiasticus.[11] The 'neutral snake' is often linked with both solar-fire and lunar-water symbolism. So, too, is the rose. There are also many images of religious personages with rose flowers springing from the forehead, much like the wisdom of the Uraeus, the Egyptian cobra seen on the forehead of the pharaohs. Our discoveries led us to conclude that the rose was the flower symbol of the snake, as mistletoe was the plant symbol. The rose has thorns and yet is beautiful; it inflicts wounds and yet saves. The Greek word for the grape, from which we get wine (a metaphor for the 'vital energy') is *rax*, which equates with *rex* or king. It also resolves into 'raisin' (meaning 'source-centre'), 'reason', 'horizon' and 'rose'. The fruit and flower associated with the serpent are etymologically linked to the kingly attributes of the serpent protectorate and an indication of the ancient truth itself.

Other Serpent Motifs

As we have already mentioned, the ivy is linked with the snake, and some believe this is due to the shape of the ivy leaf resembling the head of the snake. Bacchus/Dionysus both have the ivy on their brow, signifying the serpentine third eye, thus sharing the symbolism of the Uraeus worn by the ancient Egyptian pharaohs.

Symbolism also links the ivy with the *cornucopia*, the 'horn of plenty', with images of ivy coming from the brow of Ceres, the 'Ivy girl'. Ceres, whose name is possibly linked to *ceras* ('cross') and *Keras* ('anointed'), is the goddess of growth and the giver of increase. She is Isis or the Greek Demeter and related to the Earth Goddess or World Mother, and is therefore Mary, the mother, sister or wife of Christ. (If the Biblical Jesus is based on the Egyptian god Horus, as many say he is, then the mother of Horus/Jesus is also his wife and sister from his former incarnation as Osiris, hence the Three Marys, who, it has been suggested, are really one person.) The Naga snake deities of India – which we know as 'cobras' – are known as *chera* in some parts of India. *Chera* is similar to both *ceras* and the name 'Ceres'. Worshippers term themselves *Cherus* or *Cheras* and are related etymologically to the English 'cherry', which is itself associated with the colour red and the Hebrew *Cherub*.

The cherub is the cherub of Babylon, of Assyria, of the Orient. It is a fabulous beast, a winged animal like the gryphon or dragon. As we discovered, cherubs also keep watch over the Tree of Life (Hom) situated in Eden (Heden). Surely there is a connection here with the four Cherubhim, the 'serpent angels' who the Bible tells us guarded the Tree of Knowledge and Immortality in Eden where the serpent or snake resided. According to Greek legend, this apple-bearing Tree of Life was in the Garden of the Hesperides and was guarded by a serpent or dragon named Ladon. Indeed, the Hindu Mount Meru is also said to be guarded by a dragon. The Chinese tell of a great tree bearing apples of immortality which is also guarded by a dragon. This dragon is the symbol of immortality and of wisdom.

There are printer's marks showing the Tree of Life entwined with a serpent and with the word 'Brasica' written underneath. 'Printer's marks' were originally used as a secret method of passing Gnostic information among the brotherhood of the Guild of Printers and stem from the same period that saw the growth of Freemasonry.[12] Only when held to the 'light' were these symbols seen with the eye, and they were only seen with the heart by those with the 'eyes to see'. The Chinese equated the Persica

(*Brasica*) tree with the Tree of Life. Gnostics held a 'sacred life' rite called the Persica, a symbolic ritual intended to bring the power of preservation or immortality. In etymology, 'Persica' is related to Jasper, the Persian name meaning 'treasure master'. In the Biblical Book of Revelation we find a reference to Jerusalem: 'And her light was like unto a stone most precious, even like unto a jasper stone, clear as crystal.'[13] Jasper is also the colour of the Philosopher's Stone and is associated with the serpent. Although it has been defined as an 'opaque quartz, usually red, yellow or brown in colour', the ancient term for it, as described in Revelation, meant that it was clear and therefore void of colour (i.e. non-influenced) and a perfect symbol for the Void or gateway.

'Philosopher Stones' also have peculiar meanings that relate back to our earlier discussion about the hiding of the serpent under the auspices of the stone. *Philo* means 'love' or 'love of' and *sophy* means 'wisdom' or 'wise serpent'. 'Philosophy' can therefore mean either 'lover of wisdom', which is symbolized by the serpent, or 'lover of serpents'. It also recalls the way the Greeks included this same idea in the story of how Medusa, the Gorgon sister with the hair of snakes or serpents, could turn people into stone with just one look.

In the preceding pages we have presented a great deal of evidence from classical and ancient history, mythology and legend to link the serpent to the Elixir of Life. The Egyptians, Babylonians, Greeks and many other ancient peoples mixed a number of truths together to give us some fantastic tales. But a universal truth runs like a great string through them. At times we wanted to pull hard on this string to see what was tied to the end, or indeed the beginning. But the age-old question always arose: how long is a piece of string? Here one could give the amusing but cryptic answer 'Twice as long as from the centre to one end' – and in this answer there is a clue to the life-force behind all the serpent mythology. For everything, both past and future, stems from the centre and the

'Alpha-Omega' point of time, the Eternal Now. The beginning of the story of the snake was tied to the string many thousands of years ago, but our story could have begun anywhere. We shall never know just who first discovered the healing properties of the snake. We do know, however, that it was the serpent people, the Shining Ones, who spread the teachings associated with the snake/serpent all over the globe. We can follow the story of the snake through history and see where those who still held the truth moved to, and we can try to discover for ourselves who originated the concepts we now see in the stories of Arthur. We can also see the ideas associated with the snake in other cultures, and how they created their own protectorates and Grails. One of the cultures where the snake has been of paramount importance is Asia, and it is to this magical part of the string that we now travel.

CHAPTER EIGHT

Asian Myths

If our discoveries about the Grail were true, then what had appeared in classical Western mythology also had to appear in one form or another in the East. We were not to be disappointed. Asia was not just a confirmation of our theory, but also a fertile land of information. The serpent was at the very heart of the peoples' beliefs, their way of life and their royal lineages.

The Chinese date their dragons/serpents back to around 5000 BC and believe strongly that they are descended from them. The goddess Nu Kua, like Fuxi, her male consort, was half-mortal and half-dragon. Also referred to as a 'water being', she gave birth to shapeshifting human dragons from which the Chinese emperors were said to descend. As in Korea and Japan, Chinese dragons were generally beneficent and were held in the highest esteem. We found ourselves asking the question 'Why?' Why is the serpent/dragon always perceived as the giver and taker of life? Why is the dragon in the bloodline of the Chinese royal family, as in Egypt, Europe and elsewhere? The 'blood' of the serpent simply *must* be symbolic of something greater. That 'something greater' is immortality.

Serpents and dragons appear throughout Chinese mythology. The Chinese god of immortality, Shou-hsien, is represented by a white stag known as the 'celestial stag'. In fact it is not a stag at all, but a dragon. Then there is the famous legend of Madam White Snake, who is so distraught at her husband's death (which she herself has caused) that she travels to the Kun Lun mountains to steal a magic herb which brings her husband back to life. This peculiar little story became the subject of many films and operas across Asia, and bears many similarities to stories told about the Greek healing god Aesculapius.

The *Pan Tsao Kang Mu*, a Chinese *materia medica* dating from the sixteenth century, is made up of extracts from nearly 800 authors. It was first printed between the years AD 1573 and 1620 and contains some peculiar references to dragons. The book says that physicians who wish to use the dragon's bones ought to make themselves aware of the likes and dislikes of the dragon. Apparently it has a fondness for beautiful gems, especially jade, a green jewel like the emerald. Dragon's bones are to be found in watercourses and earth holes. There is no particular time of day useful for collecting the bones. The white and flesh-coloured bones are said to be the most efficacious in curing disease and of all the bones the spine is said to be the best. The brains make the 'white earth' which, when applied to the tongue, is of great virtue.

In the section on crocodiles (like the serpent, a member of the reptile family), the *Pan Tsao Kang Mu* states, 'The crocodile's flesh cures quite a host of diseases … but the tail, like the serpent's flesh, is very poisonous.' Under the heading 'The Jan She' or 'Southern Snake' (the 'hidden head snake'), we are told that the snake reveres woman, wrapping itself around her dress. We are also told that its fat and gall (poison) can be mixed together. This must be for medicinal purposes, for why else would it appear in a medical text? But as it is, the purpose is not specified and the mixing of fat and poison could be most dangerous unless prepared by an expert.

The *Shan Hai King*, a Chinese text from around 2000 BC, says that the 'Pa snake' can eat an elephant. This must be a reference to the boa, because of the boa's immense size. It also states, 'Gentlemen that eat of this snake will be proof against consumption.' The boa is caught by men who put flowers on their heads to draw its attention. Once it has been caught, they chop off its head and eat it.

In his *De Natura Animalium*, Aelian, the second-century AD Greek historian, states: 'They hung before the mouth of the Dragon's den a piece of stuff flowered with gold, which attracted the eyes of the beast, till by the sound of soft music they lulled him to sleep, and then cut off his head.'[1] We also found that Mercury, one of the two constituent parts of the Philosopher's Stone, is called the dragon.

Perhaps the most powerful snake symbolism is to be found in India. Placed uniquely between East and West, India appears to have been the breeding ground of serpent ideas. It was therefore not surprising to find just about all the myths from the Far East and West were cultivated in this single but large country. For instance, the great Indian goddess Kali originally came from Sumeria, where she was Kalimath, and by tradition the sister of Cain's wife Luluwa. Kali was a primary princess of the 'Dragon house', who, with her consort Shiva, was the goddess of time, seasons, periods and cycles. These details are what we would come to expect after looking at the significance of cyclical phenomena in shamanic lore. As the World Mother, Kali was the controller of immortality. She was later to be worshipped by the Thugees, the descendants of the Assassins, of whom we spoke earlier in connection with the Knights Templar.

We always see a courting couple in Indian myths, who may represent the shaman and the *shamanka* or shamaness who empowers him to enter the Underworld which is itself represented by the body of the archetypal shamaness or Goddess.

But most intriguing of all was the peculiar 'royal dynasty' of the Indians. This family was said to descend from snakes and to possess the immortality given to them from the blood of the snake. Was this why it was also important for Western royal families – for instance, the Merovingians – to be seen as the 'descendants of the serpent', the enlightened Shining Ones who protected the secret of the Elixir of Life?

Like the Chinese goddess Nu Kua, the Hindu serpent goddess Kadru is said to have given birth to the 'cobra people' or 'serpent people' known as the Nagas, who retain immortality by drinking Kadru's divine and lunar blood. As we were to discover, the reason why the blood of the snake or serpent was called 'lunar blood' and was thus associated with the feminine principle was that the venom of the snake was already associated with the masculine principle, as expressed in the internal processes related to the Kundalini enlightenment experience.

The Naga Serpents

The Sanskrit term *Naga* or *Naja*, meaning 'serpent' or 'cobra', became the name for various groups of serpent deities and demi-god humans who dwelt in the beautiful Underworld or Patalas in the city of Bhogravati and guarded great treasures, sometimes bestowing them on their human subjects. The Nagas were said to be 'underwater serpents', a reminder of the 'fish deities' who came to Mesopotamia from the sea and the Merovingian kings who claimed descent from a 'sea serpent'. Here we also have a remarkable similarity to the later Arthurian and pan-European myths of healing waters and serpent and dragon guardians of great treasures.

It may be that India, along with Egypt, is at the root of much of the serpent worship in the West as well as our ideas of the Grail. Many have said that Aryan (Iranian) myths of the Grail came to England with the Roman conquest. Serpent worship was rife in India way back into at least the third millennium BC, before Vedic-Aryan intrusions into India, and without doubt influenced the ancient Hindu texts of the *Vedas*, *Upanishads* and *Mahabharat*.

The Nagas are said to have three kings, the greatest of whom is Sheshnaga ('eternal cobra'), who was born from the remains of creation. He has 1,000 heads formed into a giant hood – a reminder of the crown chakra symbolized by a lotus flower with 1,000 petals. Many have said that this was the origin of the halo now seen in images of Christian saints.

The second Naga king is Vashuki, who is a more important god for our purposes. The story runs that gods were weak because they were divided between *Devas* (angels or Shining Ones) and *Asuras* (demons) and so Lord Vishnu came up with an idea. His plan recommended 'churning the cosmic sea of milk', the *Kurma* of Hindu tradition which is an aspect of Vishnu himself. Vishnu's purpose was to dredge up the elixir of immortality from the bottom of the sea. This would bring strength back to the angels and enable them to defeat the demons. However, the task in hand was far too great for the angels alone and so they enlisted the help of the demons with the idea that they would share in the elixir. Vishnu then dived into the cosmic sea with Mount Meru on his back. The serpent god Vashuki was then wound around the mountain and the gods and demons pulled at both ends of this giant snake, thus churning the great ocean. Back and forth they pulled until Vashuki started to feel nauseated and belched fire into the demons' faces. Eventually Vashuki was so ill that he vomited up a great poisonous cloud that threatened to kill all living things. Shiva saved the day by swallowing up the poison and thus saving the world. The allegory extends further than this, however, for the gods were also dredging up the Elixir of Life. Eventually they got their elixir and fooled the demons out of their share. The snake Vashuki was thus the tool used to acquire the elixir. It was also an extremely dangerous creature, issuing poison – life and death. But without the serpent or these 'serpent energies', the elixir would not have been discovered.

If we look to Sumeria and the Babylonian Epic of Gilgamesh, we find the story of the 'plant of eternal life', which resides at the bottom of the ocean. Gilgamesh dived in and recovered the plant. However, while he was resting on the shore a snake came along and ate the plant, providing us with a further illustration that the snake is believed to hold the key to immortal life.

The third Naga king, Taksaka, is more of an earthly being than a god. His story begins the *Mahabahrat*. There are stories of more poisoning and the idea of the 'wisdom of the serpent king' is introduced. The story that the Nagas retreated to the Underworld, where they reside to this day, is similar to the hero legends we find all around the globe. It is also in keeping with the growing belief that these ancient cultures may have disappeared beneath the sea due to a global catastrophe of some kind. As Jung points out, most of the world's heroes have snake legends attributed to them, in symbolism or in myth, and most of them disappeared into an 'underworld' of one kind or another. This agrees with what we have been saying about shamanic entry into the Underworld, the collective unconscious, and the process that grants enlightenment to the individual and through which one is 'reborn'.

One of the most interesting points about the Indian Naga myths is the idea that the women of the race, the *Nagin*, are strikingly beautiful. They have the shamanic ability to shapeshift and have a precious gem (an emerald) that grants them magical powers embedded in their skulls. These 'female snakes' marry earthly princes. Indeed Arjun (John), the hero of the *Mahabharat*, marries the Nag Princess Ulupi, who provides him with protection from all underwater creatures. Their marriage recalls the Chinese and Japanese myths of royal dragon descent. Indeed, several royal families in India claim descent from the Naga. The royalty of Manipur in north-eastern India trace their lineage back to AD 33 and the union of a 'serpent princess' with a human. The same can be said of the southern Indian Pallavas.

There are possible links here with the story of Jesus, especially when we consider that the Hindus influenced the Essenes. In *The Wonder that was India*, A. L Basham points out similarities between Essene and New Testament texts and the Pali scriptures. The Essenes, a group who encoded information relating to the Grail, had their own Ophite cult and 'snake medicine' texts. It could be that Jesus was seen as the serpent king who resulted from the union of a serpent (the vital life-force or Holy Spirit) and a snake princess, who, theoretically, would be a 'virgin' (the serpent mother). The date of AD 33 fits remarkably well with the time that Jesus is said to have gone to the 'heavenly kingdom', which, after all, is also the realm of the Nagas.

One Indian story tells of a farmer who accidentally kills a group of young snakes. The mother snake returns and in anger bites the farmer, his wife and children whilst they are asleep. She then goes in search of the farmer's daughter who is already married and lives out of town. However, when she arrives she finds her worshipping an image of the snake and asking for forgiveness for the errors made by her and her family. The mother snake then feels so bad that she gives the daughter some nectar or elixir, which is used to bring her entire family back to life. The first part of this story illustrates the effects of the venom of the snake, the second part the effects of the blood or antidote. Once again, the snake is presented as the purveyor of life and death.

There are also many stories of Naga 'snake maidens' residing near water and offering all manner of healing remedies, including marriage. Similarities with the Grail-related Arthurian legends, the Lady in the Lake and the many Celtic Lady in the Lake images are obvious.

The Guardian and the Treasure

Although the royal serpent lineage of ancient India is well hidden within Hinduism, Jainism and Buddhism, it is nevertheless a profound element of Indian mythology, but the lineage's possession of unique 'snake elixir' secrets was watered down with the passage of time.

Close by in Vietnam there is a similar tale about Po Nagar, the first Empress, who united the Cham people and taught them how to cultivate rice. More importantly, she also taught them how to use medicine. So, the idea of the Naga spread, especially in connection with the snake, medicine and a royal lineage.

As with Egyptian shrines of Isis, the cobra is said to still haunt Hindu temples. At the sound of the priest, it issues from a hole to accept oblations of milk. This snake is said to be the special keeper of concealed treasure, as it was many hundreds of years ago. The idea of a serpent guarding great treasure is worldwide and has come down to us in stories of a sleeping guardian dragon that must be overcome by a hero before he can receive the treasure. The sleeping dragon, however, is really only a reflection of the 'sleeping' hero or heroine representing their unconsciousness of the Source, which is itself the 'treasure' they must win in order to 'awaken'.

The guarded treasure is always gold and when mixed with the 'lunar oil' of silver, the *aurum potabile* or 'solar oil' of gold was held to be a 'Great Arcanum' fit to be used on most diseases. Indeed, dissolved gold was held to be the Elixir of Life, the divine antidote to disease and death. However, gold is not really gold, nor is 'lunar oil' oil from the moon or silver. They are metaphors used by the serpent people to communicate their secret teachings. A clue to their symbolic meaning lies in the 'guardian'. Serpents or dragons *always* guard the treasure, and only the serpent is seen as both a solar and lunar symbol. Quite simply, the serpent not only guards the treasure – it *is* the treasure. Where better to hide the secret than in the very thing which is said to guard it?

We find evidence for this in folk tales from other parts of the world. For instance, in the tale of Mindia the 'Snake Eater' from the mountainous regions of Georgia, Mindia was taken prisoner and noticed that his captors ate snake meat, from which they derived great supernatural powers. Hunger drove Mindia one day to steal and eat a piece of the meat, from which he acquired great physical and mental abilities. When he escaped, he took this idea back to his tribe, which became wise and strong.

In many myths, the Elixir of Life – the *Ambrosia, Soma, Amrita* or 'deathless drink' – is said to reside within the blood of a monster with dragon or snake-like features. The snake medicine of the Chinese is but a residue of this ancient knowledge. *Ambrosia* literally means 'food' or 'nectar of the gods'.

Amrita or *Amrit*, which means 'deathlessness' or 'nectar', is a form of drink used by Sikhs in their rituals. It is a solution of sugar crystals dissolved in water by stirring with a double-edged sword in similar fashion to a phallus, lance or spear stirring the 'primordial waters' of the Void, or the 'churning of the oceans' in Hindu mythology. The mixture is probably nothing like its original form, which we believe to have been both the venom and the blood and the related enlightenment experience. Nonetheless, the fact that only initiates drink it indicates its importance and reveals that even now it remains the remit of the 'chosen few' to receive the elixir. It is therefore little wonder that only a select élite can undertake the journey of the Grail and that the initiation rituals of the Grail-related myths are so difficult. To tread the path of the 'Serpent Grail' meant being part of the correct bloodline, i.e. being 'pure' and being ultimately prepared to face your own death should that purity be lacking.

One Asian legend of Garuda, a deity who is half-man, half-bird (similar to Quetzalcoatl of the Toltecs), describes him as the offspring of Kasyapa and Diti, and recalls the legend of the Phoenix who laid a mystical egg. It is said that after 500 years Garuda sprang forth from the egg and then flew to the 'Abode of Indra' and extinguished the fire that surrounded it. He then conquered the guards (the *devatas*) and took away the *Ambrosia* which he used to liberate his mother. When a few drops of this elixir fell upon the grass known as *Kusa*, it was consecrated for all eternity. (This legend is similar to the story in which the Norse god Odin transforms into a falcon or eagle and flies from the mountain cave – the Abode or Underworld – back to his kingdom. On the way, some of the mead he is carrying spills from his beak onto the earth and manifests as hallucinogenic mushrooms). It is said that the snakes received their 'forked tongues' as they licked the *Ambrosia* up from the grass, thereby bringing attention to the mid-point at which the duality of opposites is cancelled out. More importantly, the serpents – i.e. the shamanic 'serpent beings' – were said to have gained the secret of *Amrita* (immortal life) from this process.

Mistletoe, the 'all-healer' of European culture, and the herb brought by the snake in the tale associated with Aesculapius, was also said to correspond to *Soma*, the Indian god of the moon and the drink taken by shaman. In his book *Hindu Mythology*, W. J. Wilkins quotes the following lines from Hindu folklore in praise of *Soma*:

> This Soma is a god; he cures
> The sharpest ills that man endures.
> He heals the sick, the sad he cheers,
> He nerves the weak, dispels their fears;
> The faint with martial and our fears;
> With lofty thoughts the bard inspires;
> The soul from earth to heaven he lifts;
> So great and wondrous are his gifts,
> Men feel the god within their veins,
> And cry in loud exulting strains:
> 'We've quaffed the Soma bright,
> And are immortal grown;
> We've entered into light;
> And all the gods have known.
> What mortal now can harm,
> Or foeman vex us more?
> Through thee, beyond alarm,
> Immortal god, we soar.'[2]

This *Soma*, 'the moon', was the 'food of the gods', and was said to have kept them immortal. The 'manna' of the Israelites, described by the Rabbis as being 'like pearls' and in the Old Testament as 'honey-like', fell during the night like moonlight.

Among other mythological symbolism associated with the moon, *Soma* is seen as a crescent-shaped bullhorn. In the Druid festival of mistletoe cutting, bulls were brought in as sacrifice. The pearl-like berries of the mistletoe are also said to symbolize the semen of God. Sin, the crescent moon, was associated with Thoth. ('Sin' = *san* = 'saint' or 'shining'.) Indeed, *ophis* (Greek for 'serpent') may be equated with Apis, the sacred bull of Memphis who represented the god Osiris, and the bull Mnevis or Om-on-ephis, the 'one living, serpent light of Heliopolis'. The Merovingian dynasty of priest kings were supposed to have descended from a 'bull-serpent', the Quinotaur, which suggests that they possibly descended from the House of Osiris at whose head is Atum-Ra, the Egyptian father god equated with the Greek Zeus and the Sumerian Anu.

Milk and Honey

Honey is closely associated with *Ambrosia* or the Elixir of Life, the substance that gives eternal life. The Greek term for it is *meli* or *melissa*. 'Melissa' is one of the names given to Isis and occurs in the European legend of Melusine, who is half-mermaid or possibly half serpent (*see plate 29, and Melusine and the Count of Anjou, page 158*). Melusine is therefore thought to be another form of Melissa (Isis) who brings clusters of blossoms to the honey-drinkers. The term 'mermaid' may come from the Persian *mar*, which, according to Gould in his *Mystical Monsters*, 'may be supposed the same as that serpent which guards the golden fruit in the garden of the Hesperides'.[3] *Mer*, meaning 'place of ascension' and 'everlasting life' was a name given to the pyramids.

Britain was once known as the 'Honey Isle of Beli'. At Avebury we find Melsome Wood, with Milk Wood close by, and there are several close associations of the 'milk myth' with the area. This could relate to the widespread ancient and traditional practice of milk offerings to the Nagas of India. Milk and honey are always closely associated as symbols of the elixir. Solomon said of his Sophia: 'Thy lips, O my spouse, drop as the honeycomb: honey and milk are under thy tongue', which is where we find the venom sack in the snake. It is therefore worthwhile spending some time looking into the lactating aspect of various female deities.

Lactating Goddesses

The wisdom and immortality of the serpent are symbolized by the feminine form, especially in the East. When the serpent goddess is symbolized in this way, it makes a great deal of sense for her fertile aspects to issue the elixir. What comes across, however, is that the symbols for the elixir are white (milk) and red (menstrual blood). For instance, we find in the *Rig Veda* and the *Upanishads*:

> O goddess of waters. You have within you the life-giving sap. May you feed us with that even like mothers giving breast milk…

> Your inexhaustible breast, Sarasvati, that flows with the food of life, that you use to nourish all that one could wish for, freely giving treasure… [Sarasvati is the wife of Brahman]

> Putan placed the child on her lap and gave him milk from her breast full of deadly poison … he held her breast with both hands and in anger drank in the very life juices of the Asura woman.

In Mesopotamia, the early Sumerians described themselves as being constantly nourished by the milk of Ninkhursag, the great mother goddess who was also known as Ninlil. She and her consort, Enki were known as Shining Ones and serpents, and later became the biblical Adam and Eve. Ninlil is probably the source of most mother goddesses. She was also known as Ki or Ninti/Nintu and was a double-headed or double-eyed serpent goddess of the Earth. She has been linked with Ashtoreth (Asherah), the Phoenician goddess of love, whose symbol was also the double-headed serpent. She also merged with her daughter Anath to become the wife of Jehovah as Matronit or Shekinah. This was a goddess of health and fertility worshipped by Sarah (Sarasvati), Abraham's wife. The Syrians knew her as Atar Gatis, the mermaid. In Egypt, Ninkhursag was called Isis, the ultimate mother of the messianic line.

According to some, Ninkhursag gave the most potent of all life-forces, the venerated Star Fire or 'Moon-Fluid', otherwise known as menstrual blood. However, we need not go so far as to say that the secret of the elixir lay in the milk and blood of a woman. The symbolism is double-edged. At a literal level, the milk of the serpent goddess symbolizes the poison or venom; the Star Fire, the blood. Because Isis is equated with Ninkhursag, the double-headed serpent goddess, it is now obvious why there are many images of her feeding the sons of gods – the pharaohs – with her sacred milk.

The idea of the 'lactating mother goddess' passed into Christianity, where Mary's milk is said to have healing powers similar to the milk of Isis. The imagery takes on a new slant with the Gnostics. In the first-century AD *Odes of Solomon*, we find that the Holy Spirit opened her bosom and mixed the milk of the two breasts of the father.

The Greek goddess Demeter also had wondrous milk. She wandered the Earth looking for her daughter Kore, who had been carried off by Hades, god of the Underworld. Disguised as an old hag, she arrived at a village where the household of King Celeus befriended her. She nursed Demophoon, the king's son, taking him to her breast. Her milk aided the child to grow like an immortal being. It is said that Demeter anointed him with *Ambrosia*, the food of the gods, and that the boy grew beyond his age, although not for eternity, due to the sin of his mother.

The lactating goddess image can therefore be interpreted in a couple of ways. As a symbol of the human struggle to survive, she is the fertile pinnacle of womankind. Alternatively, and in most cases, she symbolizes the elixir-producing snake. On the one hand she bestows plain fertility; on the other, immortality. Further variations are brought into play by location and cultural differences.

The snake, then, is deeply entrenched in the ancient culture of Asia as the dragon in the Far East and the Naga cobra in India. In both cases it is the creator of the royal lineage, the guardian of secrets and treasures and the giver of immortality. But can we draw anything from the Eastern traditions in our journey to find the Grail? It is a well-known fact that our modern European languages emerged from an amalgamation of ancient Indian and European tongues. If language could be influenced in this way, then so too could beliefs and culture. Religion or faith could not have been separated from commerce and industry. Life was religion, and commerce was life. The two spread with each other. And just as our language is an amalgamation of the older European and Indian tongues, so too are our legends. We now turn our attention to see which great Western legends were once found deep within the traditions of the East.

CHAPTER NINE

Celtic and European Myths

In this chapter we are very much coming home again and heading inland, towards the mystery of the Holy Grail we know so well. We all have a wider knowledge of the Celtic and Pagan European myths than we may imagine, for most of us pick up small amounts along the way. Yet these ancient myths and legends have become so deeply embedded within our culture that we no longer recognize them as ancient. Also, they have changed along the way. The tale of Robin Hood, for example, is no longer what it was even in the medieval period. We have added our own fantastical modern-day effects and imagery, but when the feats of Robin Hood were recounted in the fourteenth and fifteenth centuries, the tale was already an old one that had been much altered, and with every passing day was altering even more.

With folk tales like Robin Hood, the question is not 'How far do we have to go back to discover its origin?', rather 'How do we know when to stop?' Did it all begin with the Norman Conquest? Or was Mr Hood really a goblin from pre-Celtic times? Nobody will ever really know for sure. Yet somewhere behind all the myths and legends there was an initial truth. What that truth was can be the most perplexing and difficult question to answer. Sometimes we can infer from the strongest thread of a particular story what it may have been. At other times it has been buried, for the story has been stolen, used by one propagandist or another and altered to meet the needs of the rulers of the day.

The Arthurian myth is very much like that. Even today, Arthur's story is used to promote a particular belief or point of view. One minute he is a great Englishman, the next a Welsh leader, a Scottish warlord or an ex-Roman soldier. There may even be some truth to the idea that he is all things to all men. However, the fact remains that people such as Robin Hood and King Arthur are amalgamations of older legends, of ancient gods and people. They are the guiding ideas from another time, incorporating the beliefs and hopes of days gone by, and with each passing generation acquiring fresh elements that produce an ever-evolving storyboard.

What is true for the legends of Robin Hood and King Arthur is true for many more legends. If we look at a strange festival that happens every year in Italy, we can see how a myth can alter over time, especially when influenced by the moving tide of imperial religious power.

The Snakes of San Domenico

On the first Thursday in May in the town of Cucullo, Italy, a festival is held in honour of Saint Domenico. What is unusual about this festival is the part played by the snake. Italy has a large number of snakes, and on this particular day in May they get everywhere. They are draped over the saint, held aloft by devoutly religious followers, roam the streets and even participate in the Mass, being held above the heads of the congregation as the chalice and Host are elevated.

It is said that in times gone by the snakes were killed and sold to pharmacists who made them into cures and ointments. Nowadays they are simply let loose or killed.

Christian tradition claims that San Domenico came to Cucullo when the town was infested with snakes and, like the Pied Piper with the rats, he charmed them from their nests and led them out of the area – an obvious allusion to the time when the serpent cult was replaced by

Christianity. The background to the story is as follows.

Long before San Domenico arrived in the area, the Etruscans had established a cult dedicated to the snake goddess Angiza, who was said to live in the nearby woods and to have been a serpent healer goddess, similar to the healing goddesses of the Celts. The tradition in present-day Cucullo of decorating poles with entwined snakes symbolize healing dates from the worship of the serpent goddess and recalls the Staff of Aesculapius and the Caduceus. You can still buy local treats and sweets made to look like serpents. Further elements illustrate the widespread worship of snakes in Italy. As part of private worship within the family, each household contained a shrine or *lararium*, where offerings were made to the ancestors in the hope of bringing good fortune and health. The ancestors were believed to take on the form of a serpent, and only then were they given the power to keep the family healthy. This is clearly another allusion to the fact that the ancestors were serpent worshippers, the same serpent worshippers who were displaced by Christianity.

Similar traditions are to be found everywhere and hide the real identity of the original culture – a shamanic-related Pagan culture – which was almost wiped from the face of the Earth by the spread of Christianity, but which survived within Gnostic serpent cults such as the Ophites. In our view, the powers behind the Church sought to exploit the serpent 'son of God', but at the same time had to do away with the serpent lest their congregation benefited from the enlightenment and 'serpent power' that lay within themselves.

Cultural links of the kind just described not only transcended time, they also crossed continents. But we have to look for these links in local tradition and folklore. One such link is the original French myth of Melusine, whose name is associated with honey. Her story recalls the Indian tradition whereby the royal lineage claimed to come from serpent deities.

Melusine and the Count of Anjou

The story goes that the Count of Anjou, who had links with the Templars, was unmarried and lonely. One day he mysteriously brought home a beautiful woman called Melusine. They married and were very happy. Melusine was kind, and a good mother, and the people loved her even though no one knew anything about her background. However, one thing about her confused the people: although she attended church on Sunday, she never took the Eucharist – the 'body' and 'blood' of Christ. When this was brought to the Count's attention he ordered his guards to ensure that she stayed for the whole service and took the Eucharist. The next Sunday, Melusine attempted to excuse herself from the church just before the Eucharist, but the guards stopped her and, just as the priest was about to administer the holy rite, she let out a loud shriek, turned into a dragon and took off with her two children.

This is a very strange story indeed. Where did its various elements come from, and where did the Count find this mysterious woman? We have no answer to this, other than to suggest the Count might have brought back some element from the Middle East that gave rise to the story, especially when we consider the links between Melusine and Isis. Why did Melusine turn into a dragon? Could this be a link with the Indian tradition that the royal lineage has 'serpent blood' in its veins? Is Melusine's refusal to take the Eucharist a Christian addition to the story to reinforce the belief that the dragon/serpent is evil? Or is it that she herself is the 'body' and 'blood' of the resurrecting serpent god, in which case to take the Eucharist would be for her a kind of cannibalism? Whatever its original meaning, it remains a very strange folk tale. One further point, however: it is said that the children of Melusine went on to be part of the royal lineage of Europe.

There is another possible explanation for this story. The Count of Anjou, who came from a family intricately linked with the Grail, was in possession of a profound secret. The historical René d'Anjou, an alleged Grand Master of the now infamous secret society known as the Prieuré de Sion, is said to have owned a Grail-style cup inscribed with the inscription 'He who drinks deeply will see God. He who drinks it all in a single gulp will see God and the Magdalene.' In our story, the Count of Anjou went out in his sadness and came back with Melusine, a 'dragon/serpent being', who fled the church. Could this be an allegory for the Church expelling the Count's secret, along with the children or off spring of the secret? Moreover, this secret somehow relates to blood and dragons/serpents and is symbolically linked with a royal bloodline.

The lords of Anjou were members of the Plantagenet family who became rulers of much of Europe. Some authors have recently claimed that this family, which was of the Merovingian bloodline, is the real Holy Grail. Other authors have pointed out that there were 'protectors of the Grail' or 'guardians of the secret'. The bloodline is only part of the secret. The real secret of the Grail family is what they protect – the venom and blood of the serpent – which together provide us with the Elixir of Life. It simply cannot be that the bloodline of the royal families of Europe, said to be the direct descendants of Jesus, is the true Holy Grail.

A clue to the real truth behind all of this lies in the name 'Europe'. Bryant and Faber, two distinguished writers on ophiolatreia (serpent lore), claim that the name 'Europe' is derived from Aur-ab (the 'solar serpent'), which is etymologically linked to the word 'aura' and contains the word ab, meaning 'wisdom', as attained from the Underworld. Indeed, the first inhabitants of Europe are said to have descended from a mother goddess of serpentine form, a formula that normally means the people of the area were members of the ancient shamanic snake cult. With this in mind, we searched through the various strands of Celtic and Pagan European literature and folklore to try to discover the role of the serpent in the religious and medical life of ancient times.

First, it has to be said that northern European snakes are less deadly than their counterparts in Egypt, Greece, Africa and Asia. Moreover, there are fewer of them and they are certainly not as impressive to look at as their brothers and sisters in hotter climates.

Second, we need to define what we mean by 'Celtic'. The term is generally applied to cultures in Wales, Scotland, Ireland, Cornwall, Brittany and the Isle of Man. There are arguments about the fringes of Celtic culture being elsewhere, but for our present purposes we shall stick to the traditional understanding. In those lands just mentioned, especially in the more rural areas, remnants of Celtic history can still be found today.

The Celts themselves can be split into two linguistic and cultural groups – the Brythonic and the Goidelic. The former is associated with Wales, Brittany and Cornwall, the latter with Ireland, Scotland and the Isle of Man. In all these areas we find that Catholicism established itself after a brief struggle with the Celtic Church and then Christianized the names of local deities so that, for instance, Brigid became Saint Bridget. The names may have changed, but the traditions of the Celts remained alive, for the renaming of deities and holy places, such as wells and ponds, helped to preserve them. Now, years after this mini-reformation of the Pagan Celtic Church, the vestiges of Celtic culture are still there for us to explore.

There was another benefit of this peaceful takeover. The Celts had been poor recorders of their history, for they were inclined to pass on their traditions orally from bard to initiate. Then the Church came along and started to write things down, even Pagan beliefs, thus giving us a unique insight into the past. Now, due to this remarkable preservation of Celtic culture, we are able to look back and discern certain myths, even beneath their Christian overlay.

The greatest contribution that Celtic culture made to the Grail quest was the addition of the concept we now know as the 'chalice'. Although in all cultures there had to be a container for the true Grail, it was not until the coming together of Christianity from the eastern Mediterranean and the Celtic fertility religion of north-western Europe that the sacred vessel took on such great significance. We can thank the very ancient idea of the cauldron for this. Although the cauldron is by no means uniquely sacred to the Celts, it is in Celtic culture that all the related concepts are brought together.

The Cauldron of Rebirth

The magical motif of the cauldron is not unique to Celtic legends. It also appears in African, Asian and Native American folklore, where it shares a similar symbolism. However, the most famous cauldron, and the one most clearly linked with the Grail myths, is that of Bran the Blessed.

As mentioned earlier, the Welsh *Mabinogion* tells of Bran's 'wondrous cauldron' which has the virtue of restoring health, even to the fatally wounded. (We find an almost exact parallel for this in the Greek story of Demeter.) Bran's cauldron was said to date from ancient times and to have come originally from Ireland, a country which, according to Lorraine Evans in her book *The Kingdom of the Ark*, had close links with ancient Egypt. If indeed there were these close links, then it is possible that the secret elixir of the Serpent Grail was used as a bargaining tool for power, possibly seeping its way into popular British folklore veiled as the cauldron that was already resident in its myths. The possible link with Egypt is also interesting in that serpent worship in one form or another was rife in Egyptian myth, legend and religion.

As a side-note, the connections we made earlier imply that, due to the internalized nature of the trance state by which one enters the Underworld, Bran's head could be described as his 'cauldron'. In terms of the related enlightenment experience, his head both contained the Grail (the divine spark of immortality) and represented it. It was cut off at his own bidding and buried beneath a tower in London, facing France to protect the people of Britain. However, King Arthur dug it up as a sign that the people no longer needed Bran's protection now that he was king.

Much like the Celts, the Norse also have a strong tradition with a cauldron, in this case the Odhrerir cauldron, which is said to have contained a potion concocted by dwarves from the blood of the wise Kvasir. (Note the use of the term 'wise', a term universally applied to the serpent.) The potion imparted occult knowledge and ancient wisdom, and was deeply coveted by the god Odin himself. He managed to get hold of it by turning himself into a snake and drinking the cauldron dry. He then took it with him to Asgard, the home of the gods, where he is said to have spat the potion into a vessel.

Let's think about this. All the elements of our theory, from the snake to the blood, are brought together here in a small and almost insignificant tale about a god who has to turn himself into a snake to gain possession of a 'wise' potion, which he then spits into a vessel.

The most famous example of a cauldron within the historical and archaeological context is the Gundestrup Cauldron. Although this unique artefact is described as Celtic, it originates from the culture of south-eastern rather than north-western Europe. We only mention this because it can be misleading to see the cauldron as being typically Celtic when it clearly shows evidence of outside influence. The Celts associated with the Gundestrup Cauldron are from the region of the lower Danube (named after the god Dan). They had migrated eastwards into Transylvania during the fourth century BC, and even ventured as far as Greece and Thrace, hence the Thracian influence on the cauldron.

The Gundestrup Cauldron was discovered in 1891 in a peat bog at Gundestrup in Jutland, Denmark. It was thought to have been deposited in the bog as a votive offering, although pollen analysis has shown that it was originally deposited on dry land and not buried. Archaeologists believe that it was probably made by several skilled craftsmen between the first and second centuries BC. It is 96 per cent pure silver and was originally gilded. Both the style and the craftsmanship show distinct Thracian influence, if indeed it was not made in Thrace. There is much dispute over its origin, with some saying that it may have even been made in the Balkans.

If anything, this wide-ranging argument over the origin of the Gundestrup Cauldron reveals one thing – the style of the artefact would have been almost universally recognizable. Does this indicate that of all religious artefacts the cauldron, as the giver of life, was the most important? Was it therefore purposefully intended to be acceptable to many cultures? Other cultures would certainly have recognized the images of their own deities on the cauldron. They would also have understood the story it told because they would have known the meaning of its symbolism.

The images on the cauldron are from a mixture of cultures, ranging from Greek to Persian, from Celtic to Indian. The gods portrayed on it can be cross-referenced to each culture. It also depicts exotic animals, such as elephants, and mythological beasts, such as the griffin. But only one creature draws the attention of both today's archaeologists and yesterday's makers of the Gundestrup Cauldron – the snake.

The deity most frequently referred to by historians and archaeologists on the cauldron is Cernunnos, the 'Horned God', sometimes known as Herne or Orion the Hunter, Osiris or Dionysus. Others have linked Cernunnos with Lugh Lamhfhada, or 'Lugh of the Long Arm', the Irish version of the Indian 'Savitar of the Wide Hand'. According to F. Graham Millar of the Halifax Center, Royal Astronomical Society of Canada, 'The other images on the panel are neighboring constellations – and, subject to artistic licence – they are in the right place.'[1] Ursa Major is facing the 'Horned One', Leo Major and Minor are there also, as are Hydra, Bootes, Hercules or Ophiuchus with horns, the Ass (now obsolete), Ursa Minor, Delphinus and Capricornus. This linking of the Gundestrup Cauldron with the heavens is relevant to our Grail theory because it links the most important figure on the cauldron with the ancient serpent god of healing, Aesculapius. As Millar points out:

> The maker of the Gundestrup Cauldron depicted the staff as a mythical serpent and very anciently, the 'Horned One' was resident in the constellation of Menat, which was Hercules plus Ophiuchus. As precession continued, the sky position of Menat ceased to signal the autumnal equinox, so the Horned One moved into Bootes … snakes were used to mark important circles on the celestial sphere; for instance, Hydra marked the equator. Around 7,500 BC the colure (meridian) of the autumnal equinox was marked by Serpens Caput, the snake in the hand of Menat. By 5,000 BC the colure had moved to the staff in the left hand of Bootes … Lugh was a manifestation of the ancient Cernunnos, formally dwelling in Menat, but later in Bootes.[2]

Normally not much of this would have been very important. However, Cernunnos, the main figure on the Gundestrup Cauldron who is often portrayed with the torso of a man and splayed serpent legs, is none other than the 'Horned One' of much of the wider world, who is also Lugh, who is also Ophiuchus. And Ophiuchus is none other than Aesculapius, the Greek serpent healing god and the Egyptian Imhotep. We have already referred to the Thracian and Greek influence on the cauldron, and now this further Greek influence reveals that the Celts understood the deeper significance of the snake and depicted it on their cauldron.

The Horned One on the cauldron is depicted surrounded by various beasts, which has led experts to consider that Cernunnos was a 'master of beasts'. He is sitting in a Yoga position, and Yoga is associated with Kundalini, especially the practice of Kundalini Yoga. He is also holding the binary symbols I and O in such a way that his spine could be said to represent the point at which these two opposites become one. In his right hand he holds a torque (the O), and in his left he holds a ram-horned snake (the I) by the neck, which links him yet again to Aesculapius, the snake-staff wielder. He who wields the snake is master of all beasts. The torque, which is usually worn around the neck, symbolizes the Ouroboros. Through its connection with the neck, it could also represent the fifth or throat chakra, the demarcation point between physical reality (the body and the four 'lower' chakras) and mental reality (the head or mind and the sixth and seventh 'higher' chakras).

The next most important image on the cauldron has been the subject of much argument. On the left is a tall man with a peculiar headdress, like a woolly hat with a tassel or a serpent emerging from his head. He is holding a smaller man upside-down over a basket or cauldron. And this is where the arguments begin. Is the man being thrown into the cauldron or basket, or is he being pulled out of it? Taking into account the many tales of Celtic cauldrons of resurrection and rebirth, we believe that if the vessel in the image is indeed a cauldron, then the smaller man is being 'resurrected' and sent back into battle. The question is, is the vessel a cauldron or basket? We are of the view that, amongst other things, it is the cauldron of 'rebirth' or 'plenty' referred to in so many Celtic myths. We are not alone in this.

In 1954, the historian Gricourt suggested that the scene depicted dead warriors marching in as spearmen below and riding away as horsemen above. Our own theory, backed by the substantial similarities within European mythology, is similar. In the first instance, the warriors are marching from the right towards the cauldron and the figure of a dog or wolf, both of which are situated on the left. The shaman is usually depicted with a dog or wolf as his companion, and this image has been drawn in the sky as the constellation of Orion (the shaman) and Canis Major (the dog). The latter constellation contains Sirius, the brightest star, also known as the Dog Star. In ancient Egyptian mythology, Orion is said to represent Osiris, the shamanic god of the Underworld. Sirius, the wolf or dog, also associated with Isis and Horus, could represent the Egyptian dog or jackal god Anubis, a deity of the Underworld, or, more likely, the dog-headed Thoth, signifying the gateway to the Underworld, the land of the dead. And here, on the Gundestrup Cauldron, the dog or wolf is guiding the dead souls towards rebirth, jumping upwards as though directing the men towards the cauldron. The men then re-emerge from the Cauldron (the Underworld) as the greater horseback warriors (the horse being a symbol of power). As they ride away from the cauldron and back into battle, they are led by a slithering snake. They have been reborn. The image on the cauldron is therefore communicating the abstract shamanic concept of rebirth via the Underworld or universal Void.

In the context of our Grail Triad, what we are really dealing with here is a second-level mythical image of the transformation process. As such, the image conveys two truths – one practical, the other mystical – relating to the first and third levels of the Triad. On the first level, the cauldron is now a tangible physical artefact, an original symbol of the Grail, which at one time may have held the potion of the snake, the Elixir of Life. On the third level, the cauldron represents the 'enlightenment experience' through which one is 'resurrected' psychically – that is, one is 'reborn' with a greater wisdom and knowledge.

This first-level concept of the cauldron as a container of potions is now seen in the witch's cauldron of Western folklore. Although witches' potions are generally deemed toxic and vile, they almost always contain toads or snakes, which is surely a folk memory of the original mixture of snake venom and blood. Today's image of the 'wicked witch' dates from a time when those in power within the Christian Church sought to undermine the Pagan Wicca religion which was associated with the ancient serpent cosmology. For, as the historian B. Deane states, ophiolatreia prevailed in Britain in ancient times:

Our British ancestors, under the tuition of the venerable Druids, were not only worshippers of the solar deity, symbolized by the serpent, but held the serpent, independent of his relation to the sun, in peculiar veneration. Cut off from all intercourse with the civilized world [something now hotly disputed] … the Britons retained their primitive idolatry long after it yielded in the neighbouring countries to the polytheistic corruptions of Greece and Egypt. In process of time, however, the gods of the Gaulish Druids penetrated into the sacred mythology of the British and furnished personifications for the different attributes of the dracontic god Hu. This deity was called The Dragon Ruler of the World and serpents drew his car. His priests in accommodation with the general custom of the Ophite god were called after him Adders.[3]

The word 'adder' is derived from Gnadr, who according to tradition stated, 'I am a Druid; I am an architect; I am a prophet; I am a serpent' – a statement that links the Druids to the 'Dionysiac architects' of Freemasonic fable. Many of the ancient gods and goddesses of Britain can be matched up with those of Greece and Egypt. Ceridwen, the goddess whose car is drawn by serpents, is said to be Ceres of Greek myth. Ogmius is a compound of Hercules and Hermes/Mercury. One particular Bardic poem, *The Elegy of Uther Pendragon*, describes one of their religious rites and identifies the ophiolatreia with Druid ways:

> With solemn festivity round the two lakes;
> With the lake next my side;
> With my side moving round the sanctuary;
> While the sanctuary is earnestly invoking
> The Gliding King, before whom the Fair One
> Retreats upon the veil that covers the huge stones;
> Whilst the Dragon moves round over

The places which contain vessels
Of drink offering;
Whilst the drink offering is in the Golden Horns;
Whilst the golden horns are in the hand;
Whilst the knife is upon the chief victim,
Sincerely I implore thee, O victorious Bell.[4]

The poem contains several clear references to the ancient serpent cult. The title 'Gliding King' derives from the snake's gliding movement. It is also an epithet given to Sleipnir, Odin's eight-legged horse which took him into the Underworld and whose name means 'Gliding One'. Another reference is the 'Fair One' who retreats to the 'veiled stone'. In other words, the serpent is moving around the stone sanctuary. Note also the drink offerings, which are in 'Golden Horns'. Gold is a symbol of immortality, and horns symbolize the venom and therefore the male serpent or snake. It is known that the 'drink offerings', similar to those of the Bacchantes, were of blood. But the association of gold with immortality informs us that the horns help to make the blood contained within them more potent as an elixir. Golden horns have been found elsewhere in Europe, at Tundera in Denmark, for example. The poem is thus a clear allusion to the older serpent cults which prevailed over Europe for centuries and an insight into widespread dissemination of the Elixir of Life. In this 'serpent Eucharist' we have a key to the search for the Holy Grail.

As we researched more deeply into the history of the Celtic people we found a great and once powerful race emerging from the mists of legend. They were said to have come to Ireland from the Far East. They had been 'banished from heaven', like many a great serpent angel. They were tall and beautiful, like the Naga serpent people of India. They were skilled in magic, poetry and hunting. Today they are regarded as semi-divine beings, half-human, half-angelic. They are known as the Tuatha dé Danaan, which translates as 'folk of the god whose mother is Dana'. The goddess Dana or Danu has been linked with the ancient Egyptian goddess Isis, the mother of Horus. Does this mean that these mysterious people who landed in Ireland and possessed magical powers and profound wisdom are the equally mysterious Shining Ones, who were also known as the Shemsu Hor, the 'Followers of Horus'?

When they invaded Ireland, the Tuatha dé Danaan brought with them four treasures, each of which is associated with the magical items of the Grail romances. These were the Sword of Lugh, a magic spear, the round Stone of Destiny (a dish) and the cauldron of their god Dagda. These four items became the Swords, Wands, Disks and Cups of the Tarot, and the Spades, Clubs, Diamonds and Hearts of our modern playing cards.

The chief of this great tribe was the god known as the Dagda, the 'All Father', who is equated with the Pagan god Pan and the Egyptian god Atum-Ra. His name brings to mind the 'fish-being' Dagon of the Philistines, who is otherwise known as Odakon or Oannes the fish or serpent. Dagda possessed a remarkable cauldron which, according to Grimm, 'spewed forth porridge – that great and ancient all-provider'. He also possessed a staff that could kill with one end and restore life with the other. Folklorists say that Dagda must be a cultural memory of an ancient agricultural deity, and that his association with wine and fruit betrays this fertility concept. The similarities between the Tuatha dé Danaan and the Naga, and the etymological links in the name given above, suggest that the god Dagda was either imported from the East or a universal deity. The tradition according to which St Patrick is said to have ordered the snakes out of Ireland also reminds us of the similar tradition associated with Rhodes. Could it be that in both cases the large numbers of snakes that were said to possess these islands were in fact the followers of the serpent cult?

We mentioned in a previous chapter the legend of Dian Cecht, who killed Meich, who was said to have had three hearts, each of which contained a serpent. Dian Cecht was a god of healing who was said to have dipped the Tuatha dé Danaan into a cauldron of regeneration to save them. Are we being told that he saved them by transforming them in some way? It is also possible that this story of being dipped into the cauldron (the Underworld) is related to the survival of the 'fish beings' or 'serpent people' after a worldwide catastrophe. We also asked ourselves whether the dipping into the cauldron linked the ancient rite of baptism with the snake. Perhaps the answer to this would be found in the 'healing waters' from our Pagan past.

To folklorists, the divine 'healing water' is known as the Water of Life, or more pertinently as the Water of Youth. This very title suggests that water – whether in the form of a lake, pool or river – was seen by our ancestors to have restorative powers. The Water of Youth is normally to be found in a far-off land and in all fables is said to have the power to restore youth, health and wholeness. In general, it is found during some great quest, usually with the aid of an animal or supernatural beast. More often than not, it is guarded by an underwater serpent.

The fable of the Water of Youth is found worldwide. In Babylonian myth, for example, Ishtar took the 'water of life' into the Underworld to restore Tammuz. The stories were so powerful that people actually searched for the real spring or pool in places as far-flung as the New World of the Americas or Australia.

In all probability, the serpent is associated with water because in all cases it appears as the creator god and the rain god. In many places it is also associated with the rainbow and, as the Rainbow Serpent, is found in America, Australia, Africa and even ancient Persia. This particular image of the snake can be likened to the Cosmic Serpent, arching in the sky to obtain his sacred drink of eternity at the head-end of the rainbow. This serpent is revered by many as the all-healer god, a culture hero and sustainer. There are many tales of this rainbow god and its peculiar initiation ceremonies, in which initiates are vomited up by the snake into a new life.

Around what is believed to be the site of ancient Nineveh, a city associated with Jonah, plaster bosses showing a man emerging from the mouth of a watery beast have been found. Could the initiation ceremonies just mentioned be linked in some way to the initiation undergone by Jonah in the Old Testament? Jonah, otherwise known as Oannes and linked with the name Janus, is clearly a serpent deity. Today, the beast that swallowed him is described as a whale, but in fact the Bible describes it as 'large fish' in a context that recalls the Leviathan, the great serpent associated with Kundalini, the Earth power and underlying force of the universe. The fish and the serpent have been interchangeable for centuries. Indeed, the Mandorla or oval symbol of the vesica piscis, now used by Christians as the 'fish' symbol for Christ, was originally the symbol of the serpent cult.

Sacred Wells and Springs

We found another link with the 'sacred spring' in Greece. As we mentioned earlier, Dionysus, who is linked inextricably with the worship of the healing serpent, gave King Midas the gift of turning everything he touched into gold. But poor old Midas even turned his daughter into gold. The only way he could 'cure himself' of this gift of the serpent was to bath in a sacred spring. In this analogy of healing the link between the symbolism of the serpent and the water is paramount, for the story tells us that the gifts of the snake are not always to be desired. The same is said of the Grail: those who desire it shall never have it.

Holy wells are to be found across the length and breadth of Europe, sacred places of a bygone age, now Christianized beyond recognition. At many of these places sacrifices from Pagan times, both animal and human, have been found. Today some of these wells are still decorated with offerings from the Earth, such as flowers or vegetables. 'Well dressing' may now be regarded as a quaint old English custom, but for our ancestors the practice was carried out solemnly and had a deeper meaning. The well contained the spirit of the serpent god, and to offer a sacrifice to this god would bring fertility and healing.

Researchers from the late nineteenth and early twentieth centuries give us an insight into this ancient practice. In his *Tour in Wales*, which was published in 1784, Thomas Pennant wrote about the village of Llandegla, where the church was dedicated to St Tecla, a virgin and martyr who suffered at the hands of Nero:

> About two hundred yards from the church, in a quillet called Gwen Degla, rises a small spring. The water is under the tutelage of the saint, and to this day held to be extremely beneficial in the falling sickness. The patient washes his limbs in the well; makes an offering into it of fourpence; walks around three times; and thrice repeats the Lord's prayer.[5]

Pennant himself made the link between the well and the serpent god of healing, for he wrote that 'if the afflicted be of the male sex, like Socrates, he makes an offering of a cock to his Aesculapius, or rather to Tecla'.[6] It appears that Pennant felt he had almost made a blunder by mentioning this Greek serpent god of healing, but he was right to do so, for the wells of Europe were linked in their entirety to the serpent-healing gods and goddesses of the past.

At many of these sacred watery spots, archaeologists have also discovered offerings of cloth or scraps of cloth. This is something that happened up until World War I and possibly beyond. It seems the locals symbolically offered bits of themselves when they were in greatest need of healing. It is like healing by association. The same practice is carried out in Africa and other parts of the world for exactly the same reason, although there the scraps are pinned to a sacred tree. This very human approach to the unknown reveals the unique attributes of the 'tree' and the 'water' that we have already discovered in the worldwide serpent mythology. It is the serpent god who – like Odin, Jesus and others – is pinned to the tree as a sacrifice, a motif later taken up by the alchemists.

We were still looking for a clear link between the serpent cult, the Grail and water when Noel Rooney, a friend of Philip's, sent an e-mail drawing our attention to a strange Hebridean tale. At first it seemed of little consequence, but as we investigated further it provided us with evidence that the Grail was indeed closely connected with the serpent/water worship of the past.

High up in the northern Hebridean Islands of Great Britain is a beautiful well, situated on a croft above the sea in the village of Melbost Borve, north-west of Lewis. The well is known to be a place of healing and is dedicated to St Bride, the name given by the Catholic Church to Brigid, the Celtic mother goddess, who is also known as Bridget, Brighid and Brigit. In local tradition there are still strange and ancient rituals associated with this enigmatic deity. Brigid or Bride has a white wand of birch, broom or bramble, called the 'sacred wood', which is stripped of all bark. She is also associated with healing and good health, and was indeed the Celtic goddess of the life-force itself. Although the precise origin of her name is still much discussed, it is etymologically similar to 'bright' and may thus be connected with the Star Fire – the menstrual blood or taboo 'Moon-Fluid' – which itself is possibly linked with the healing element of the blood of the snake.

Mary Beith, a well-known expert on the subject, has linked Brigid and other mother goddesses to the serpent gods and goddesses of ancient times. She also links Brigid with the Libyan snake goddess Neit, who was adopted by the Egyptians. Neit is associated with weaving, for she wove the world with her divine shuttle, and weaving is a common theme amongst serpent gods and goddesses because the zig-zag movement of the snake resembles the back-and-forth movement of the shuttle. Weaving is also part of ancient Gaelic healing rituals and traditions. The *t-snaithein*, or 'charms of the threads', involved the use of the alchemical red, white and black threads. The entwined threads of Brigid were used in a sacred ritual to bring about healing. The *barr a'chian*, or 'top of the head' ritual, involved winding the red threads about the neck while reciting a charm. Brigid was also said to have been raised by a white red-eared cow and, as we discovered, milk is of paramount importance with other serpent mother goddesses.

But to return to the Hebrides, these islands lie across a stretch of water known as the Minch, a wild sea at the best of times. The links between the Hebrides and Celtic Ireland are strongly rooted in Norse culture, the Hebrides having been invaded several times by the Vikings, who held the lands for quite some time. So what does this group of islands, culturally exclusive and ancient, with links to the snake cults, a surviving female healing deity and peculiar traditions now lost elsewhere, have to do with the context of this book?

In the eighteenth century, a certain Monsieur de Longueville Harcovet produced a peculiar work entitled *Histoire des personnes qui ont vécu plusieurs siècles, et qui ont rajeuni*, a work all about people who lived extended lives. He referred specifically to the Hebrides:

> In the Hebrides islands, west of Scotland, the people are so long-lived that, it is said, there is a cruel custom of putting to death those who, after a hundred and fifty or two hundred years, have become so decrepit that they are considered useless.[7]

On its own this little extract could sound fanciful. However, when we take into consideration the links between the Hebrides and the highly revered deity Brigid, serpent deities, colours (red, white and black), wands, healing and the unusual exclusivity of Hebridean culture, then we can discern the first-level practical application of our Grail Triad at work behind Harcovet's observation. It would be a fascinating project to exhume a few of the inhabitants of the Hebrides from the eighteenth century – and even earlier – to see if there are any traces of snake venom, enzymes, proteins and the like.

At this point we wondered whether there were any links between Brigid, King Arthur and the Grail. If Brigid were in some way connected with Arthur, then we might hope to discover a hidden link. Alternatively, if she were connected to the Grail, or indeed a chalice of healing, then this could point directly towards a serpent connection with the Grail through real historical references and an actual place.

According to Celtic scholars, Brigid, the Irish version of the Welsh Ceridwen, is the original Lady of the Lake. Yet when we went through the original Arthurian tales, written in the twelfth century in Wales, we could find no mention of a Lady of the Lake. Nor could we discover her origins in French literature, as we would have expected. It seems that this sub-aquatic pseudo-deity may very well have originated in Celtic legend and been incorporated into Grail lore later on.

Further research revealed that when the Romans came to the shores of Britain they associated Brigid with the wise Minerva, a Gorgon. Minerva's symbol is the snake, and she is associated with healing and sacred springs, wells and waterways, as can be seen at the Roman spa at Bath in England (*see plates 34 and 35*). Brigid also displays that unique duality we have come to expect from our serpent gods and goddesses, as she is also seen as 'fire', especially in the Kildare Brigid. This links her to the 'magical arts', as they were then known. These arts are also known as the 'Smithy', and it was the Lady of the Lake who gave Arthur his magical sword, Excalibur, which had obviously been made by a powerful smith.

Another strange association that has links with our story is the idea that Brigid owned a magical orchard of apples. Obviously, we could do no more than link this with the Avalon of Arthur's tale, the 'Island of Apples' that would keep Arthur perpetually youthful, awaiting our call as the 'once and future king' – a strange fact, since the owner of this orchard is Brigid, a goddess of healing associated with the serpent.

This fitted together so neatly, but as yet we did not have any link with the Holy Grail. There was plenty of information about the healing properties of Brigid and the serpent, but nothing to link this ancient snake-cult deity directly to the sacred chalice. Then we had a breakthrough ...

We were investigating the various legends about Brigid and her Welsh counterpart, Ceridwen, when we stumbled across the story of Brigid's Well and Ceridwen's Cauldron in the *Mabinogion*, the great Welsh folklore tradition.

According to the legend, Ceridwen lived on the shore of a lake named Lyn or Lake Tegid and had a son named Morfran (meaning 'Great Cow'). The name 'Lyn' is another version of the word 'Lin', which means 'snake'. Her son was so hideous that it was deemed the only way he would make it in the 'world of man' was to become a prophet or prognosticator. In order to make this happen, Ceridwen brewed an elixir that would give him great wisdom. Ceridwen and Brigid were also said to be keepers of the cauldron, chalice or cup, and to 'drink' from the chalice was a metaphor for receiving great healing, fertility and sustenance. The cauldron was also known as the 'cauldron of rebirth'. From our research, we concluded that Ceridwen and Brigid were serpent deities from the pre-Biblical snake cults. Their mutual association with wisdom, healing, cauldrons, chalices or cups, as well as sacred healing wells and springs, suggest that they were one and the same.

The Hebridean link and M. de Longueville Harcovet's eighteenth-century observation point to a belief that 'extended life', whether understood literally or symbolically, came from the serpent. The layers of legend over hundreds of years have all but eliminated the snake from the story. But it is still there, concealed beneath the symbolism, myth, legend and later initiation rituals. Sometimes it just takes a different pair of glasses to see it. And sometimes it takes a friend's e-mail.

Plate 1: The Grail Chalice depicted in stained glass. St Mary's Church, Scarborough, England.

Plate 2: A Naga serpent deity. Manipur, India.

Plate 3: The Ouroboros encircling the Holy Spirit as a dove. The illuminating rays of the sun emerge from the Spirit. Lichfield Cathedral, Staffordshire, England.

Plate 4: The infamous Uffington White Horse, England. In myth the horse is linked to the serpent. In science it carries the antidote to snake venom. Uffington may derive from Eff, the Egyptian hieroglyph for serpent.

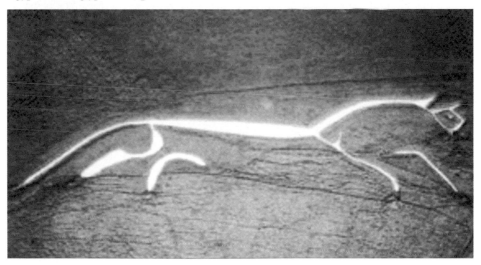

Plate 5: Hygeia, the healing daughter of Aesculapius, shown here with the serpent. York Minster, England.

Plate 6: The male and female stones at Avebury Stone Circle, England, showing the duality implicit in these ancient monuments. Avebury is linked to the serpent cult of ancient Britain.

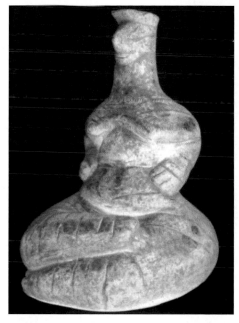

Plate 7. An example of serpent-worship as the Mother Goddess, related to Mary the Mother of God and Sumerian and Egyptian serpentine Mother Goddess images suckling the infant saviour.

Plate 8: Parisian medical doctor's tomb. Note the use of the serpent at the foot of the tombstone. Cimetière de Montmarte, Paris.

JÉSUS
Tombe la 3ème fois.

Plate 9 *left*: The Station of the Cross depicted here with the Roman caduceus in the background at an angle with the cross of salvation. The Dome Chapel, Paris.

Plate 10 *below*: Egyptian stylized winged orb of enlightenment with protective serpents. Cimetière de Montmarte, Paris.

Plate 11: Adam, Eve and the serpent tempter. The earliest record of the serpent in the garden reveals that it gave wisdom, knowledge and eternal life. Lincoln Cathedral, England.

Plate 12 *above*: St John with his dragon chalice. Winchester Cathedral, England.

Plate 13 *left*: Adam and Eve with the serpent which, unusually, has a human head. York Minster, England.

Plate 14 *above*: Serpent-headed column at the Pantheon in Rome. These miniature winged images are also to be found at the head of every column in St Peter's Cathedral in the Vatican.

Plate 15 *below*: Author Philip Gardiner with human skulls on show in a holy place - a practice dating back many thousands of years. Capela dos Ossos (Chapel of Skulls), Faro, Portugal.

Plate 16 *right*: A Grail Maiden depicted here with a broken chalice revealing the inside of the Lorraine Cross, a symbol for poison. Sainte Chappelle, Paris.

Plate 17 *left*: The Green Man within five circles, symbolic of the 'perfect man'. The Green Man is a symbol of fertility in Europe and derives from archetypal serpent gods. York Minster, England.

Plate 18 *below left*: Fifteenth-century Armenian wall painting showing St George killing the dragon. The defacement may be an expression of anti-Christian sentiment over the centuries. Byzantine Museum, Nicosia, Cyprus.

Plate 19 *above*: The Baptism within the Grail. Baptism - from baphe (to submerge) and metis (wisdom) - means to be submerged in wisdom. Kykkos Monastery, Cyprus.

Plate 20 *right*: St John the Baptist's head on a platter or chalice. The worship of the head is important to the story of serpent cults for it is where wisdom truly resides. Kykkos Monastery, Cyprus.

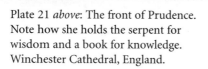

Plate 21 *above*: The front of Prudence. Note how she holds the serpent for wisdom and a book for knowledge. Winchester Cathedral, England.

Plate 22 *right*: The reverse of Prudence, revealing a bearded male head, suggesting that real wisdom comes from a balance between the inner male and female. (As above.)

Plate 23 *right*: Obelisk, Paris. The Obelisk derives from Basilisk, the serpent; Obelisk means light of the serpent. The Obelisk was symbolic of the upright spinal column or djed pillar of Osiris with the pyramidion or ben-ben capstone representing the head.

Plate 24 *below*: Isis, Queen of Heaven holding the Sistrum from *Mosaize Historie der Hebreeuwse Kerke*

Plate 25 *right*: The Asp and the Mirror, photographed outside an ordinary building close to the Louvre in Paris. Note how the serpent looks within, as we must.

Plate 26 *above right*: IHS – in hoc signo, the ritual cry of Bacchus or Dionysus, now also of Christ, here depicted upon the sacred chalice of the Eucharist, giving symbolic eternal life. Lichfield Cathedral, England.

Plate 27 *above*: Angels with the Grail chalice collect the blood of Christ from both sides, suggesting the dual process we must undertake to gain true wisdom and immortality. Lichfield Cathedral, England.

Plate 28 *middle right*: The serpent gnawing at the roots of the world tree, as in Scandinavian myth where the great serpent gnaws at the roots of Yggdrasil upon which Odin is crucified. Here we have the same scene, but with Christ crucified. Lichfield Cathedral, England.

Plate 29 *below right*: An image of the shapeshifting serpent Melusine, sadly eroded by time. The name Melissa was also given to the Egyptian goddess Isis, and derives from meli (honey), the nectar or Elixir of the gods. Newstead Abbey, England

Plate 30 *above*: The serpent Ouroboros encircling the image of time which has wings of flight, suggesting that we can escape this cycle and attain immortality. St Giovanni, Rome.

Plate 31 *below*: The Ouroboros. Note the rose at the centre, a flower closely associated with serpent history. Cimetière de Montmarte, Paris.

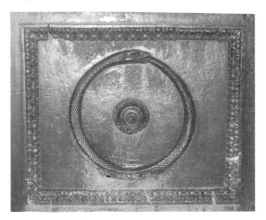

Plate 32 *right*: St Patrick eradicates the non-existent serpents from Ireland. There were in fact no snakes in Ireland. This alludes to the Christianizing of Ireland and the destruction of its serpent-worshipping cults. Salisbury Cathedral, England.

Plate 33 *above left*: A Christian Bishop's headdress, taken from the ancient worship of Dagon or Oannes, the fish deity – the wearer becoming the fish god. Algarve Museum, Faro, Portugal.

Plate 34 *above right*: The head of a Gorgon from a Roman bath. Minerva was a Gorgon and these strange deities are always linked with the serpent, and with healing and watery places. Bath, England

Plate 35 *above*: The Roman bath so important to Minerva the wise and associated with serpentine watery deities. Bath, England.

Plate 36 *right*: The dog-headed dragon slayer, depicted here at Mdina Cathedral, Malta. The Celtic god Dagda relates etymologically to the dog. In myth, the underworld is often guarded by a dog-like creature who slays the serpent to allow passage.

Plate 37 *below*: Moses and the Brazen Serpent – the central panel of the stained glass window. Here the serpent shall be lifted up in the wilderness to save the people from snakebites. Salisbury Cathedral, England.

Plate 38: And Christ shall be lifted up as the Brazen Serpent of Moses. Both images of Christ and the Brazen Serpent healer are depicted here, but the serpent takes the higher position. Lichfield Cathedral, England

Plate 39 *above*: Two snakes taking up opposing positions on either side of the tree of life which grows below the cross of Christ. Cimetière de Montmarte, Paris.

Plate 40 *below*: Seventeenth-century pharmacist's sign, Paris, showing a serpent rising from the chalice.

Plate 41 *left*: Stained glass window with the grail at the place of the skull (Golgotha). Winchester Cathedral, England.

Plate 42 *right*: This serpentine column or pillar may be linked to the Scandinavian Yggdrasil, or the Asherah poles of the Temple of Solomon, which were entwined with serpents for the serpent goddess in the Temple. Rosslyn Chapel, Scotland.

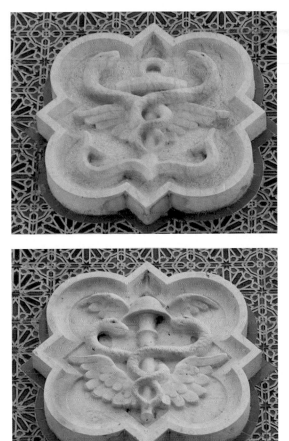

Plate 43 and 44 *above*: Two depictions of the caduceus. Note how in one image there is the Anchor (from the Egyptian Ankh which gave new life to the spirit) and in the other the winged Rod or Staff of Mercury. Faro Portugal

Plate 45 *right*: The Knossos serpent goddess with outstretched arms controlling the dual aspects of the serpent. Knossos, Crete.

Plate 46 *above left*: The serpent of St Paul who overcame their venomous poison on the Island of Malta and went on to heal people himself. Here the serpent rises from the flames – not destroyed in them as the Christian myth proposes. St Paul's Shipwreck Church, Valletta, Malta.

Plate 47 *above right*: The serpent upon the sword, shown here on a government and Museum building in Bastion Square, Mdina, Malta. The sword is linked in many ways to the serpent and also to King Arthur, the Pendragon or head dragon.

Plates 48 *left* and 49 *above*: Here we have two alchemical representations including the serpent in many symbolic poses from Figarum Aegyptiorum Secretarum, 18th century, from *Alchemy and Mysticism* by Alexander Roob, Taschen, 2001.

Plate 50 *above*: The Last Supper, Notre Dâme, Paris. Note how the 'sleeper' or the one in the hypnagogic state is directly above the Grail image and below that is the doorway or gateway to the Otherworld.

Plate 51 *left*: The solar serpent with the life-giving ankh. Luxor, Egypt

Plate 52 *below*: A Thrysos (serpent on a rod or staff) shown here on the exterior of Notre Dâme within a bowl, perhaps a mixing bowl.

The snake/serpent was not only well established within the Western tradition, it was central to it. In the East, the Americas and Africa, the snake is 'one with the water', and this was no different from Western and European folklore, for here too the snake was seen as part of our ancient waterways. However, all across Pagan Europe these healing water shrines were rapidly Christianized and Mary, the Mother of God, was installed as the new deity in charge. Mary, as we were to discover, was already intrinsically linked with the snake healing and water concept. In fact her very sign became a 'boat on the waves'.

We now know that the feminine water serpent is a metaphor for the *Ida* nerve channel and is represented by one of the entwined snakes on the Caduceus. However, when we were first looking into this area our question had been: Was it due to the water containing a serpent that the water was seen as so important? Or was it simply that since water was one of life's essentials the ancients had associated their most beneficent deities with it? At the time we had decided that the question was not important enough to support our discovery of the practical application of the Grail. We did not know that it would raise its head again. So, we continued our research through literature, folklore and tradition, hoping to find other clues.

We have already seen that 'Avalon' means 'Island of Apples' (from the Welsh *aval*, meaning 'apple') and that Brigid was by tradition the owner of the orchard. She is also said to have been raised under an apple tree and this links her to the biblical heroine of the Song of Solomon, of whom her lover says, 'I will climb the palm tree, I will take hold of its fruit stalks. Oh, may your breasts be like clusters of the vine, And the fragrance of your breath like apples.'[8] She says of her lover that he is 'like an apple tree among the trees of the forest, So is my beloved among young men.'[9] The apple tree is frequently linked with the tree of life and the tree of knowledge. The apple is the giver of immortal youth and the fruit guarded by the snake in the Garden of Eden, even though it is a

European fruit tree and not indigenous to the Middle East. A small link in a vast landscape. But why was Brigid the owner of the apple orchard?

A Slav story tells of an apple tree that bears the 'fruit of everlasting youth'. If one of its apples is 'eaten by a man, even though he be dying, [it] will cure him and make him young again', which reminded us of the saying 'an apple a day keeps the doctor away'. It also reminded us of the words of Wolfram von Eschenbach, from whose work *Parzifal* we quoted earlier: 'There never was a human so ill that, he one day sees that stone, he cannot die within the week that follows... Such power does the stone give to a man that flesh and bones are at once made young again.'[10]

A Greek myth tells how the tree was found with no flower or fruit growing upon it. A messenger was dispatched to the Palace of the Sun, where Apollo was asked by his mother, 'What can be done for the tree which would restore an old man to vigour and youth?' Apollo replied, 'The means are not difficult. A snake hidden among the roots destroys the sap. Kill the snake, transplant the tree and the fruit will grow as before.' Here the snake is related yet again to the 'tree of everlasting life', albeit in an opposite fashion (*see also plate 39*). Nonetheless, the snake/serpent is still the key to eternal life, for it is the bringer of both life and death. In stealing the life-giving sap, the snake in this myth is given possession of the Elixir of Life.

We find a further allusion to the 'new life' given by the apple tree in the popular story of *Cinderella*, in which Cinderella says, 'Little golden apple tree, with my vase of gold have I watered thee, with my spade of gold have I digged thy mould; give me your lovely clothes I pray, and take my ugly rags away.'

From Russia comes the story of Dobrynja and Gornytch. One day Dobrynja, the hero of our story, decided to take a bath in the river even though he had been warned not to. Suddenly the waters turned black and Gornytch – a huge three-headed dragon with seven tails and claws of iron – appeared. The dragon knew that this young warrior might try to kill him and, seeing that Dobrynja was unarmed, decided to attack first. The young warrior's horse bolted, taking his entire armoury with him, except a helmet with which Dobrynja fought valiantly and knocked off one of the dragon's heads. The dragon pleaded for mercy, saying that he had some young dragons that needed tending, so Dobrynja set him free. This was a mistake, for the dragon then stole a maiden. Dobrynja felt so bad about this that he saddled up his grandfather's horse and, taking a seven-fold whip, set off. In a fearsome battle Dobrynja killed all the hatchlings and managed to take off the dragon's two remaining heads with his whip. Before the poison from the dragon's bites had time to take hold, he bathed for three days in the blood of the dragon. He then released all the dragon's captives and rescued the maiden from the dark lair.

In this story, as in so many others, the dragon 'guards the prize'. We also find the poisonous venom and the blood mixed together, bathing the brave of heart. But this tale from the fringes of Europe moves us into a difficult realm, that of the dragon slayer.

Dragon Slayers

Although the dragon is clearly associated with the serpent, it is some-times difficult for folklorists to see the two as one. Yet we were loath to enter this complex part of the story for the simple reason that there did not seem to be any link between the dragon being slain and the healing serpent. How wrong we were.

Experts maintain that in all probability dragon slaying originated from the mythical concept of the sea serpent. The sea serpent is a leg-endary beast that frequents the high seas and also large lakes. Legends such as that of the Loch Ness Monster are remnants of such stories. In many ancient mythologies the sea serpents are said to have been defeated by the gods on high. From early days, the motif of the dragon slayer crept into the stories of these water serpents, as for instance in the

Hebrew story of Baal and Leviathan in which Baal, a progenitor solar deity, becomes one of the first dragon slayers.

The idea that dragon slaying was initiated from the legend of sea serpents is borne out by the fact that dragons themselves were originally seen as water beasts. They were benevolent animals that guarded treasure and can be linked to the Indian Nagas. These too were serpents from the underworld, water born, that guarded great treasures. The dragon slain by Perseus was a water beast and in Celtic literature it is said that St Patrick drove all the snakes out of Ireland but left behind the Peists (i.e. 'pests') – a general term for serpents – ordering them to remain in their watery abyss. It was not until later medieval times that the dragons left the waters behind and became creatures of land or even air. One explanation given for this change of abode is that the water needed to be Christianized and so the creature that had come to symbolize the Devil had to be banished.

Dragon slayers have come in all shapes and sizes, from St George to the fabled Beowulf. And it is in Beowulf's story that we discovered the glimmer of a link. Beowulf was a great Anglo-Saxon hero and probably the most famous of dragon slayers. His story was probably composed about AD 700 and is set around modern Jutland. Beowulf's third and final conflict was with a terrible dragon that had been roused from slumber when a slave stole its most precious treasure. The treasure is significant: it was a cup. Why would a dragon with huge quantities of treasure, much of which was assuredly of greater value than a cup, be so upset at it being stolen? This is one of the oldest European legends in which we find the dragon-slaying motif, and it features a treasured cup.

Another element of the dragon-slaying motif was already familiar to us: to kill the dragon, the dragon slayer generally chopped off its head (*capella* or 'cup'). This was so similar to elements we had already discovered that the link between the serpent and the treasure must surely contain a hidden clue. The treasure, the fertility of the land, the saving of the people could only be obtained by decapitating the serpent. The head of the serpent must therefore contain a special power.

The Jewel in the Serpent's Head

The power that resides within the head of the serpent is known in folk-lore as the 'jewel in the head'. This magic talisman is both ancient and universal, although the virtues of the jewel differ from one locality to the next. For some it is a tool for working spells, for others a love potion, but for the majority it is an antidote to poison. Even early Greek writers told of this powerful jewel and Pliny himself said that the serpent had to be alive when its head was cut off. Whatever this 'jewel in the head' was, it required the life-blood of the snake still to be flowing and was therefore a 'living substance'. Could the dragon slayers personify the initiates who knew the secret of the serpent, for the outcome of their exploits is to save the people and restore the fertility of the land?

The 'jewel in the serpent's head' is said to be green, like an emerald. We are told that Lucifer, the 'serpent god of the sky', came down to Earth and brought the Emerald Jewel, which became the Philosopher's Stone. According to many Gnostics, Lucifer is the true saviour, and any research into ancient secret societies will reveal this belief, which is one of the secrets of Freemasonry. The 'jewel' is known as the dewdrop essence of the rose, the 'Ros' or 'moon dew' of the alchemists. According to the Hindu tradition, the Ros or dew of the rose is also the *Om Mani Padme Hum*, which translates as 'jewel in the heart of the lotus'. Flowers – in particular the rose, lily and lotus – are metaphors for the Hindu chakra vortices, and since the flower is located at the top of the plant, the eso-teric flower represents the head at the top of the spine. Within the human head are the pineal and pituitary glands and the thalamus, which are symbolized by the three (sometimes 'golden') apples – the 'fruit of the spinal tree'.

In the next chapter we cross from Europe to the New World of the Americas. When the Europeans crossed the Atlantic, they not only took with them disease and warfare but also a culture that erased much of the history of the Native American peoples and left behind a complex mystery which, with the aid of our new theory, we can now begin to unravel.

CHAPTER TEN

American Myths

In the previous chapter we investigated the role of the serpent in European and Celtic mythology. We traced it back in time and space to the Middle East, where its origins were to be found in pre-classical and pre-Biblical times. But we were intrigued to know whether the same attributes were associated with the snake in other parts of the world. If they were, this would indicate that at some time in the past an ancient group of people had disseminated the myths about the serpent. It could also show that the healing properties of the snake were universally understood. Theoretically either scenario could be true, but evidence needed to be found. Therefore we journeyed, in literary terms, to the Americas, in the hope that we would find similar myths about the snake as the bringer of immortality.

We were not journeying blind. We both had previous knowledge of the American myths. Many years ago Philip had spent time with the aboriginal Indians, discovering their spiritual way of life. He had always been keen to understand their unique relationship with the Earth and the universe around them. Although neither of us would consider ourselves 'spiritual' in a religious or New Age sense, we could see that the reverence the Native Americans showed towards their environment was something we could learn from. Whereas our Westernized world thrives on modern technology and a capitalist infrastructure that has little genuine regard for the natural world, indigenous peoples have learned over thousands of years to respect their natural environment. They appreciate what they take from it and show that appreciation in their sacrifices to their gods and their mock replacements of the gifts they have received. Knowing that they revered the world in this way, we also knew that if there were any truth in the healing properties of the snake they would have discovered it a long time ago and possibly left clues in their myths and stories. However, the culture of the Americas is so very different from our own that we also knew we would not find direct links with a chalice, a lance or an American 'Holy Grail'.

We began by familiarizing ourselves with the history and mythology of this vast continent, and what we found initially was that, in spite of its size, the mythologies of its different cultures were relatively similar. By contrast, the diversity in Europe is extreme. In each country there are hundreds of localized deities, all of whom probably share common origins, though they now present very different aspects to the outsider. In the Americas, however, the deities retained similar names and identities over longer periods. There are some differences, of course, but not many.

We found that in the Americas the snake has been a popular folk symbol in both art and literature. For thousands of years it was seen as the creator god, healer and 'all things to all men', as elsewhere in the world, and would have remained so had the European invaders not demonized it and Christianized the religious culture of the indigenous people. Even today, however, the snake remains a symbol of transformation and healing for Native Americans. Moreover, they are rediscovering their heritage and reinvigorating their ancient ways. They have many important ceremonies that link the snake to healing and have developed unique ways of transmuting the poisons of a snakebite, or even multiple snakebites. The ability to overcome this onslaught on the human immune system has given the shaman or medicine man a unique position within his tribe, for he appears to possess magical, god-like powers.

For Native Americans the snake was thus much more than the

'creator of life'. It could also save and bring apparent immortality. This idea was not new, nor was it unique to the Native North Americans. There is evidence to suggest that it had travelled northwards from the more ancient and snake-oriented culture of Middle and South America.

In South America we have the Aztec/Toltec *quetzal* (meaning 'bird') and *coatl* ('serpent'). Putting them together gives us Quetzalcoatl, the Plumed Serpent god of Central America, also known as the Lord of the Dawn or Morning Star, but more especially as the Master of Life. This feathered serpent was even eaten in a ceremony similar to the Christian Eucharist. The Maya had their equivalent in the god-like heroes Kukulcan and Gucumatz. Quetzalcoatl, (as Votan), was said to have founded a great city called Nachan (Palenque), which means 'city of snakes'. Note the remarkable similarity in the language of different cultures in connection with the snake: Nachan, Naga, Nasorean, Acan, *nacash* and more. Like Dionysus and Bacchus, the Mayan god Acan is also a god of wine.

A peculiar tale, a kind of post-invasion story, is told about this great snake god. It is said that Votan visited the Hebrew King Solomon. As part of his expedition he was admitted into a 'snake's hole' because he was the 'son of snakes', which probably means that he was an initiate in the snake cult. The 'snake's hole' – the shamanic 'wormhole' in consciousness – led him to the 'root of heaven' (the source-centre), which recalls the worldwide motif of the serpent residing at the foot of the Tree of Heaven or Tree of Life. Votan then returned home and built a great underground treasure store over which he appointed a woman chieftain. The treasures were said to be strange jars, and nobody knows what they contained. The Spanish claimed to have found these treasured jars and, taking them to be of no material value, burnt them in 1691. If to Western eyes these treasures appeared to be of no material worth, then just what kind of treasures were they? Did the Spanish burn one of the last remaining secrets of the snake-medicine cult?

Obviously this story did not exist in its present form in pre-Christian times. The great Solomon must have replaced an ancient American serpent god, for Solomon was called 'the wise' and wisdom is inextricably linked with the serpent. Indeed, they are one and the same. Upon hearing the stories of the missionaries, the natives simply inserted Solomon into a slot that had until then been occupied by a snake god. A similar thing had happened in Europe when Pagan deities were renamed as Christian saints.

The links between Christianity and the native gods were never greater than with Quetzalcoatl, who was often replaced by Jesus. Like Moses, he carried a staff, and Mexican paintings frequently depict the 'raising of serpents' in an image similar to that of Moses lifting up his Brazen Serpent in the desert (*see plate 37*). There are other stories, such as the 'parting of waters', that betray the presence of links between Christianity and pre-invasion folklore.

Quetzalcoatl belongs to the Golden Age of the Toltecs, but according to their legends their end was near. The fabled Tezcatlipoca, whose mother was a serpent, presented himself in the guise of a physician to the ailing Quetzalcoatl and gave him a beverage that was claimed would restore him to health and prepare him for the long journey ahead. Today, the native people of South America still follow the order of Montezuma, their lost king, and look towards Quetzalcoatl for extended life because of this myth and its reference to the healing power of the serpent. The myth also tells us that the Elixir of Life was given to the serpent god by the 'son of a serpent' so that he might not only attain immortality himself but also bestow it on others. We discovered an even more remarkable link between Quetzalcoatl and the Grail romances. Quetzalcoatl is said to have left the country on a barge or raft supported by snakes, floating away across the water and promising to return as a 'once and future king'. Arthur, too, is said to have floated across the water on a barge to Avalon, whence he will one day return as the 'once and future king'.

One particular theme in South American folklore is a concern about the rains coming – a common problem the world over. Here, however, this theme is about more than fertility; it is a need for the continuation of life and the key to immortality. One of the most popular gods of Mayan mythology was Chac (or Chac Mool), a dragon beast. He ruled over bodies of water and, like Yahweh, was known as the 'rain bringer'. Chac required sacrifices from his people. In return he shed his blood so that there would be rain – the sacrifice being the 'death' element, the blood 'the life'. Although this rain motif should not necessarily always be attributed to the serpent, in the Americas the associations are striking.

In the myths of both North and South America, as in those of Australia and Africa, the deep association between the serpent and water is evident in the fact that the rainbow is seen as the serpent. It is also seen as the bringer of peace, a culture hero, the creator and, more importantly, as a healer and the giver of immortality. Many readers will be familiar with the popular saying that the end of the rainbow conceals a buried treasure or pot of gold (a golden cup or chalice?) in much the same way that the serpent is said to guard a treasure. And we shall always search for this treasure in vain, just as we search in vain for the treasure of the Grail. The serpent is the guardian of both.

We never expected to find Grail myths or motifs in the Americas. But we were surprised at the similarities we discovered. For instance, within many Mayan structures there are images of the Grail, or what we were coming to believe was the Mayan version of the Grail. In the Mayan world, blood was all-important and great blood-sacrifices and bloodletting were widespread. The lineage of the god-kings was in the blood and the gods received their blood with great joy and brought fertility to the land – a similar scenario to that found in many other parts of the world. Our research uncovered a link between the blood-associated beliefs of the Mayan peoples and the popular perception of the Grail as a bowl or cup.

On what is known as Structure 23 in the ancient city of Yaxchilan there are remarkable images of a bloodletting ritual. They are quite gruesome to our modern eyes, but were clearly of a highly religious and spiritual significance to the people of the time. Although the chronology of the events shown is much debated, the content is not: it depicts the preparations for a 'holy war' and unfolds in a number of scenes across several lintels. Shield Jaguar, the blood-lord of the city, stands holding a flaming staff. Below him is Lady Xoc (meaning 'shark'), who is performing a unique and disturbing sacrifice. She is kneeling, dressed in sky-ornamented clothing with a headdress showing the god Tlaloc, the rain god of Teotihuacan, thus indicating her lineage and blood to be of the gods, with life-giving powers. She is pulling a rope or vine strung with thorns through her tongue and the blood is dripping down it into a bowl/basket decorated with serpents at her knees. The design on the bowl/basket, known as the 'step-fret', represents water, waves, wind, sun, light and, most importantly, life. It is a known symbol of the serpent and a magical talisman against death. Her blood is also splattering upon white paper placed in the bowl/basket to collect and somehow enhance the power of the sacred offering, so that the vessel only becomes a life-giving symbol after the paper has collected the blood. Like the Grail, the vessel is a receptacle for blood. Furthermore, the alchemical colours red and white that are mixed in this sacrificial scene are the same as those the bread and wine of the Christian Eucharist: the paper and bread wafer are white; the blood and wine, red. The vessel then changes into an unadorned ceramic, the serpent image having now come to life following the offering of blood.

In the scene on Lintel 24, Lady Xoc's head tilts back as she beholds the 'new life' rising from the bowl. Amidst the plumes of smoke is the war-snake Waxaklahun-Ubah-Kan and emerging from within the bowl are Tlaloc, the god of both rain and the war, as required by the ritual, and Yat Balam, the founder of the royal bloodline. Following this remarkable conjuration, Lady Xoc is transformed and the step-fret serpent design now appears around her clothing. She too has become like the serpent and has conjured the 'protector blood lineage' of the bowl. Her ability to perform this magical ritual comes through her sacred bloodline, for only those of the correct lineage can both utilize and protect the power of the bowl. Lady Xoc now bestows a magical helmet – a 'jaguar helmet' – upon Shield Jaguar, symbolizing yet again the power associated with the head. Another small point we noted was the similarity between Lady Xoc's fantastic headdress and the Uraeus of the ancient Egyptians.

So, in the mythology of the Americas, the snake was not just seen as the healer, but was also associated with a vessel. We also have a goddess called Shark (a fish-like deity) who is closely linked with the serpent, drips blood into a vessel and produces a life-giving elixir. In fact, we have a sacred mixing bowl – the Grail – in which the red and white, (the colours of the snake's blood and venom), are mixed together to create the Elixir of Life, the key to immortality.

The universal nature of the healer-snake myths of the Americas is further evidence that the snake has been associated with healing since ancient times. The snake was also a healer in the literal sense, for it was utilized by the medicine men in the healing of people. This means that on the first, practical level of our Grail Triad, the Grail is the snake, and the snake the Grail.

Having explored the role of the snake/serpent in the mythologies of the ancient world, it was now time for us to return to the Grail story of the West. We also needed to investigate the origin of the idea that the blood of Jesus was the liquid contained in the Grail. If the blood and venom of the serpent were constantly being presented as the original Elixir of Life, it seemed to us that Jesus was indeed a 'serpent deity'.

PART THREE

The Serpent Grail

CHAPTER ELEVEN

The Serpent in Religion

W e began our research into the role of the snake/serpent in religion by following up any available mention of the snake. In this way we hoped to discover any clues that might help us to unravel the confusion of reinterpretations and symbols. As already mentioned, we had found evidence for the existence of the serpent cult in Egypt, where it was known as the Shemsu Hor ('Followers of Horus'), the Akhu or Shining Ones. We had also discovered that the origins of the serpent people lay elsewhere, but finding their place of origin was not going to be an easy task because they had effectively been written out of history.

So far we knew that there was a worldwide cult of the serpent that had spread from its place of origin to prehistoric Mesopotamia, then through Egypt and Greece into the West. We had found hundreds of place names associated with the serpent people. There were also messianic 'sons of serpents', and sacred cups or chalices utilizing both the venom and blood of the snake. What we needed to do now was to see whether these serpent legends had crept into Christianity, Islam and Judaism. If so, had they then merged with the pre-existing serpent myths of Celtic and Scythian origins to become the Holy Grail as we know it today?

The most obvious place for us to begin was the biblical Book of Genesis, a source to which all three faiths look for their origins. A cause for much debate in theological circles, Genesis tells us where we came from and why we are what we are, but the origins of Genesis itself lie in ancient Mesopotamian sources, in localized pre-existing myths such as the Sumerian epic of Gilgamesh. Since we were looking specifically for mentions of the serpent, we moved quickly through the brief tale about the creation of the universe and the Earth to the story of Adam and Eve in the fabled Garden of Eden.

The figure of Eve is based upon much older mythology and may be traced back to the ancient Mother Goddess or World Mother and the serpent cults of the pre-biblical period. Closer examination of the name 'Eve' revealed her serpent origins, for the Hebrew for Eve is *havvah*, meaning 'mother of all living', but also 'serpent'. Likewise, the Arabic words for 'snake,' 'life' and 'teaching' are closely related to the word or name 'Eve'. Early Gnostic texts regarded Eve as a serpent guarding the secrets of divine immortality and wisdom. They taught that the Hebrews had been jealous of her role and so had taken the creation of humankind away from the serpent and attributed it to Yahweh. At other points in tradition, the Mother Goddess myth of Eve takes on a masculine edge when she is married to Ophion, Helios or Agathodaemon. These were all great serpent deities and thus provide further evidence to link the early stories of Genesis to the serpent cult.

Gnostic mysticism eventually transformed an amalgamation of the female and male principles of these great serpent deities into what we now call the Ourobos or Ouroboros, a mighty dragon or serpent that resides in the Underworld and is shown eating its own tail, symbolizing the cycles of time and eternity. It seems that this ancient Gnostic symbol first appeared in Egypt, although it is now a worldwide symbol.

The serpent appears again in Exodus 4:3–4, where we are told that when Moses cast down his rod it turned into a snake, and when he picked it up it became a rod again. According to some etymologists, the name 'Moses' means 'emergent snake', and it is interesting to note that the princess who adopted Moses was called Thermuthis, which is the name of a serpent deity, although the Bible does not record this name. However, writing in the first century AD, the Jewish historian Josephus states:

> Pharaoh's daughter, Thermuthis, was walking along the riverbank. Seeing a basket floating by, she called to her swimmers to retrieve it for her. When her servants came back with the basket, she was overjoyed to see the beautiful little infant inside ... Thermuthis gave him the name Moses, which in Egyptian means 'saved from the water' ... Having no children of her own, she adopted him as her own son.[1]

In Exodus 7:10–12, the Rod of Aaron (the high priest and older brother of Moses) also turned into a snake during the brothers' confrontation with the Pharaoh and the magicians of his court, whose rods were similarly transformed. This incident clearly associates snakes with magic. As if to demonstrate the superiority of Yahweh over the Egyptian deities, Aaron's snake devours the snakes of Egypt, and in so doing possibly earns the 'chosen people' the title of 'the Immortal Race'.[2] The rod/snake is then used to bring plague upon the Egyptians, release water from rock, and part the Red (or Reed) Sea, and is an object so sacred that it is placed in the Ark of the Covenant.

Although Moses later rebuked Aaron for erecting a 'golden calf' in honour of Hathor (or even Horus), Moses himself raised a pole or pillar with a brass serpent on it (*see plate 37*):

> Yahweh sent seraphim [fiery serpents] among the people; their bite brought death to many in Israel. The people came and said to Moses, 'We have sinned by speaking against Yahweh and against you. Intercede for us with Yahweh to save us from these serpents.' Moses spoke for the people and Yahweh replied, 'Make a fiery

serpent and use it as a standard. Anyone who is bitten and looks at it will survive.' Moses then made a serpent out of bronze and raised it as a standard…'[3]

It was not until the time of King Hezekiah (719–691 BC) that this Brazen Serpent was broken into pieces, but the above passage illustrates the strong connection between the serpent and the power to heal. The Brazen Serpent also established the crucified serpent as a symbol of the saving faith of Israel – a symbol that would later come to signify the alchemist's illumination or enlightenment. St John's Gospel equates this symbolic serpent with Jesus, 'As Moses lifted up the serpent in the wilderness, even so must the Son of Man be lifted up; so that whoever believes will in Him have eternal life' (John 3:14–15).

In ancient Judaism, the sceptre of the Annas priest was similar to the Rod of Aaron. Called the *kentron* (meaning 'sting'), it was used to excommunicate. If you were 'stung', symbolically speaking, by the *kentron*, you were no longer one of the chosen people. For the Jewish writer Philo of Alexandria (*c.* 30 BC-AD 50), the serpent was both the bringer of death and the cure, and he described it as 'the most spiritual of animals', which is in stark contrast to the later demonization of the snake.

The name of the very ancient god Baal Tamar means 'Lord of the Palm' and the New Testament tells us that when Jesus rode into Jerusalem he was greeted with waving palm fronds. This possible link would normally have passed us by, since it makes no overt mention of the serpent. However, the serpent is closely connected with Baal Tamar and the local Phoenicians held the palm in high esteem. Coins from the period show the palm tree with a serpent coiled around it. We also found that a useful chemical called oleoresin, which is usually dark red in colour, is also known as Dragon's Blood and is derived from the coat of ripe fruit, particularly from the rattan palm. It is also obtained from the peculiarly named Dragon Tree. This remarkable substance is employed in photoengraving and is sometimes used in colouring varnishes. What intrigued us was why this useful red substance taken from the palm would be called Dragon's Blood. Theoretically speaking, it could have been called anything, but the fact that it was given this name would seem to reinforce the link between the dragon/serpent and the palm tree.

Earlier we mentioned the Phoenix's symbolic association with resurrection. This wondrous bird is also linked with the serpent, for in the Garden of Paradise that features in various world mythologies it is associated with the rose, and the rose is the flower of the serpent. Like the Hindu lotus flower and the Egyptian blue lily, it represents the chakra vortices associated with the serpent energy of the Kundalini. This is why the head of Jesus – a shamanic serpent resurrecting god – is sometimes depicted as the rose at the centre of the cross, an image that symbolizes the third-eye chakra in the head. The baptism of Jesus – his symbolic rebirth – is graced with the appearance of a heavenly dove, which combines the rebirth of the ancient Phoenix with that of the Egyptian *ba*, the soul.

The rose of Jericho, which is red in colour, was also called the 'rose of the Virgin' or 'Mary's rose'. The horticultural name of this rose is *Anastatica hierochuntia* and it is native to Arabia, Egypt and Syria. When exposed to moisture it uncurls slowly like a snake, hence its association with the serpent. Its thorns and flowers provide natural parallels with the wounding and healing properties of the snake.

The rose not only became the secret symbol for the serpent but also came to symbolize secrecy, as in the term *sub rosa*. The Golden Rose, which symbolizes immortality, was blessed by the Pope and was taken up by the Rosicrucians, whose other symbol was the red cross on a white background, which combines the alchemical colours of red and white again. The Rosicrucians, or people of the Rosy Cross, are linked with the secrets of the Grail and have been linked to the Templars, Cathars and Freemasonry as well.

In Ethiopia and the surrounding lands, a strange oral tradition known as the Snake in the Grove is told with relation to Mary, who is called the Queen of Snakes. The story relates how Mary came to Ethiopia with Joseph and the baby Jesus after their flight to Egypt. They stayed for many years at Axum, the capital of Ethiopia, a place now said to hold the secret of the Ark of the Covenant. Before returning to their homeland, Mary ordered the snakes never to hurt the women of the area. She was thus seen, mythically at least, as the Queen of Snakes.

According to Baigent, Leigh and Lincoln, the authors of *The Holy Blood and the Holy Grail*, the Virgin Mother is identified as Mary Magdalene. As they point out, the Leo section of the paper *The Red Serpent* (a poem of unprovenanced origin that may be as recent as 1967), states: 'To others, she is the Magdalene, of the celebrated vase filled with healing balm. The initiated know her true name: Notre Dame de la Croix [Our Lady of the Cross].' How could Mary simultaneously be the mother of Jesus and Mary Magdalene, the supposed wife and partner of Jesus? In this context Mary is linked with the serpentine Isis, the mother of Horus, who was also his wife and sister in his previous incarnation as Osiris, the father of Horus. If we apply this same archetypal relationship to Mary and Jesus, Mary is sister, wife and mother to Jesus, and Jesus is her brother, husband and son. These relationships make two complementary triads – one male, the other female. Here, though, in *The Red Serpent*, we note that Mary Magdalene is the bearer of a healing balm in a vase or vessel – a detail that accords with our theory linking the serpent to the Grail.

Hebrew words for the snake are *akshub* ('coiled serpent'), *epheh* ('hissing or venomous'), *Livyathin* ('the Leviathan' or sea serpent), *nacash* ('hissing serpent'), *pethen* ('python' or 'twisting snake'), *seraph* (as in Seraphim, 'burning or shining serpent'), *shephiyon* ('snapping serpent' or 'adder') and *tsepha* or *tsiphoniy* ('tongue-thrusting snake'). The Hebrew word *nacash* also means 'to be wise', and wisdom is an integral part of snake symbolism and mythology. As mentioned in the previous chapter, the Hebrew *nacash* is very similar to 'Nachan' ('city of snakes'), the Mayan name for the city now known to us as Palenque.

Sophia, meaning 'wisdom' or the 'Virgin of Light', comes from *is ophis* (the 'light of *ophis*' – i.e. the serpent). The 'light of the serpent' is thus synonymous with 'wisdom', and according to the apocryphal *Wisdom of Solomon* it is Sophia/Wisdom who grants immortality. The Ophites ('worshippers of snakes'), the late-Judaic and early-Christian cult already mentioned, taught that Sophia and the Christ entwined together like serpents in the person of Jesus and thereafter he became Jesus the Christ – that is, the 'anointed' or 'Christed One'. In this context, Sophia represents the sacrificial blood offering of the Mother Goddess or World Mother (the subconscious self) while the Christ represents the male positive energy force (the conscious self). When the serpentine (i.e. subtle) energies personified as Sophia and the Christ fused together in the person of Jesus, they were embodied in him. Symbolically speaking, he *became* the Serpent of Wisdom.

There is an ancient allusion to the idea of a messianic serpent becoming a man in Phrygia, where it is said that colonies of 'Ophiogeneis' or, more correctly, the 'serpent breed' were sent out far and wide. The notion prevailed among them that the heroic or messianic figure who had led them had in fact turned from a serpent into a man. This is the idea of a sacred serpent bloodline, which is also encountered in the legend of Aegeus of Athens (the first king of the country and the father of the hero Theseus), who is said to have been a 'dragon'. Of course there are those who see Cecrops as the first Greek king, but even he was said to have been the result of the blending of a serpent and a human being

The Gnostic Ophites

In the early years of the first millennium AD, the beliefs of the Gnostic Ophites were the norm. By contrast, it was the later ideologies of St Paul and others that were considered unusual. The Ophites, otherwise known as Sethians, saw the serpent as 'light' and 'shining knowledge', and regarded Seth, the third son of Adam and Eve, as the first of the race of 'perfect ones', the 'sons of god' and 'sons of the serpent'. He was equated with Set, the 'healing serpent god' of Egypt and later cults.

In both Judaism and Christianity, the character of Seth is in strong contrast to that of his brothers Cain and Abel. He was said to have been a great prophet of the Gnostic world, and the Gnostics took him as the first amongst them instead of Adam, who, having been created directly by God, was considered to be a god himself. The sons of Adam were therefore the 'sons of a god', and the enlightened Seth was appropriately seen as a 'son of the serpent'.

This Gnostic concept of the enlightened or illuminated ones being the 'sons of a god' tends to confound the 'royal bloodline' interpretation of the Holy Grail myths. The idea that the Holy Grail is confined to the bloodline of Jesus is indeed limiting when we understand that all human beings have the potential to become the 'son of a god' or 'son of the serpent' through the attainment of enlightenment.

In the days of the worldwide serpent cults, whole nations were called 'sons of serpents'. It is even said there were some beings who were bred from a serpent and a human, but we have to understand this in a symbolic sense and not as the literal cross-breeding of humans and reptiles, as some authors have claimed. The pharaohs had to be 'sons of a god', as did the Roman emperors and Greek kings, to enable them to lead and be worshipped by their people. Alexander the Great even claimed to have been born of a serpent god. In fact, the idea of being the 'sons of serpents' seems to have existed since earliest times and is generally associated with extremely good health and longevity.

In his *Antiquities of the Jews*, the Jewish historian Flavius Josephus wrote:

Adam had indeed many other children, but Seth in particular. As for the rest it would be tedious to name them... Now this Seth ... became a virtuous man ... so did he leave children behind him who imitated his virtues... They also inhabited the same country ... and in a happy condition, without any misfortunes falling upon them, till they died.[4]

Writing of a tradition that was already ages old in his own time, Flavius here points out that these ancient people, whom we have seen described elsewhere as 'sons of serpents', lived in a 'happy condition'. This suggests that they had some secret knowledge of how to live an extended life and that this knowledge was later assimilated into popular culture.

Worship of the serpent or wanting to be like a serpent seems to go back to a time when the shamanic serpent beings or Shining Ones were present on the Earth and had some influence over human affairs due to their wisdom.

In her book *Isis Unveiled*, the Theosophist Madame Blavatsky wrote, 'The wickedness of Cain is repeated in Ham. But the descendants of both are shown to be the wisest of races ... and they are called on this account snakes, and the sons of snakes.'[5]

There is now little doubt that early Christian sects venerated the serpent. St Epiphanius seemed to put his finger on it in *Adversus Haereses* (Against Heresies), when he stated that the serpent worshippers 'venerate the serpent because God has made it the cause for Gnosis'. Here he is unwittingly passing on the secret knowledge of these early sects. That is, we cannot attain the wisdom and immortal life associated both symbolically and literally with the serpent without first experiencing the state of profound enlightenment (i.e. Gnosis) by which we become a 'son of the serpent'.

The suggestion that certain early Christian sects venerated the snake/serpent would seem preposterous had we not the evidence of their rituals – rituals that were eventually to become part of traditional Christian Sunday worship. As Jean Doresse explains in *The Secret Books of the Egyptian Gnostics*:

> The Ophites made a very special cult of these reptiles [snakes]: they kept them and fed them in baskets; they held their meetings close to the holes in which they lived. They arranged loaves of bread upon a table, and then, by means of incantations, they allured the snake ... only then did they partake of the bread, each one kissing the muzzle of the reptile they had charmed. This they claimed as the ... true Eucharist.[6]

This Eucharist ritual, which emerged from the same place of origin as the Grail, was 'borrowed' from Egypt. The same is true of Seth or Set, as Murray Hope explains in her *The Temple of Set*:

> When the Hebrews emigrated from Egypt during the XIX Dynasty ... they took with them the caricature of Set: Satan (from the hieroglyphic Set-hen, one of the god's former titles).[7]

Seth is also known in Islam, and there is evidence that Seth/Set was assimilated into the Islamic tradition as the Agathodaemon, a figure of great Hermetic influence whose image is a snake. The prestige with which he was endowed is still to be found even now within the realms of mystical or Gnostic Islam. According to Jean Doresse, this deeper meaning of the serpent deity is retained within Shi'ite groups, but chiefly those in Iran.

But, as we have previously pointed out, there was still a feminine element to this strange survival in the world's religions of a serpent god who gives life, heals and provides knowledge. This was Sophia, the 'light of the serpent' or 'wisdom', who was venerated by the Naaseni and equated with Jesus 'of Nazareth' or Jesus 'the Naaseni', even to the point of calling him the 'good serpent'. This balance between masculine and feminine simply had to be part of the sacred teachings. It was as old as Gnosticism itself, and without it the story of Jesus – an archetypal 'resurrecting serpent god' – would not have had the powerful force it did.

The Nazar

According to Hippolytus, the Naasenes – a Gnostic sect that existed under Hadrian (ad 110 40) celebrated the mysteries of the Great Mother. Furthermore, it is believed that every Naasene temple (*naos*) was secretly dedicated to the serpent. The names 'Naas' and 'Naaseni' are affiliated with the word *Nazar*, whose meanings include 'keep', 'guard', and 'protect'. The 'Nazar' or 'guardians', who were serpent worshippers, could well be the true guardians of the Grail, for in the same way that the serpent was the guardian of treasure, so the serpent bloodline was the guardian of the secret of the Elixir of Life. It was not the bloodline itself that was the secret.

The word 'Nazar' is also linked with the Nazarenes and Nazoraeus, which, according to Dr William Benjamin Smith are not derived from a city called Nazareth since that did not exist at the beginning of our era. 'Nazoraeus' was the appellation of a snake deity and meant 'Yahweh the guardian'. The Nazarenes may therefore have been the guardians of the secrets belonging to the serpent-worshipping Naaz, Naas or Naaseni, who also worshipped Sophia/Sophis (Isis), the 'wisdom goddess' or 'light of the serpent'. The 'Nazarene', a title given to Jesus, is closely related to *nacash*, the Hebrew for 'serpent' from the root NHSH. This root alludes to the serpent as the 'bringer of wisdom and enlightenment', and implies to 'decipher' or 'find out'.

The original stories of the serpent-worshipping Nazarenes would have been adapted and changed over the centuries. For example, in later European and more specifically Arthurian legends, we find stories of battling dragons. These are often believed to be a play on the battles between the invading Saxon armies and the Romano-British. However, we discovered similar tales in the culture of these much earlier Judaic and pre-Judaic peoples. As we have already mentioned, these 'battling dragons' mirror the opposing aspects associated with the division in human consciousness and the belief that this division must be healed for an individual to become a 'shining serpent'. Our research revealed that these 'duelling dragons' were an integral part of the beliefs of the ancient Naaseni, the followers of the 'shining serpent' which they identified with the figures of Jesus and Sophia who together embodied the balance of opposites.

While researching the above etymological links, we came across the place name 'Naase' (meaning 'the one light') in Kildare, Ireland. According to *The History and Topography of Ireland* by the twelfth-century historian Gerald of Wales (Giraldus Cambrensis), this is the very place from which the stones for Stonehenge originate. He relates that Stonehenge was also known as 'the Giants' Dance' because a race of giants had taken the stones from Africa to Ireland, where they had built a monument on Mount Kildare, but Aurelius Ambrosius, King of the Britons, later instructed Merlin to take the stones to Britain.[8] We have already discussed the matter of the 'serpent' or 'serpent's head' in connection with Stonehenge, and it seems significant that the stones are said to have been moved by Merlin, the Celtic version of the ancient Egyptian Thoth, the wielder of the Caduceus staff. The idea that the stones originally came from Africa is possibly an allusion to the origins of the serpent god.

But to return to the Naasenes, we discovered that this sect had links with the Essenes, who were themselves linked with Isis by Herodotus, who is said to have called them Issedones, or 'Followers of Isis'. Now, as we had also discovered, Isis, Eve and Sophia all shared the identity of the serpent goddess. The Naasenes and Essenes were also both closely connected with the Ophites, who were part of the Egyptian Therapeutae in

Karnak and Qumran. The Therapeutae (from whom we derive the word 'therapy') were renowned as healers and worshipped the 'sovereign beast' (i.e. the snake) as a divine emblem of the pharaohs. They are also known to have used elements of the snake in their potions.

From our research it was becoming evident that there were very strong links between the Essenes and the Ophites and that these cults drew on older traditions that incorporated the 'messianic serpent' or 'descended king'. For these cults, Jesus was the 'son of a serpent', because in terms of both lineage and symbology that is precisely what he was. It has been suggested that Jesus was trained by the Therapeutae in Egypt, and the gospel stories indeed tell us that he was taken to Egypt as an infant to escape from Herod. There is even a suggestion that he visited the Great Pyramid and was initiated there.

The Naasenes claimed that the Gospel of Thomas contained the secret sayings of Jesus. These sayings provide further evidence for the connection between Jesus and the 'Sophia Light':

> There is light within a man of light, and it illuminates the whole world. (Saying 24)
> I am the light which shines upon all. (Saying 77)[9]

This linkage of Jesus to the serpent through the Sophia Light reminded us of the symbolism of the horned serpent. Ancient coins from across the classical world carry images of snakes with horns, and these images have come down to us in the horns depicted on the heads of dragons. The Hebrew word for 'horn' also means 'light' or 'to shine', so the serpent was the 'creature of light'. These horns are often given the form of thorns, which reminded us of the crown of thorns (or 'horns') worn by Jesus in the ultimate sacrifice from which we derive the symbolism of the Elixir of Life and the Grail – the blood and the chalice.

The crowns worn by rulers are not merely symbols of their authority, but also represent the seventh or 'crown' chakra. Both the crown chakra and the head are said to 'light up' like the sun during the enlightenment experience. And so, in wearing the crown of thorns, Jesus was truly wearing the headdress of the enlightened serpent king.

Sweat and Blood … Gall and Vinegar

The above link between the serpent and the 'King of Kings' provides a direct connection to Arthurian myth and the Grail legend, for an ancient tradition relates that Joseph of Arimathea carried to England the Grail that had collected the blood shed by Jesus while he hung on the cross. A tradition associated with King Maelgwyn of Gwynedd (c.540) states that 'Joseph had with him in his sarcophagus two white and silver cutlets filled with the blood and sweat of the prophet, Jesus.'

Sweat, or more properly 'swote', is generally produced when the body gets too hot or experiences a trauma or anxiety of some kind. It has been used by alchemists in mixtures of poison. The human body does not produce a poison as such, but sweating is a way of getting rid of the toxins in the body, so could this element of human sweat symbolize the poisonous venom of the serpent, in contrast to the healing element of the blood?

The New Testament Gospels tell us that Jesus was given a mixture of wine and gall while he hung dying on the tree. (According to some Gospels he was given vinegar, which is soured wine.) What the Gospels do not tell us, however, is that the gall was snake venom and the wine symbolized blood. Therefore, poison and blood were both given to Jesus and issued from him. It was only after the arrival of Nicodemus with aloes and myrrh, a pain-relief and purgative mix, that the poisons could be expelled from the body of Jesus while he was in the tomb. It is not surprising to find these highly scientific methods being utilized to recreate the symbolic 'death' and 'resurrection' myth associated with the 'son of the serpent', especially when we consider that the Essene were healers and experts in the use of herbs, healing remedies and snake venom.

If, as has been suggested, this sequence of events did not really happen, there are two possible explanations for them. Either they were devised for some symbolic reason associated with Gnosis and the third level of our Grail Triad, or they were some kind of alchemical and medical recipe related to the first level of the Triad.

Another point worth noting is that Jesus left his shroud behind in the tomb. In many of the world's mythological traditions, the theme of resurrection is represented by the snake's sloughing of its skin: the snake goes into a cave or 'other world', where it sheds its skin, and then re-emerges 'born again'. Jesus, as the Serpent King, did exactly the same thing when he was placed in the tomb and was resurrected, having left behind his shroud or 'dead skin'.

This raises the matter of the Turin Shroud, which is said to have been the burial cloth wrapped around the corpse of Jesus. If this cloth was seen, either literally or symbolically, as the 'sloughed skin', then its significance would have been known to the Gnostics of the time, or indeed to the medieval alchemists who are said by some to have created the image on it.

The early Christians certainly had knowledge of the healing properties of snake venom, as suggested in Acts 28:3, where we are told that Paul was bitten by a snake while he was collecting logs on the island of Malta. The snake fastened itself to Paul's hand, but he shook it off. The people waited for Paul to start swelling or even fall down dead, but instead he went and healed the father of Publius and other islanders who were diseased.

Looking at the essential elements of this incident, is there another possible interpretation other than the literal one? Paul was bitten by a snake and then healed not just one person but all the islanders who were sick. At one level, this biblical story would seem to be based on the fact that a person who has been subjected to several snakebites builds up an immunity to the effects of snake venom. At another level, it appears that

Paul needed the power of the serpent in order to be able to heal. The latter interpretation coincides exactly with 'the way' of the shaman.

Earlier, we discussed somewhat briefly the Nazareans, also known as Mandeans. The Nazareans, who still exist today in the Lower Euphrates, are said to possess a great secret. Walter Birks, author of *The Treasure of Montségur: The Secret of the Cathars*, claims to have had numerous discussions with these people during his stay there in the Second World War. According to Birks, their rituals seemed to centre upon the use of a sacred chalice and their history includes some tenuous link with the Cathars. Although the Nazareans refused to give up their secret knowledge, Birks claims that one of the priests told him that their greatest secret was that the Grail symbolized the doctrine taught by Christ to John the Beloved (the Evangelist), a doctrine they claim to hold to this day.

It is now known that the Templars met up with the Nazareans and, according to some authorities, secret knowledge was passed between them. However, John the Baptist also features in Templar literature and is associated with the Templar head known as Baphomet. The name of this head is linked etymologically to *baphe*, an Attic Greek word meaning 'to dye' or 'to dip something in'; the latter action is similar to the initiatory rite of baptism. If our theory is correct and the original Grail was indeed a mixing bowl in which the Red and the White were mixed together, then the act of 'dipping' something into it – as the gods dipped their dead soldiers in the cauldron to resurrect them – could be part of the secret knowledge retained by the Nazareans. The Nazareans/ Mandeans claim that their secrets originated in Egypt, although they themselves come from Palestine. They also claim that their sect was led by John the Baptist, who taught them the secrets that the Christ had taught him. However, the Christ referred to here is the Christ of Gnosis, not the Christ of history. Earlier in this book we discussed Dionysus, the great 'snake god' of healing, also known as Bacchus. Dionysus/Bacchus is linked with

Oannes or Dagon, the biblical Jonah. Oannes was a 'merman' identified with Hea, Ea or Enki, the only member of the Babylonian trinity who was symbolized as a serpent.[10] Oannes was also a craftsman, like Jesus. The Gnostics identified Christ with the serpent or fish gods Dagon or Oannes. Indeed, Matthew 12:41 tells us that Jesus was greater than Jonah, and he is therefore greater than Oannes: 'The men of Nineveh shall rise in judgement with this generation, and shall condemn it: because they repented at the preaching of Jonas; and, behold, a greater than Jonas is here.'

Dionysus/Bacchus is the god of wine, and the vine is a symbol of both the serpent and Christ, whose flesh and blood – as given in the Eucharist – bring the promise of immortality. In Hereford Cathedral and many other churches, there are images of St John's chalice with a dragon, dragons or serpents rising from within (*see plate 12*). The story goes that a priest of the temple tested the superiority of John's God by giving him and two others a poisoned cup or chalice to drink from. When John made the sign of the cross over the cup/chalice, the poison emerged in the form of a snake. John drank the contents and then brought back to life two others who had drunk from it before him and had died instantly from the effects of the poison. In linking the power to heal with the snake/serpent, this story is similar to that told earlier about Paul and the snake on Malta, for following the appearance of a snake both men went on to heal and, in the case of John, to bring back to life.

Moses, whose name means 'the emergent snake', is said to have worshipped at the Temple of On (the 'Mansion of the Phoenix') – i.e. Heliopolis – the very place associated with Oannes, one of whose names is 'On'. Could it be that this biblical figure was a priest of the snake cult? Could this be the real reason why his Brazen Serpent was such an effective healer? After all, according to the Bible, the Brazen Serpent was used to prove the power of God.

The Bible also provides evidence that the ancient Israelites may have practised more than just snake worship. In Deuteronomy 32, Yahweh (one of the Elohim or 'Shining Ones') becomes upset by the Israelites' idolatrous ways and, through his servant Moses, makes the following accusation against them.

> For their vine is of the vine of Sodom, and of the fields of Gomorrah: their grapes are grapes of gall; their clusters are bitter. Their wine is the poison of serpents, and the cruel venom of asps.[11]

Here, Yahweh (the Shining One) accuses the Israelites of not understanding the correct use of the snake. Why else would he refer to their use of wine and snake venom? If the 'wine' remains poisonous, the Elixir of Life has not been prepared properly, and so the Israelites must listen to Moses, God's 'chosen one', who knows how to prepare it.

Moses' Brazen Serpent recalls the ancient symbol of the 'creator snake' that was pinned to the tree in sacrifice. In later centuries, the Cathars believed that a similar symbolism applied to Jesus, as the spirit pinned to the cross, in a sacrifice that represented the self-sacrificing of the ego whereby the division in human consciousness is healed. The Cathars were accused of worshipping a beast named Agathadaemon, which means 'good serpent', or 'good demon'. Agathadaemon is also part of the mystical Islamic pantheon, which is not surprising when we consider the links between the Cathars, the Templars and Islam.

For the civilizations of the ancient world, the cross was the symbol of the water deities, who were almost always serpentine in form, and the association of healing with water led to the adoption of the cross as the ultimate symbol of healing, fertility and immortality. This symbol appears in Genesis as the 'mark of Cain'. Cain was the 'son of Enki' (Adon, Adam, Osiris) and the brother or husband of Ninkhursag (Eve, Isis), the double-headed serpent goddess and giver of immortality and health. His mark was dignified as the 'Cup of the Waters', and Egyptian and Phoenician records describe it as being an upright red cross in a white circle, a similar motif to that found on the Eucharistic wafer. This symbol was taken on by the Templars, who wore it on their breasts, and it became a symbol for the later Masons.

The red cross was also associated with the Ormus cult (from 'orm', meaning snake or serpent). We are told by the authors of *The Holy Blood and the Holy Grail* that 'Ormus was an Egyptian sage, who around AD 46, amalgamated pagan and Christian mysteries, and in so doing, founded the Rose-Croix.'[12]

Ormus is not only said to have been the originator of the red cross symbol and the Rose Cross or Rose-Croix of the Rosicrucians, but also of the Illuminati, those who were said to draw their power from the one known as Lucifer, who was symbolized as a serpent. According to Jan van Helsing, a prolific author on all things associated with secret societies, the term 'Illuminati' came into common usage in fourteenth-century Germany, where it was applied to the high initiates of the Brotherhood of the Snake. These initiates claimed that they were here to propagate a spiritual knowledge given more than 3,000 years before Christ, at around the same time that we believe the idea of the Grail emerged in Sumeria and pre-dynastic Egypt. 'Illumination' is synonymous with wisdom and enlightenment, qualities that are associated with the snake. In light of this, we asked ourselves, why did the Red Cross symbol become associated with modern medicine? Why is the snake the other symbol?

The red cross on a white background also became the national flag of England, also known as the 'cross of St George'. The popularity of St George can be traced back to the Crusades, just prior to the formation of the Templars. It was said that he had come to assist the Crusaders at Antioch in 1098 and the Normans, under the leadership of Robert Curthose, had taken him on as their patron. The real St George, if indeed there was one, seems to have originated in about AD 300 as a Roman officer near Lydda during the Diocletian persecution. Whatever the truth might be, the utilization of the red cross and the symbolism of the Christian rite of the Eucharist originate from the pre-Noah period, as Laurence Gardner points out. He suggests that the symbolism derives from menstrual blood, but we believe it points to the serpent and the Golden Age of the serpent people, the Shining Ones.

The goddess Ninkhursag may have been the symbolic progenitor of the royal bloodline, but it was the blood of the serpent Ninkhursag (the Egyptian Isis) that was important, not the bloodline. Indeed, Ninkhursag's brother/husband Enki (the Egyptian Osiris) had a familiar insignia: a serpent coiled around the Tree of Life. So not only was the mother of the royal bloodline a serpent, but Enki, the father, was also associated with the serpent and with an insignia closely linked with the healing serpent emblem of the Caduceus. The latter, in associating the snake/serpent with the Tree of Life (a symbol of immortality), reveals the ancient understanding that the snake was intrinsically linked with longevity. Immortality was gained by 'digesting' the Tree of Life, and it was the role of the wise serpent, as guardian of this most sacred treasure, to protect the Tree. In fact, the serpent people were alone in knowing how to utilize the healing power of the symbolic Tree.

The so-called Star Fire, which symbolized the hidden blood of the serpent, only became menstrual blood when the Scarlet Priestess of the temple took on the symbolic form of the serpent. Likewise, the venom of the snake was often referred to as 'milk', and milk was a sacred offering given to the temple snakes at Delphi. When understood in this context, it can be seen how the symbolic 'blood' of the menstruating goddess and 'milk' of the lactating goddess (which was also claimed to be an agent of longevity) were further symbolized by the Red and the White. In order for the secret knowledge to remain secret, it was concealed beneath the veils of symbolism.

Leviticus 24:12 refers to a special bread called 'shewbread', which was made from fine flour, or more correctly a fine powder, said by the Gnostics to be white powder. In Egypt this bread was known as 'scheffa cake' and was conical in form. (The cone has symbolic associations with the serpent.) But what was the 'powder' from which the bread was made?

The 'manna' that sustained the Israelites during their wandering in the desert is described as 'God's Shewbread' or *Shem-an-na*. The Sumerians called it 'Firestone' or the 'Highward Firestone', and in the Book of Revelation we find, 'To him that overcometh, I will give to eat of the hidden manna, and I will give him a white stone.'[13] Moses, the wielder of 'snake magic' and the Caduceus, is said to have burnt the Golden Calf to a fine white powder. Some have seen this transformation of gold into a white powder and then into a stone as the origins of alchemy. In fact, gold is a symbol of both fire and blood. It is also a symbol of immortality, being the 'blood of the immortal gods'. Furthermore, the Golden Calf was the symbol of the Egyptian goddess Hathor and the god Horus, and Moses is said to have learnt his magic whilst in Egypt. If the 'bread' were literally made from the powder of a golden calf, it would have caused serious stomach problems, and so there must be another explanation. Let us take it apart.

Since Egyptian times there has been a group known as the Great White Brotherhood, who are said to have founded many mystery schools and who emerge today as the Masons. But before reaching our doorsteps in their modern guise they first founded the mystery schools of Thoth and, more importantly, initiated the Egyptian Therapeutae, who were linked with the Israelite Essenes. The Therapeutae are known to have been closely linked with the Ophites and to have had a deep knowledge of medicine and snake poison. As we have already said, many of today's scholars believe that Jesus had dealings with this group and learned many of his healing techniques from them. Indeed, we believe that this group created the myth of Jesus, a new Osirian god-man.

The Golden Calf presented us with a problem. We knew that gold was a symbol for many things, including immortality, the sun, fire and blood. But why a calf? The symbol of the Egyptian goddess Hathor is a golden calf, but in the Temple at Serabit el-Khadim, on the Sinai Peninsula, Hathor is identified as a serpent goddess. The calf is also a symbol of Horus, who was also often associated with the serpent. From this we concluded that Moses was not turning gold into powder, but into the symbolic blood or immortal aspect of the serpent goddess Hathor or the god Horus. We then found the reason for Hathor being portrayed in this way. It was said that Hathor was a lactating goddess, and it was the milk from her breast that gave divinity to the Egyptian pharaohs. So Hathor's 'blood' gave sustenance and immortality and her 'milk' bestowed divinity, which is also immortality. Hathor was a serpent goddess, and the mixture of her divine Red and White was reduced to a white powder that sustained the people – a gift from God, and an early allusion to the Philosopher's Stone, which has often been compared to white powder. We had here a clear link from ancient Egypt, via Moses, to Judaism, and from there to the modern era.

Earlier in this chapter we retold the story of St John the Evangelist and the poisoned chalice. St John supposedly lived to the extraordinary age of 98 and by tradition dug his own grave. He also outlived all the other Apostles. An altarpiece in the cathedral of St Bavo in Ghent depicts him holding the chalice in his left hand – an image repeated in many churches and cathedrals across Europe. In alchemy, a dragon or serpent rising from a chalice represented pharmacy (*see plate 40*) and indicated that the bearer was a 'true initiate'.

For many Christians, the Grail is the chalice used at the Last Supper and is the same cup that caught the blood of Christ. According to a certain oral tradition, that chalice was a wonderful object that had been kept in the Temple for a long time and therefore predated both Christ and Christianity. The tradition relates that this holy vessel, which had been made from some unknown compound, could not be melted down or destroyed. It was lost, supposedly sold by Temple priests, but was eventually bought by Seraphia and made use of by Jesus on several occasions. It had a spoon that could be pulled out inserted into its base, was highly polished, adorned with jewels and, more importantly, ornamented with a serpent and a small bunch of grapes – the snake and the wine yet again. In fact, the chalice was said to have been in the possession of Abraham and even Melchizedech, who had brought it with him from the land of Semiramis, which points to a very ancient snake cult that may have had a role to play in the fabled extended lives of these early chosen people. We do not make any claims as to the veracity of this little oral tradition, but where there is smoke there is always fire.

In the Islamic tradition we found an accumulation of Judaic and Christian interpretations of serpent secrets, as well as African and mystic influences. We also found a most remarkable instance of healing in the tradition of the Prophet Mohammed's illness. The tradition relates that a malevolent Jew acquired a strand of the Prophet's hair and worked magic with it to bring a terrible illness to him. The pain was so severe that Mohammed sanctioned the use of magical prayers to counteract this 'evil eye'. He also sanctioned the use of snake poison in the treatment of diseases.

This was yet further evidence of the role the world's religious traditions ascribe to snake venom as an all-curing elixir. It was now time to examine the archaeological evidence for the existence of the Grail and perhaps even discover one of the original mixing bowls for the Elixir of Life.

CHAPTER TWELVE

Archaeology and Imagery

The evidence we have produced to support our theory has, up until now, been largely circumstantial, faint vestiges of a once worldwide serpent cult buried within mythological and religious traditions. What we needed now was tangible evidence – something that could be seen, perhaps even touched – that would confirm the widespread existence of serpent worship and the healing powers associated with it.

We soon discovered that prehistoric mounds in serpentine form are to be found the world over, almost always on top of mountains or near rivers. The mountaintop locations are very important, since these were places the ancients associated with the heavenly realms. Placing the serpent atop a mountain simply implied that this was the serpent's home. Yet archaeological discussion seemed to suggest that the importance of the serpent was due either to its solar attributes or to its phallic symbolism. Not once did we come across a 'textbook historian' questioning whether the serpent had anything to do with the actual rather than the symbolic snake.

One particular factor that links together ancient cultures is their striving for the stars. They built and built until they couldn't build any higher – mounds, pyramids and phallic towers. These tall monuments were the pinnacle of human achievement, man-made mountaintops, and the association of the serpent with these ancient buildings as well as the high places of the natural world is evidence of the importance of the snake/serpent in ancient religion.

As we have already mentioned, Jesus was nailed to the tree on top of a mound or hill called Calvary or Golgotha, the 'place of the skull'. The name 'Calvary' is from the Latin *calvaria*, meaning 'skull', and is derived from the Greek *kranion*, from which comes our word 'cranium'. Calvary/Golgotha shares the same 'primordial mound' symbolism that we find in the Great Pyramid and other sacred monuments and earthworks associated with the serpent. Indeed, as the 'place of the skull', the hill of Golgotha recalls the recurring theme of the 'serpent's head'.

Further evidence for the association of the serpent with high places came from the Egyptian *Book of the Dead*, which mentions a 'Hill of Bat', where heaven rests. Upon the brow of the hill is a snake about 30 cubits long (there are 30 degrees between each sign of the zodiac, hence the measurement). The name of the snake is 'eater of fire'. In symbolic terms, fire refers to pain and poison, and therefore to 'eat fire' is to take away the pain and poison. This 'eater of fire' could therefore be one of the earliest mentions of the 'fire-breathing' element associated with dragons. It is also revealing that it was the snake/serpent god who took away the pain and the Chaldean name for 'serpent' was *acan*, meaning 'fire'.

In Argyllshire, Scotland, there is a 300-foot serpent mound at Glen Feechan, a name which, according to some etymologists, sounds like *acan*. The serpent winds along in a pattern reminiscent of the shamanic path of resurrection and rebirth, which suggests that it may have been used for an ancient ritual associated with immortality.

A whole range of ancient serpent-related architecture is to be seen at Avebury, England, where there is also possible evidence for serpent shrines or healing activity. At Avebury the form of a serpent once extended over three miles in length and was so impressive that even the antiquarian John Aubrey thought it grander than Stonehenge. A drawing produced in 1740 by Dr William Stukeley, an antiquarian and scholar of sacred history and cabalistic science, still shows the circular sanctuary coiled within the folds of the eternal serpent. Avebury's twin circles were almost three times larger than the entire circle of Stonehenge. At the centre of the south circle is a huge stone known as the Obelisk, a word that comes from 'Basilisk', the great serpent said to be the most venomous of all, and is linked to the oracular god of Canaan, Ob or Oub. From the sky, Avebury appears like a great 'serpent trail' that takes one on a journey, as told in many myths, through the snake and out of its mouth to resurrection and eternal life. The stone circle with its two smaller stone circles looks like an egg, or a cell in the process of dividing, a process known as *meiosis*.

We do not know the name under which our European ancestors worshipped their serpent. However, Avebury could resolve into 'Haie barrow' with *haie* being the Arabian for 'serpent'. Aubrey might also have found its origins in the Canaanite term *Oub*, or 'Ave' from the root *havvah*, the Hebrew for 'serpent'. Such etymological links open up the possibility that the ancient Europeans may have known their serpent deity under names similar to those used by their brothers and sisters in the Middle East. Nor must we forget that the head of the Avebury serpent stood upon a ridge still known today as Hackpen. *Hack* is the old English term for 'serpent' and *pen* is 'head', so Hackpen is associated physically and etymologically with the 'serpent's head'.

Near Avebury one finds a Bowood, a Bay Bridge and a Bytham. It is possible that these place names are related to the 'boa' and 'python', for there were strong links between mainland Europe, England and the Mediterranean, where such snakes were worshipped, for example the Pythoness of Delphi. The prefix 'Uff-' in Uffcot and Uffington, noted for the white Celtic horse cut into its chalky hill (*see plate 4*), possibly derive from 'Eff', the Egyptian hieroglyph for the serpent. The horse is also linked with the serpent, possibly because the horse carries the serpent shaman into the Underworld, as in the case of Odin and his eight-legged steed Sleipnir.

As well as serpent links between continents, we discovered links across time. In India, for example, we have the Naga dynasties that we discussed in Chapter 8. We found that these serpents often take the form of twin pillars guarding the entrances to temples and shrines. This brought to mind the pillars of Boaz (Severity) and Joachin (Mercy), the two divine pillars from Solomon's Temple that were possibly rediscovered during the Templars' excavations in Jerusalem and exported to the West as part of their secret treasure. (The similarity between the words 'Boaz' and 'boa' is obvious.) These twin pillars are found in many sacred places around the globe. At Rosslyn Chapel in Scotland, they are serpentine in form with a Caduceus effect running up them – clear allusions to the secret of the serpent (*see plate 42*). Also at Rosslyn we found two peculiar figures flanking the entrance to the north door. To the left is an image of Melchizedek, who holds the chalice or Grail. To the right is Moses, that wielder of snake secrets, who is holding the Brazen Serpent. So on one side of the entrance to this sacred and highly secretive building we have a recognizable symbol of the Grail and on the other we have the hidden Grail symbol of the dragon or serpent.

On the other side of the Atlantic, we found stylized snakes on similar entrance columns at Chich'en Itz'a, the Mayan 'temple of the warriors'. As with the Middle East, the Mayans associated the serpent with wisdom and knowledge, and also with time, the key to unlocking immortality. It is for this reason that many of the world's ancient monuments and temples are intricately linked with the mapping of time and with the serpent. As already mentioned, the word 'temple' itself comes from *temos* or 'time'.

Walking the Path of the Labyrinth

The labyrinth is not only a symbol of immortality, it is also the 'lost' or 'hidden' way – the Gnostic journey – which is symbolized by the Grail.

Furthermore, the labyrinth is similar in form to the coiled serpent, and is therefore possibly linked to the ancient practice of employing snake's entrails as a method of divination. Either way, the labyrinth is a tangible means of travelling the path of the Grail.

In ancient Babylonia and Egypt, the symbolic labyrinth was used in the mystery cults associated with the serpent, and especially in initiation rituals. It has been suggested that early ritual dances predate the labyrinth itself and symbolize the motion of the serpent, thus enabling the initiate to obtain immortality, either on Earth or in the afterlife. The fact that the serpent emerged from under the ground gave birth to the idea that it came from the Underworld, and so the labyrinth was the dance towards the magical immortality of the afterlife.

Aesculapius, the serpent-healing god mentioned in previous chapters, had his temple sanctuary at Epidaurus, in Greece. The temple dates from the fourth century BC and is made up of a square and circle formation, intrinsically linked with the number eight. The original temple housed a gold and ivory statue of Aesculapius with one hand resting upon the head of the divine serpent. People who came from miles around to this great centre of healing were sometimes instructed to meditate, but at other times were given strange unknown potions, which, it is said, would heal them body and soul.

One of the most intriguing buildings at Epidaurus is the Temple of Tholos, meaning 'earth'. It is a wonderful round building with circular columns forming an inner and outer circle like Stonehenge. However, the most important part lies beneath the floor where there is a labyrinth said to be similar to the Cretan labyrinth of Daedalus. To move from one circle to the next it was necessary to traverse the entire circuit. The structure is believed to have been an initiation temple in which the inner path was a symbolic representation of the Underworld. It is also believed to have housed snakes, which were sacred to Aesculapius.

As initiatory devices, the labyrinths of the ancients symbolized the path that the serpent shaman or initiate had to traverse. But what about later times? What was the significance of the labyrinth for the Templars, the alchemists and great Gnostic thinkers of Europe?

Chartres Cathedral in France has strong connections to Egyptian Isis cults and serpent ideologies, and so it is no surprise to find that it also possesses what is probably the world's most famous labyrinth. This remarkable labyrinth fits exactly into the great rose window that sits above it in the west wall of the cathedral and is said to represent the path of the soul upon Earth as it progresses towards the ultimate goal of immortality at its centre. Walking the convoluted path through the labyrinth to the centre and out again is to emulate the ancient path of the serpent, entering the snake's tail and emerging from its mouth (like Osiris and the serpent at Avebury), having been born again. Whether or not the architects of Chartres understood the real truth behind the snake and the Grail is debatable, but the fact remains that the snake was intrinsically linked with the journey to eternal life.

The Sumerian Grail

In 1929 L. A. Waddell published a book entitled *The Makers of Civilization in Race and History*. Much of it has either been debunked or superseded by new evidence, however we should not throw the baby out with the bathwater, as there is a great deal that has not been satisfactorily explained and requires further investigation.

Waddell went to great lengths to prove that the ancestors of modern Europeans originated from the Aryan and Sumerian civilizations – something we are inclined to agree with, as do many scholars. He also tried to prove that these ancient civilizations were the originators of the Grail myths, a point that has been overlooked by many modern researchers in their quest for the Holy Grail. Waddell claimed that a genealogical list of the first Sumerian dynasty agreed with both Indian and Nordic mythical genealogies. The list was inscribed upon a stone bowl known as the 'Stone Bowl of Uda', since it was inscribed by King Uda and dedicated to King Ukishi of the city of Kish, the first king of the Aryan dynasty. Waddell links the bowl to one captured by Her-Thor in the Nordic *Eddas* and states that its original title was the 'Serpent-Stone-Bowl'. He also claims that it is the Holy Grail.

King Uda or Dur, after whom the bowl is named, is also known as King Sagg or Sakh. This is the same king who is said to have fathered Bakus or Bacchus, who we now know was intrinsically linked with serpent healing and the Grail. So in Waddell's 'Grail' we have a positive link between an actual Grail-like object and one of the central characters of the serpent myth – a link, incidentally, that Waddell did not himself make.

There is also a second link that gives us an insight into the underlying significance of the head in ancient times. *Sag* or *Zag* means 'leader', and the pictoglyph for it is a 'capped head', for which the sign name is *saggu*. Like the head of Bran the Blessed, who was also known as Uther Ben, the primary meaning of *saggu* is 'head' or 'first', which suggests that the 'source' is inside the head. So King Sagg's head, like the heads of many 'anointed' or 'Christed' avatars, is itself the Grail that contains the source. For instance, the name of I-em-hetep (Imhotep), the ancient Egyptian mythical son of Ptah, means 'Come in peace' and was given to him because he brought with him the art of healing. As already mentioned, he was later equated with the Greek Aesculapius. Like King Uda or Sag, Imhotep is depicted wearing a skullcap, indicating that he too is the 'head', or that, like the heads of other serpent people, his head contains the *activated* 'stone'.

The name of the second king listed on the Stone Bowl of Uda is Gin, which is a dialectic form of Gan or Kan and a synonym for Bacchus. *Gan* also means 'to increase' or 'make abundant'. *Kan*, a derivative of Gan, means 'serpent', and is also the name of the Masonic set-square which symbolizes the male shaman's head, the 'serpent's head'. So Bacchus could very well have been a real king with a knowledge of the true secrets of the Grail and the serpent myths of healing. Was it the product of this bowl/Grail that brought him such renown as a healing deity?

Significantly, the Stone Bowl of Uda is believed to have been the principal cult object of the Chaldean/Babylonian serpent worshippers, the originators of the worldwide serpent cult. A reference to it is made in the following Sumerian hymn:

> Men altogether have proclaimed his name [Adar]
> for sovereignty over them.
> In their midst like a great wild bull [the sun]
> has he lifted up his horns.
> The Shu [vessel] Stone, the precious,
> the strong stone, the serpent-stone of the mountain stone,
> That warrior – the fire stone…

'Fire stone' in this instance could be a reference to the Star Fire mentioned earlier. However, this small section of the hymn portrays the stone vessel as being the 'serpent-stone', and Waddell points to a stone bowl which, according to the Nordic *Eddas*, was captured by the god Thor. Thor also bore the titles Adar (which is closely linked with 'adder') and Sign (which is dialectically the same as Sagg). In effect, we have here identical myths and etymological links making their appearance thousands of miles apart and referring to the same magical object which, in both cases, is linked with the serpent, for the Nordic bowl was also said to have been part of the ancient serpent cult. This 'life-giving' bowl was stolen by the newly proclaimed sun cult, which is how its connection with the serpent has been hidden for such a long time. It is highly probable that similar Sumerian influences found their way, either directly or indirectly, into western Europe and from there into Arthurian myths.

The Stone Bowl of Uda has other connections too. It is said to have been sacred to the ancient Egyptian goddess Hathor, the 'Cow Mother', who has strong links with the serpent myths. Incidentally, Waddell connects Hathor with Her-Thor of the Nordic myths. We previously spoke of the Mandeans and the Druze, the followers of John the Baptist. The founder of the Druze was Ad-Darazi, an etymological connection with 'Adar'. They believed the Grail to be a 'chalice of light' and that each recipient has a different capacity to 'hold the light'. This 'light' is not only the enlightenment associated with the third level of our Grail Triad, but is also the shining serpent elixir of the first level. In our view, the etymological connections between these individuals associated with bowls and chalices show that their names were either adopted or added later.

Whether or not the Stone Bowl of Uda is the original Grail, it remains a very important element of our research, for it associates a vessel of some kind with the earliest serpent cult. It also becomes more important than those named upon it, just like the Grail in the Arthurian mythos. It bestows life and, like the cauldrons of the Celts, is fertile and abundant. It is called the 'treasure' and is guarded by serpents. If it is not itself the original Grail, then it is surely one of the very first Grails in imagery and style, and therefore possibly the oldest Grail on Earth. But there is also a more modern link which demonstrates that the idea of inscribing the Grail with the names of the 'kings' or 'protectors' filtered down through the ages to medieval European Christianity. In his epic poem *Parzival*, Wolfram von Eschenbach writes:

Hear now how those called to the Grail are made known. On the Stone, around the edge, appear letters inscribed, giving the name and lineage of each one, maid or boy, who is to take this blessed journey ... When life dies for them here they are given perfection there.[1]

The guardians of the Grail shall therefore be inscribed upon the 'stone', just like the Stone Bowl of Uda.

This 'Uda of the Vase' (Uda-vasu) is also equated with the Indian king Ishvatu Indara, Dar or Dur, the king who captured the sacred stone bowl of the serpent cult. According to Waddell, Uda is identified through his Eddic title as Bur-Mioth, who in turn is identified with the Greek Prometheus. (Bur-Mioth may also be connected with Baphomet, the Templar icon.) Such similarities and cross-associations are not uncommon. As we know, when Christianity spread through western Europe it superimposed the image of Mary over that of Isis and her related goddesses and their ancient traditions and rites. Yet it is highly likely that Mary (whether the Magdalene or the mother of Jesus) was indeed a version of the original ancient shamanic World Mother or Mother Goddess. Equally, these deities were localized symbols of universal ideas, which would further explain the associative nature of their names.

Prometheus, whom we have just mentioned, was a bestower of knowledge, and in *Prometheus Bound*, by the Greek poet Aeschylus (500 BC), we find the following interesting inference:

> To soothe the ills of man's ephemeral life.
> Nor healing food nor drink,
> Nor unguent know they (humans), but did slowly wither
> And waste away for lack of pharmacy,
> Till taught by me to mix the soothing drug,
> And check corruption mark.[2]

To what 'mix' was Aeschylus referring? Nobody knows. But 500 years before Christ, a deity who had profound links to the original serpent grail was said to bestow life and be the holder of the secret to the potion.

There are now only two remaining fragments of the Stone Bowl of Uda, yet it raises the following questions:

1. Could this ancient artefact be the very first mixing bowl/Grail of the serpent cult?
2. Did it bestow such wondrous riches and 'extended life' by means of the mix held within it?
3. Was this mix a product of the serpent, the secret of which was stolen by the new sun cults and then lost?
4. Did this secret knowledge continue as an underground movement?
5. Was this secret knowledge hidden behind intrigue and protected by a special 'family' whom some modern authors claim to be the serpent bloodline itself?
6. Were there copies of this stone bowl? Could the Knights Templar have brought these copies back from the Holy Land?

It now seemed to us that subtle links between the Templars and Grail myths could be traced back to ancient Sumeria and beyond. One such link was the pictoglyph of the head on the Stone Bowl of Uda and the Templar Baphomet. However, as Robert T. Mason points out in his paper *The Divine Serpent in Myth and Legend*, the image of the serpent was combined with an image of the human head even in pre-Sumerian times.[3] Pre-Sumerian vases have been discovered with snakes winding around and over images of the cosmos or linked with images of the ancient Mother Goddess or World Mother, herself an image of fertility and immortality. These images of winding snakes are echoed in the spirals to be seen on ancient monoliths and cairns across the globe.

This universal spiralling image of the snake is frequently associated with solar symbolism, which, since the sun cults of Sumeria are said to have stolen the serpent bowl, suggests that they were in fact just a continuation of the earlier serpent cults. In esoteric terms, however, we suggest that the link between the serpent and the sun refers to the inner sun, the source-centre of what we today would call the 'collective consciousness' from which we receive the energy of the life-force. This source-centre is also the centre of the spiral maze or labyrinth, which itself represents both the Grail and the human head.

Since the Mother Goddess was associated symbolically with the moon, we have a remarkable cosmogony in which the serpent is associated with the fiery red of the sun and the Mother Goddess with the white of the moon. The Red and the White in unison again, but this time projected onto the heavens.

From Australia to Africa, from the Americas to Europe, the spiral is a symbol of the coiled serpent that lies 'asleep' at the base of the spine from where it begins its ascent through the energy vortices aligning the spinal column to the centre of the head. In the Middle East, the region in which we suggest the Grail originated, we have probably the earliest images of the spiralling serpent coiled around the heads of gods, or moving up the back or spine towards the head. The traditional view is that these images depict the superhuman nature of the gods. In our view, however, they represent the enlightenment experience by which one becomes 'as a god' or a 'son of a god', a 'son of the sun'. And we suggest that this is the origin of the link between the serpent and the human head: it is the serpent that bestows the power of deity (i.e. immortality) on both the gods and humankind.

Similar imagery is found in China, associated with the whirlwind or the ascending dragon. This ascending dragon is associated with fire and represents the male *Pingala* channel that ascends the spinal column in the first initial phase of the enlightenment experience.

The spiralling form of the serpent energy as it wraps itself around the spine led to the vine and ivy being associated with the serpent. Like the serpent, these two plants are frequently depicted climbing up columns, pillars and trees, and also on or around the heads of deities.

When the Egyptians abandoned their mines in the Timma Valley in the twelfth century BC, the Midianites converted a local temple into a shrine. During modern excavation of this shrine a copper serpent with a head of gold – the Middle Eastern symbol of fertility and immortality – was discovered, buried within the Holy of Holies. This was an important find as it added the serpent to the Midianite pantheon, from which it had previously been missing. It also added it right at the top, as the most sacred of objects, placed in the most holy of places. In the context of our investigations, this particular archaeological find was further evidence of a link between Egypt and Sumeria and the pre-Sumerian serpent cults.

The symbolic imagery associated with the serpent evolved into universally widespread initiation rituals. Early rituals involved the Mother Goddess as the moon and the serpent/dragon as the sun – again, the Red and the White. For instance, a Roman ritual called 'drawing down the moon' included incantations to the Great Mother moon goddess who would slink down from the heavens (the source-centre) as a serpent. The power of this serpent was then utilized for all manner of cures, potions and love spells, such as making the 'snake burst in the field' as C. J. S. Thompson points out in his book *Mysteries and Secrets of Magic*.[4]

Thompson also relates a story given to him by Lane, the Egyptian explorer of the early twentieth century. While Lane was studying the magicians of contemporary Egypt, he stumbled across a unique practice that has some bearing upon the story of Moses and his snake-staff. He recounts that the magicians had a 'method of hypnotizing a viper by compressing its head and making it appear like a rod'. A remarkable feat, and one still evidently practised today by snake charmers. Perhaps this is the same method of 'taming of the snake' that had been employed centuries earlier by the Shining Ones to extract from the snake both the 'poison' and the 'blood' without coming to any harm. It also recalls the resurrection rituals of the serpent being pinned to a tree – in this instance the snake itself symbolized the tree – and the image of the Caduceus staff.

The image of the magician-prophet-shaman holding forth the rod of the snake brings to mind a magical scene on the Leyden Graeco-Egyptian papyrus from 200 BC, in which a figure is holding two magical rods, one to either side. A similar stance is replicated in various hillside figures found in Great Britain, in particular the Long Man of Wilmington, and in the now famous Minoan snake goddess figure from around 1,600 BC found at Knossos, Crete, but whose precise provenance is uncertain (*see plate 45*). The same stance is adopted by many of the figures of the ancient Egyptian Hathor to be seen in the Louvre, Paris. The statuette of the Minoan snake goddess, which is only 34.2 cm tall, holds out two writhing snakes as if she is about to cast the magic power they endow her with. Another snake appears to emerge from the head of the goddess, thus recalling the Uraeus serpents of the Egyptian deities.

According to the archaeologist Sir Arthur Evans, the Minoans borrowed much of their culture from their Egyptian trading partners, as evidenced by the numerous Egyptian artefacts discovered on Crete. Evans linked the snake goddess with the Wadjyt snake of Egypt and the snake found in Aphroditoplis (City of Aphrodite), a city whose insignia is the feather and the serpent. She can also be linked to Asherah, the serpentine Mother Goddess referred to in Judaic texts.

The wielding of serpents, either writhing or straightened as rods, is perhaps the origin of our popular image of the magician waving his wand, for they gave the power to perform great 'magical' tricks, such as bringing people back to life. (As a historian once said, 'Religion comes from magic.') A remarkable wand in the form of a twisting bronze serpent is to be seen in the Fitzwilliam Museum, Cambridge. The wand, which is straightened in the middle where it was held, is a real piece of Egyptian magic, and we found two more like it in the Louvre in Paris. Indeed, it is evident that the entwined snakes and the tree are the real origins of the magician's wand, the magical mini-staff of serpent power. The idea that the tree or staff of the serpent is a source of power is clearly seen in the imagery of the Rod of Aaron, which when thrown down became a snake. The same rod saves the Israelites by parting waters, bringing plagues upon Egypt and drawing water from rock, and, as already mentioned, was one of the objects hidden in the Ark of the Covenant.

The Serpent as a Symbol for the Ancient Shaman

The Hebrew nation came out of Egypt around the time of the Fourteenth Dynasty and it is widely recognized that they carried with them the secrets of Egypt as well as the image of the popular serpent deity Set (Seth), who later became Satan (Set-Hen). For the Hebrews, the snake was the wisest of all beasts and had been given the gift of speech by God. It seems strange that a god should give the serpent speech: Balaam's ass is the only other biblical beast with the power of speech, but it is God who speaks through the ass, not the ass speaking with its own voice.

Nowhere in the Hebrew Bible is the serpent spoken of as being evil. This is a modern interpretation. Indeed, Set is placed in the Garden of Eden as an immortal, with the power to take away the gift of immortality with his God-given speech. The Hebrew imagery in which the snake is entwined around the Tree of Life, and later the cross, is highly Sumerian. But how and why did the snake become evil? Was it to conceal the secrets that it held? Is this why speech was taken away from the serpent? According to the Bible, its arms and legs were certainly taken away. Or was it because its association with the female principle and the Mother Goddess posed a threat to the emerging patriarchal authority? We will probably never know for sure, but the fact remains that through its power of speech the serpent that guarded the Tree of Life caused Adam and Eve to be expelled from the Garden of Eden and thus enabled them to procreate. Through the power of its speech, it was actually creating life, not destroying it. Robert T. Mason argues that the serpent knew the gift of life from God 'as if it possessed that gift'.[5]

In 1699, the definitive Jewish magical diagram incorporating the Seal of Solomon was drawn by the alchemist and magician P. Smart. The diagram subtly conceals the form of the serpent, which is not surprising since mystical Judaism, and more importantly the Kabbalah, was profoundly influenced by the ideology and the magic of the serpent.

Later, Christian verbal and visual imagery associated Jesus with the serpent. John compared Jesus to the Brazen Serpent that Moses lifted up in the desert, and early Christians believed that the crucified serpent on a rod or staff (tree) was emblematic of the crucifixion of Christ. A sixteenth-century German Christian coin, the Thaler, has on one side of it the figure of Christ on the cross and on the other the serpent on the cross, thus associating the serpent with the Saviour. As already mentioned, this image combining the tree, cross, rod or staff with the serpent symbolizes the 'enlightenment' experienced by the serpent people. Their archetypal shaman god was the model for Horus, and later Jesus. He was the original god-man who personified the sun in the death and resurrection ritual played out upon the plains of the Earth.

As mentioned earlier, the depiction of haloes on the heads of saintly figures may also have direct associations with the serpent, especially the hooded cobra, thus emphasizing the immortal nature of the saints. Some images of the Buddha depict him in this way, with the hood of the cobra itself forming the halo above his head. Such imagery identifies the head as the realm of the serpent, with the 'serpent head' symbolizing the power of the 'immortals' and recalling the pre-Sumerian coiled serpents placed around the heads of immortal and superhuman gods.

The universal image of the serpent as a symbol of immortality is closely linked to the blood of the serpent and to the bloodline of the protectors of the secret knowledge associated with it. As we have already discussed, the bloodline itself is not the secret knowledge. Rather, the 'bloodline' refers to those who protect the secret of the Elixir of Life. If the Holy Grail referred uniquely to the bloodline of the fabled descendants of Jesus, exact replications of the bloodline story would not be found in other parts of the globe. Likewise, if the elixir were a uniquely European concept, references to magical elixirs would not be found elsewhere in the world. If the Philosopher's Stone were, as we are led to believe, the invention of a few Jews and Arabs in Alexandria, we would not find similar legendary stones in both the ancient and wider worlds. But the fact that these three objects have their equivalents in cultures across the globe indicates the universal nature of their underlying truth.

Serpent Skulls and the Anthropomorphic Evidence for the 'Serpent Enlightenment'

Throughout this book we have touched on the wisdom of the shamanic adepts and priesthood who we believe were the originators of the mythical Grail. In the course of our research we noted the similarities between these 'serpent people' and the Mesopotamian 'fish deities'. Evidence to support our theory about this ancient serpent cult has come to light in the ancient temple of Hal Saflieni, Malta.

Malta is an island of extremes, with dusty, rocky and barren Mediterranean landscapes providing an intense contrast with its rich Catholic cathedrals and European cultural influence. This foreign influence did not only occur in the sixteenth century with the famous Knights of St John. It seems that Malta has been a very important place for a very long time, for over 5,000 years ago temples and burial chambers to match Stonehenge and Avebury were being erected there. But what did these people worship? And where did they come from?

On the face of it, the answer to the second question seems fairly straightforward. Archaeologists believe that early settlers came from Sicily and other islands off the southern Italian coast. Pottery shards, beads and jewellery, foodstuffs and general waste all go some way to proving the influence of these offshore settlers. However, the discovery of several large skulls means that these migrations are no longer seen as being the only influence on early Maltese culture. As for the beliefs of the early Maltese, the discovery of several hundred large-bodied Mother Goddess figurines that have been given descriptive names such as the 'sleeping lady' or 'sleeping mother' suggests that they were followers of the early fertility cults. Similar Mother Goddess figures are to be found around the world and are almost always associated with serpent worship and healing as well as fertility.

So, early Maltese culture is not dissimilar to the cultures of southern and even northern Europe of the same period. And, as we were to find on our own visit there, the island's culture has been so strongly linked to the worship of the serpent that it has lasted right up until today.

The Maltese believe that St Paul was shipwrecked on Malta, at a place now called St Paul's Bay, and stayed on the island for at least three months, although some say he stayed for three years. While he was on the island, he was bitten by a snake, which he then tossed into a fire. He suffered no ill-effects from the snakebite and went on to heal many Maltese and rid the island of snakes in a story reminiscent of the Irish legend of St Patrick. However, apart from the mention of this story in the Acts of the Apostles, there is no evidence at all that St Paul visited the island, nor that he was shipwrecked there. Indeed, there is no further mention of it in any record until the late thirteenth century, when it became politically expedient to do so. And yet, all over the island, from Valletta to Medina, there are images of a Phoenix-like serpent rising from the flames (not dying in them) in memory of the miracles of St Paul. Even on the 5,000-year-old temples found at Hagar Qim, Mnadjra and Ggantia, there is evidence of ancient serpent worship. At Ggantia, for example, an image of a snake is carved into the rock. At Hagar Qim, archaeologists found a unique altar stone depicting the Asherah Tree rising like the Kabbalistic Tree of Life from a plant pot. The temples also have serpent oracle holes reminiscent of Delphi's pythoness and other similar sites around the world.

With all this, why would a few large skulls be of interest? In fact, they would probably not even have attracted our attention had the authorities not suddenly tried to deny their existence – a denial that some believe is for racist reasons. The skulls in question were apparently still to be seen in the Archaeological Museum of Valletta right up until 1985, and so we e-mailed the authorities concerned to try and discover the reason for their removal and to find out more information about these 'large heads'. We were not even given the courtesy of a reply, and so we journeyed two and a half hours by plane to the sunny island of Malta just as autumn was taking the warmth away from England and replacing it with a blanket of golden leaves. After settling into the hotel we made our way into the bustling streets of cosmopolitan Valletta, Malta's capital. A short walk away from the euphemistically titled bus station we found the Archaeological Museum and approached an official who was sitting reading the newspaper. His response to our questions was that there were no skulls, they were never on show and he had no idea what people like us wanted them for anyway. No matter how hard we tried, we could not get any other response.

It seems that a news story run in Italy a short time beforehand had deeply embarrassed the Maltese archaeological community and destroyed any hopes of anybody else covering the story, and so we moved on to other serpent-linked sights in Malta. When we returned to England we decided that all we could do was to report the story covered by the Italian media. According to the account in *Hera* magazine, Vittorio Di Cesare and Adriano Forgione from Rome had revealed that photographs of the skulls had been taken by two doctors, Anton Mifsud and Charles Savona, and that these photographs were now the only evidence remaining of this mysterious story. The Maltese were now claiming that these skulls were just extremely ancient pre-hominids.

And yet books published by the two doctors reveal that these skulls were dolichocephalous (elongated) and similar to skulls found in the Yucatan, Egypt and elsewhere.

The skulls were discovered amongst 7,000 skeletons unearthed in a vast subterranean structure, the Hal Saflieni Hypogeum, where a sacred well was dedicated to the Mother Goddess. Wells associated with the World Mother were believed to lead into the Underworld, which is why skulls are often found in wells. The walls of the hypogeum are inscribed with spirals and circles. It was also here that a small statuette of the 'sleeping goddess' was found, along with a relic with a snake inscription on it. This suggests that the people to whom these skulls belonged were also associated with the enlightenment experience.

It is believed that such elongated skulls were created from birth onwards by placing planks of wood on the amenable structure of the head and wrapping bandages around, thus forming the peculiar-shaped heads, which, hundreds of years later, the writer Erich von Däniken and others would claim as proof of alien visitation. However, such skulls are not always an artificial creation. Some are actual genetic mutations, a condition known as craniosynostosis.[6] But one thing seems clear: as in Peru and Egypt, the dolichocephalous skulls found on Malta dated back to the temple-building period. However, what is not clear is the reason for their creation.

Looking more deeply into the effects that would be caused by this malformation of the skull, we discovered that the pressure on the brain would not only cause severe pain but would also have a profound effect upon those areas of the brain – the pineal and pituitary glands and the thalamus – that many mystics claim are responsible for the shamanic (hypnagogic) trance state. It seems as though we have here historical evidence of 'natural' shamans. But, most importantly for us, these people were linked with the worship of the snake and thus provided sound evidence to support our theory.

In his article, Adriano Forgione wrote:

Malta and Gozo were very important centres since pre-historic times, places where 'medical cures' were conducted, oracles and ritual encounters with the priests of the goddess. There, on both the islands, existed many sanctuaries and thaumaturgic centres, where priests surrounded the healing goddess, direct expression of her divinity. It is well known that, in antiquity, the serpent was associated with the goddess and to healing capacities. The snake also belongs to the subterranean world. Therefore, a hypogeum dedicated to the goddess and the water cult was the right place for a sacerdotal group that was defined, in all the most ancient cultures, as the 'serpent priests' (an epithet still in use for shamans).[7]

Perhaps the skulls found in the hypogeum, and examined during our visit to Malta, belonged indeed to these priests. As mentioned before, they present an accentuated dolichocephalous, which is particularly the centre of our analysis. The long head and drawn features must have given a serpent-like appearance, stretching the eyes and skin. Lacking the lower part of the exhibit, we can only speculate, but the hypothesis can't be far from reality, a reality worsened by the fact that such deformities certainly created walking problems, forcing him … to slither!

The lack of the cranium's median knitting and therefore, the impossibility of the brain's consistent, radial expansion in the skullcap, so that it developed in the occipital zone of the cerebellum, deforming the cranium that looked like a single cap from the frontal and occipital area. This must have certainly caused the man terrible agony since infancy, but probably enhanced visions that were considered as being proof of a bond with the goddess.[8]

As mentioned above, some similar skulls seemed to exhibit a natural deformity due to genetic mutation. Adriano Forgione continued:

> Even the other skulls we examined presented strange anomalies. Some were more natural and harmonic than the cranium that mostly gained our attention, but they still presented a pronounced natural dolichocephalous and we could assume, without fear of refutation, that it is distinctive of an actual race, different from the native populations of Malta and Gozo.[9]

If this deformity were due to genetic mutation, one of the factors that could have caused it is a high level of protein, and snake venom is pure high-level protein. So could this genetic mutation have come about through the continual taking of snake venom? It seems that even a single type of protein could cause the effect. Other things that can cause structural or bone changes are diet or environmental changes such as heat or cold, but it is a matter of debate as to how fast these mutations occur. As Adriano Forgione points out, whether these particular changes were a genetic mutation or not, they would have caused massive discomfort.

Interestingly, venom is used medicinally for the treatment of bone-related problems, since it helps to relieve pain. For example, the drug Apitox, which is made from bee venom, is used extensively as a treatment for osteoarthritis, and venom is widely used in Chinese medicine for all kinds of bone and joint problems. However, the Arthritis Society of the United States warns against the dangers of using snake venom!

The squashing of the brain would not only have caused discomfort but would have probably triggered the release of the very hormones associated with the hypnagogic state and the mystical 'third eye'. In other words, these people would have been in touch directly with the third level of our Grail Triad. Indeed, according to Forgione, they may even have had a distinctly serpentine appearance.

Are the cranium-altering rituals of later civilizations derived from the practices of these ancient serpent priests? For example, the conical part of the ancient Egyptian Atef crown – the Hedjet – worn by gods such as Osiris would seem to imitate the elongated heads of the serpent people. If deliberately self-inflicted, the deformation found in these 'serpent' skulls and its imitation in the Egyptian Atef crowns could have been associated symbolically with the seventh-chakra vortex situated at the top of the head, known in India as the *bindu*. The light bulb that appears in today's cartoons above the head of a person who has a sudden flash of insight stems from an esoteric understanding of this centre. The conical hats worn by witches and wizards also point to the location of this highest energy vortex in an individual.

According to anthropologist Lionel Sims, Stonehenge was built to 'capture' the sun and the moon via the portals or gateways created by the large central trilithon. At appropriate times of the year, people would observe this phenomenon from the location of the Heel stone, while the shaman or Pagan priest walked alone into the centre of the monument as though he were exercising his power to bring the opposing forces of the sun and moon together in fusion. According to Sims, 'The priests were masters of time. They controlled and ruled the cycle of time' and in our view he is correct. The shaman priests demonstrated their knowledge of cycles through these ancient megalithic constructions. As shaman, they would not only have been 'masters of time', they would also have been masters of that place outside time, the Eternal Now of esoteric tradition.

We have already pointed to the connection between the words 'time' and 'Templar', and a further connection is hinted at here, for these shaman-priests belonged to the same tradition as the Persian or Caucasian magician-priests known as the Magi. Author Robert Lomas tells us that the old Chinese word for 'court magician' is *mag* and that the Chinese character for *mag* is a cross with slightly splayed ends, an identical symbol to that used by the Knights Templar.

Sims says that these priests wore rocket-shaped conical hats decorated with rows of sun and moon symbols that are said to outline the Metonic cycle of the sun and moon.[10] Several of these tall golden hats – one with a chinstrap – have been discovered in Ireland and central Europe, which suggests they may be of Celtic origin. Said to date from 1500 BC, they are possibly a precursor of the traditional conical wizard's hat. A similarly shaped hat was placed on the head of a person considered to be a 'dunce', a word that derives from 'dunn' or 'dune', meaning 'hill' or an 'upwelling of energy'. By thus focusing attention (i.e. energy) on the chakra vortex above the head, it was believed that the wearer would be granted more 'brain power' or intelligence.

To return to the skulls found on Malta: having discovered that these 'non-existent' skulls really did exist and that they had been dated to approximately 2500 BC, or maybe even before, we wondered whether they originated from somewhere other than Malta. We turned to Mesopotamia as well as the 'fallen angels' of Judaism, who were linked to the 'serpent doctors' of Enki and Enlil. *The Testament of Amran*, one of the Qumran Scrolls, describes one of these angels as being 'of terrifying aspect, like a snake … His face was like a viper and he wore all his eyes.' This is not a description of a supernatural or alien being, but of a member of the shamanic 'serpent' priesthood. This is evident from the words 'he wore all his eyes', which is a reference to the eye-like spots on the leopard skins worn by the shaman. The spots symbolized the 'eyes of God', which are everywhere. In Egypt, the god Osiris and members of the priesthood – the Sem shaman priests – are sometimes depicted wearing leopard skins, thus revealing their shamanic origin. The leopard was the mount of Dionysus, the Greek version of Osiris, and his priests often wore leopard skins. The Greeks also associated the leopard with Argus, he of the 'thousand eyes', while the word 'panther' is connected to the god Pan, who, like Cernnunos, is also associated with these shamanic Pagan gods.

The myths told about these gods reflect the serpent priests' ability to access the Void or 'source-centre'. Similar stories are told about the Egyptian Shemsu Hor, the Followers of Horus. But in the end these myths and stories all lead back to Enki and Enlil and Mesopotamia, where the serpent cults seem to have originated. There, epic tales tell of serpentine races and healings. In his article in *Hera* magazine, Adriano Forgione informs us that:

Professor Walter B. Emery (1903–1971), the famous Egyptologist, author of *Archaic Egypt*, who excavated at Saqquara in the 30s, indeed discovered the remains of individuals who lived in pre-dynastic epoch.

These presented a dolichocephalous skull, larger than that of the local ethnic group, fair hair and a taller, heavier build. Emery declared that this stock wasn't indigenous to Egypt but had performed an important sacerdotal and governmental role in this country. This race kept its distance from the common people, blending only with the aristocratic classes and the scholar associated them with the Shemsu Hor, the 'disciples of Horus'.[11]

In the words of Professor Emery himself:

Towards the end of the IV millennium B.C. the people known as the Disciples of Horus appear as a highly dominant aristocracy that governed entire Egypt. The theory of the existence of this race is supported by the discovery in the pre-dynastic tombs, in the northern part of Higher Egypt, of the anatomical remains of individuals with bigger skulls and builds than the native population, with so much difference to exclude any hypothetical common racial strain. The fusion of the two races must have come about in ages that concurred, more or less, with the unification of the two Egyptian Kingdoms.[12]

According to Forgione, 'What occurred in Malta is also reflected in Egypt.' He tells us that in Lower Egypt the Pharaoh's symbol was a bee named 'Bit' and the ancient name for Malta is Melita, which, as he points out, derives from the Latin word for 'honey'. He adds that Malta's symbol was a bee with its hexagonal cells. Furthermore, Melita has its origin in *Mel* or *Mer*. As we have already mentioned, in ancient Egypt the word *Mer*, which means 'place of ascension' and 'everlasting life', was the name given to the pyramids.

The Number Eight and Other Numbers

All numbers have meanings, and different meanings within different cultures. But there is one number that seems to cross cultures, transcending religious and ethnic boundaries with its underlying meaning of immortality: the number eight.

To the Egyptians, eight was the most magical of numbers and meant 'balance' and 'cosmic order'. According to Tim Wallace-Murphy and Marilyn Hopkins, the authors of *Rosslyn*, eight sacred sites formed a great cyclical ritual performed by Egyptian initiates. The initiates were issued with a Caduceus staff. Then, with sword and shield in hand, they were led through passageways while being attacked by assailants carrying flaming torches and serpents in a mock 'dragon-slaying' exercise. In the fifth ritual, they received their degree in alchemy, having watched the slaying by Horus of Typhon, the hundred-headed dragon. In the final mysterious ritual, they were given an ambrosial drink called Omellas. The ultimate goal, after learning the healing mysteries of the serpent and how to kill one, was the elixir itself. In effect, the ritual was a re-enactment of what was later to become the alchemical quest – the search for the later Philosopher's Stone or Elixir of Life acted out in some kind of great Passion play.

The Philosopher's Ladder, or *Scala Philosophorum*, which is associated with the shaman's 'sky ladder', 'tree', 'pole' or 'spiral vine', all allusions to the spinal axis, has eight steps, as depicted in a carved relief at Notre-Dame Cathedral in Paris.

The number eight was also of great importance in Islam, evidenced in Islamic architecture and art, which influenced the Templars, who incorporated the number into their Templar Cross and octagonal buildings.

As six was the number for the imperfect man and seven was the number for the perfect man, eight was the number for resurrection and immortality, while nine was the number for 'godhood' or the Godhead (as was the number thirteen). The numbers three, five, seven, nine and thirteen are significant numbers that form different esoteric systems. Unlike numbers that can be divided – for example, two, four and six, which represent duality or polarity – three, five, seven, eleven and thirteen are prime numbers, sacred numbers that cannot be divided equally in two. The prime number represents 'neutral balance' and the singular Monad. All divisible numbers are fused and resolved in the primary One which cannot be divided.

When placed on its side, the figure eight gives us the lemniscate (∞), commonly used to symbolize infinity or eternity. It is therefore the symbol of the serpent, the eternal self-eating, self-creating Leviathan, as symbolized in the circular Ouroboros snake or serpent that is shown swallowing its own tail. As the pyramid was a three-dimensional representation of the serpent, in numerological terms it represented the number eight.

The first sheet of the pre-Columbian Codex Ferjervary-Mayer shows a remarkable Maltese Cross with Tau symbols, the number eight and serpents running up poles or trees. The main pyramid of the Mayan/Toltec ruins at Chichen Itza in Mexico is called El Castle, or the pyramid of Kukulcan, the 'feathered serpent', otherwise known as Quetzalcoatl. Originally built by the Maya in around AD 600 and later improved by the Toltecs, it was clearly dedicated to the serpent and the cosmos. It has 365 steps (one for each day of the year), 52 stone lintel panels (one for each week) and 18 terraces (one for each of the Mayan months). Its sides were originally covered with carvings, some of which we can only speculate over while others represented the main motif of the building – the undulating serpent. A feathered serpent head sits at the head of the balustrades that run down each side of the steps, and as the sun lowers in the sky the shadows it casts form the shape of a serpent slowly descending the staircase.

The most elaborate pyramid of the Mayan city of Teotihuacan is also adorned with images of the serpent and serpent heads. Different aspects of the serpent are also shown: Tlaloc (the 'storm serpent'), Youlcoatl or Quetzalcoatl (the 'feathered serpent'), Xiuhcoatl (the 'fire serpent') and Cipactli (the 'crocodile serpent'). All aspects of the religious life, including its ritual, were watched over by the heads of the serpents.

We believed that we now held the key to understanding the special power associated with pyramids across the globe. The followers of the serpent cult built their pyramids as great initiation temples linked to their snake healer in the sky. The snake also gave eternal life, and so it was only fitting that the Pharaoh, king or leader, who was seen as the 'son of the serpent', should be believed to be interred in a building that was the architectural symbol of the serpent. The pyramids were the great structural 'cauldrons', alchemical laboratories or Grails of ancient times.

CHAPTER THIRTEEN

Serpent Alchemy

Alchemy is said to be a sublime mixture of philosophy and science – a unification of our understanding of the universe and life from a human point of view. It has been practised for centuries, perhaps even thousands of years. It is said to work on both the physical and metaphysical level, being both a practical and a psychological method of attaining immortality. With the passage of time, it was reduced to the notion that it was concerned solely with the making of gold. Today's popular view is that alchemy is the search for gold, or the turning of a base substance, such as lead, into the precious metal that symbolizes the sun god. Yet we have always found it odd that alchemy evolved at a time when gold was in abundance. Why go to extreme lengths to discover a way of creating a relatively common commodity?

By the fourteenth century, even writers such as Geoffrey Chaucer (1340–1400) were showing signs of scepticism, as we can see from 'The Canon's Yeoman's Prologue' from *The Canterbury Tales*:

> They take upon them to turne upside downe
> All the earth betwixt Southwarke and Canturburie towne,
> And to pave it all of silver and gold ...
>
> But ever they lacke of their conclusion,
> And to much folke they doo illusion,

For their stuff slides awaie so fast,

That it makes them beggars at the last

And by this craft they never doe win,

But make their pursse emptie, and their wits thin.[1]

In his *Ship of Fools*, Sebastian Brant (1457–1521) dedicated the following lines to the 'impostors' known as alchemists:

And so as here not to forget

The ugly lie of alchemy,

Which conjures up silver and gold

It's only trick and jugglery.

They show a lump to you as proof,

And soon, behold, out comes a toad!

This blindness drives him from his home,

Him who was sitting soft and warm;

He stuffed his wealth in the retort

Till it as ashes all and dust –

Many a man has perished thus,

And hardly one acquired wealth.

For Aristoteles declares:

The form of things will never change'.[2]

According to the scientist and author Louis Figuier (1819–1864):

If alchemy were a reality, King Solomon would have known of it. For does not Writ affirm that in him was united all wisdom of heaven and earth? But Solomon sent his ships to Ophir, in search of gold. And he also made his subjects pay their taxes. Had Solomon known the philosopher's stone, he would have acted differently. Thus there is no alchemy.[3]

John Becher, the apologist of alchemy, responded by saying that Solomon did not possess all crafts either, whether he had wisdom or not, and that we do not know why he sent his ships to Ophir 'in search of gold'. And yet, maybe Solomon did know something of the true Philosopher's Stone after all, for Ophir means 'place of the serpent'.

The real secret of alchemy has always been the search for the Elixir of Life, the Philosopher's Stone. Indeed, the followers of the Eastern tradition – Occidental alchemy – have always maintained that alchemy is the search for eternal life, which is symbolized by gold and is interlinked with the quest for the Holy Grail. In other words, the search for the Holy Grail, the Philosopher's Stone and the Elixir of Life are simply different ways of looking for the same thing.

There is some evidence that modern alchemy came to Europe at the beginning of the second century AD. However, this is based purely on the understanding that alchemy was the art of metallurgy and the phase-transition of substances. Pliny the Elder, who lived between AD 23 and 79, wrote extensively on metallurgy but not on alchemy or the idea of changing one metal into another. The fact that he did not relate alchemy to the transformation of metals is not surprising, since this was a later addition. People such as Zosimus, Stephanus, Olympiodorus, Synesius and other writers on the esoteric and alchemical worlds were all writing after the death of Christ.

According to many, the term 'alchemy' derives from *khem*, *chem* or *qem* (meaning 'black'), a word that was used for Egypt due to the black earth of the Nile, which contrasted greatly with the sand of the desert surrounding it. However, these early post-Christian alchemists changed this, claiming instead that the name came from the mysterious originator of gold-making, a certain Chemes, and that it was the Arabian alchemists who added the 'Al' to from 'alchemy'. Any texts or writings of 'Chemes' are now lost – if they ever existed – and we are left with a simple choice: either we believe the gold-makers and plump for Chemes, or we stick with the traditional idea of *Chem* meaning 'black'. Either way, it does not matter. The real issue is whether the aim of the alchemist was to make gold or to create the Elixir of Life.

Hundreds of years have now passed since practitioners of the craft began writing down the results of their experiments. Thousands of hours have been spent in laboratories trying desperately to make gold from lead, and many have gone to their grave without ever achieving their goal. Our reading of the subject convinces us that most were blindly following false symbolism. The symbols they interpreted incorrectly are obvious to us now, but must have seemed painfully complicated to them. 'Mercury' was not really mercury and 'Sulphur' was not really sulphur. How could a snake aid the transformation of lead into gold? No wonder that their perceived goal proved misleading and unachievable.

Alchemical symbolism has been over-complicated by the addition of a whole world of different ethnic symbols, for the gold-seeking alchemists of the past 'borrowed' and adapted every available symbol, emblem and myth. However, if we strip away most of the additions, we find one basic universal symbol that has always been there: the snake. This single symbol was broken up into other symbols and overlaid with all manner of names – Dragon, Serpent, Mercury, and so on – all of which actually refer to the same thing. Regardless of what we want to believe about alchemy and what it is really all about, the fact remains that the snake is at the heart of it, and has been there from the very start.

According to some, the alchemical serpent was simply borrowed from the early Gnostics and their serpent cults.[4] But we have to ask why would the early alchemists want to do this? And why is the serpent also found in Occidental alchemy from the outset? The symbol of Indian alchemy, known as *Nagayuna*, significantly named after the serpent deities of India, depicts two entwined serpents. Similar in both appearance and meaning to the Caduceus, it is found today all over India on votive tablets, temples and stone tablets called *Nagahals*.

Also, in the Americas, where we would not expect to find alchemy, Quetzalcoatl (the plumed serpent of the Toltec) was believed to have been the product of an alchemical conception after his mother had swallowed a piece of jade. Strangely, the plumed serpent or Mercurial image of this Toltec god was said to be only achievable through an alchemical process.

Quetzalcoatl's traits were later shared with Kukulcan of the Mayapan (city of the Maya), who is said to be the same god. Kukulcan ruled at Chich'en Itz'a and was said to have come from the west. The etymology of Kukulcan is similar to that of Quetzalcoatl: *Ku* means 'god', and *can* means 'serpent', so Kukulcan is the 'serpent god'. It is interesting to note that the Irish have a Celtic god-hero named Cuchulainn, which is too similar to the Mayan Kukulcan to be mere coincidence. Like all resurrecting gods, Cuchulainn was said to have been born of a virgin and to have died, pierced by arrows or spears, while bound to a sacred pillar. His spilt blood fertilized the Earth and, like Osiris/Horus, he was reincarnated as both father and son.

With the benefit of our research, we suggest that the reason that the alchemists of both Eastern and Western traditions chose the serpent as their ultimate god and symbol of eternal life was because they all believed in the same basic truth, which was expressed by the universal symbol of the serpent. On the third level of our Grail Triad, this was the enlightenment experience and on the first level it was the snake itself, with its powerful healing and medicinal benefits and life-extending properties.

Why did the later alchemists change the true understanding of the serpent symbol? We suggest that there can only be two answers: 1) the general alchemists (i.e. those who did not know or understand the truth of the serpent) believed it to be impossible to use the snake in gold-making and therefore interpreted it as symbolizing other elements; 2) the genuine alchemists purposely hid the truth of the snake from prying eyes. Both strike us as being highly plausible and complementary.

Figure 15: Ouroboros, death and rebirth, skull and child

We found that one of the most universal alchemical symbols was the Ouroboros. An allusion to the truth behind the significance of this symbol in alchemy is to be found in the following passage from the *Musaeum Hermeticum*, translated by the occultist Arthur E. Waite:

> Most venomous is he, yet lacking nothing,
> When he sees the rays of the Sun and its bright fire,
> He scatters abroad poison,
> And flies upward so fiercely
> That no living creatures can stand before him . . .
>
> His venom becomes great medicine.
> He quickly consumes his venom.
> For he devours his poisonous tail.
> And this is performed on his own body,
> From which flows forth glorious balm,
> With all its miraculous virtues.
> Here do all the sages rejoice loudly.[5]

Painted here is a remarkably literal picture of both the third and first levels of our Grail Triad: the snake, so venomous that no creature is capable of standing before him, yet his venom becomes a great medicine, and all of this is performed on his own body, from which flows a glorious balm!

The *Musaeum Hermeticum* is a compilation of alchemical treatises published in about 1625. It also contains an etching of a scene in a library with an abbot, a monk and a philosopher. They are obviously not working. Instead, they are discussing theory. Next to the library is a laboratory where an old man, said to be Vulcan, is at work stoking the fire of his alchemical toil. Above the furnace is the result of this toil – a glass bowl or vessel, wherein lies the secret of alchemy: a snake. The abbot, the monk and the philosopher are all looking towards this secret.

The snake is in fact a remnant of an older secret that was probably lost by the majority of alchemists but retained by a sufficient number to keep it alive through its symbolism.[6] Like the Egyptians, Greeks, Toltecs and Celts before them, the alchemists saw the serpent as a symbol of wisdom, divinity, transformation and health. It was also the deity from the Otherworld who bestowed all these things. Alchemy may thus have been the modern guardian of the ancient secret.

The strict methods for preparing the Philosopher's Stone were depicted using serpent symbols in alchemical works such as the fourteenth-century *Twelve Keys*, in which images of serpents in many guises abound, or those by Basil Valentine, which is probably a pseudonym.

Problems arose when alchemists added ever more layers onto the already rich symbolism, and eventually the original truth was lost. We can see some of this complexity when we look at the strange fifteenth-century *Ripley Scroll*, said to be one of the most important alchemical treatises. With only 21 copies still in existence, it is also a very valuable document. It has been copied and translated several times, each time losing some of the original meaning.

Of the son take the light
The Red gum that is so bright
And of the Moon do also
The which gum they both trowe
The Philosopher's Sulphur vive
This I call it without strife...
But of this water thou must beware
Or else they work will be full bare
He must be made of his own kind
Mark thou now in thy mind
Acetome of philosopher's men call this
A water abiding so it is
The maidens milk of the dew
That all the work doth renew
The Serpent of life it is called also ... [7]

The language may appear strange to our modern eyes, but it is also revealing: the Red and White are all-important; we must beware of the substance, as it can be poisonous, yet it is also called the 'Serpent of Life'. With *The Ripley Scroll*, we can see that, right up to the fifteenth century, the serpent was openly named, although it would appear that Ripley has no idea why. Or could it be that he is employing obscure language in order to conceal the truth, thus passing the secret on in such a way that it remains inaccessible to those not ready to understand it?

We are not going to go into a detailed analysis of alchemical texts, as this book has already covered much that could be said to be in the remit of the alchemist. However, we are going to examine a small cross-section in an attempt to uncover the truth they contain.

Nicolas Flamel, the famous alchemist who has recently been made yet more famous by the Harry Potter books and films, claimed to have discovered the Philosopher's Stone and set up many hospitals with the aid of his wife Prunelle (Perrenelle). In the Charnel-House of the Innocents in Paris, he had an archway built with a mural said to contain the 'Great Secret', and this became a place of pilgrimage for Hermeticists of the seventeenth and eighteenth centuries. Almost every image on the mural contains the snake or serpent.

It was said that Flamel had managed to turn lead into gold and had thus become tremendously wealthy. The truth is that he actually became rich by translating the book of Abraham the Jew, not by turning lead into gold. The focus of the Philosopher's Stone was on enlightenment and medicine – respectively the third and first levels of our Grail Triad – not on material gold. Nicolas Flamel is also said to have lived for a very long time, even to have been immortal. In truth, he lived for 88 years, from 1330 to 1418, and has been venerated ever since. However, this does bring us to a very interesting point: did the secret of the Grail snake enable people to live longer? For it was said that certain 'immortals', such as the Druids and the 'immortals of the mountains', lived longer than others.

On his way back from China in 1293, Marco Polo got a taste of south India and alchemy. He recorded a meeting he had with a group of Yogic alchemists who, so it was claimed, produced a tincture of Mercury (Quicksilver) and Sulphur that afforded a life span of 150 to 200 years. As we know, Mercury (the god) was associated with Aesculapius, the serpent healer, and so the Mercury (Quicksilver) in the tincture was understood by many to be snake venom.

As we can see from the above, alchemy made much use of the serpent, whether it was in the literal or symbolic sense. Two of its principal characters, Hermes and Mercury, are equated with Aesculapius and symbolized by the serpent. The serpent is also found in the *Emerald Tablet* of Hermes Trismegistus. Hermes is the Greek god who conducts the souls of the dead to the kingdom of Hades, the Underworld. The name 'Trismegistus' simply means 'thrice greatest', which is an indication of the high esteem in which Hermes was held. Hermes, however, is not a true Greek god. He emerged from a Greek colony in Egypt, and in all probability is a mixture of Thoth and Imhotep, both Egyptian deities related to the serpent healing associated with Aesculapius. Thoth-Hermes became humanized and was said to have written many books on a wide range of subjects. In truth, these books were the anonymous writings of various Gnostics and mystics who simply signed their writings 'Thoth' or 'Hermes' in order to give them greater importance.

The passage of time and the destruction of the great library at Alexandria have meant that few of the many writings ascribed to Hermes Trismegistus have survived. One of the greatest of the surviving works is *Poimandres*, the 'Good Shepherd', in which the ascent of the soul through seven successive stages of 'being' or 'consciousness' bears a strong resemblance to the 'seven heavens' in the biblical Book of Revelation. The doctrine of the ascent of the soul originated with the Babylonian myth of Tammuz and Ishtar and was memorialized in the seven steps of the ziggurat. In addition to its appearance in *Poimandres* and Revelation, it is recorded in the royal arches of Enoch and Mohammed's Night Ascent to heaven with the angel Gabriel.

The most often quoted of Hermes' works is *The Emerald Tablet*. As we have already mentioned, the emerald is emblematic of the serpent, as the jewel found within or indeed on the serpent. The Emerald Tablet itself is said to have either been found in the hands of Hermes' mummy in the Great Pyramid of Giza or to have fallen from the head of Lucifer, the great angelic serpent. When seen as a gift of the serpent deity, it links alchemy back to the early serpent cults of Sumeria for this 'Emerald of Lucifer' has been called the Philosopher's Stone. In truth, the earliest copy of *The Emerald Tablet* is from the *Leyden Papyrus*, discovered in 1828 in the tomb of an anonymous magician in Egypt.

The Emerald Tablet, also known as the *Tabula Smaragdina*, has been at the centre of Hermetic philosophy for hundreds of years and we believe it holds important clues to the origins of alchemical thought.

For this reason we are going to quote it here in full:

> Tis true, without falsehood and most real: that which is above is like that which is below, to perpetrate the miracles of the One thing. And as all things have been derived from one, by the thought of one, so all things are born from this thing, by adoption.
>
> The Sun is the Father; the Moon is its Mother. Wind has carried it in its belly; the Earth is its nurse. Here is the Father of every perfection in the world.
>
> His strength and power are absolute when changed into earth; though wilt separate the earth from the fire, the subtle from the gross, gently and with care.
>
> It ascends from earth to heaven, and descends again to earth to receive the power of the superior and the inferior things. By this means, thou wilt have the glory of the world. And because of this, all obscurity will flee from thee.
>
> Within this is the power, most powerful of all powers. For it will overcome all subtle things, and penetrate every solid thing. Thus the world was created. From this will be, and will emerge, admirable adaptations of which the means are here.
>
> And for this reason, I am called Hermes Trismegistus, having the three parts of the philosophy of the world. What I have said of the Sun's operations is accomplished.[8]

Many alchemists claimed that this text was just a clue to the method of gold-making. However, there are many things within it that relate to the serpent. In the line 'The Sun is the Father, the Moon is its Mother', it tells us that the father and mother of the Elixir of Life are the sun and the moon, both of which are traditional aspects of the serpent gods. Does this mean that we need to mix two kinds of snake? Or two parts of the snake?

On the third level of our Grail Triad we mix two kinds of snake: the male and female energies in the body of one individual, during the trance state and the enlightenment experience. And on the first level we mix two parts of one snake: the male and female aspects – i.e. the blood and the venom, which provide the Elixir of Life.

We were aware that we were pushing the boat out into dangerous waters by suggesting that these symbols referred literally to the snake and were not just symbols of certain metals or elements. But once we had understood the purpose of alchemy to be the 'elixir of the serpent' – i.e. the fusion of its opposite aspects on both the first and third levels of the Grail Triad – then even *The Emerald Tablet* of Hermes could be seen to hold clues we were looking for. Looking at the text more closely, line by line, we may see some of its original truth showing through.

The snake was said by many to have travelled on the wind. It is called 'the One' and is the 'Creator,' both 'Father' and 'Mother'. It is nursed in the belly of the Earth, as it resides in the dark places – a metaphor for the Underworld – and Thoth-Hermes is the 'keeper of the dark Hades'. With regard to the first level of our Triad, the *Tablet* may mean that this venom should be taken from the dead serpent for preparation. It even tells us to do this gently and with care, for it ascends and descends. When a thick liquid like the venom of the snake is mixed, say with blood, and shaken up and down, it mixes together and changes colour. When left to stand, the more solid element descends. This may be a simple way of describing the process, but it fits. However, we could not claim that this was necessarily the true method for making the elixir. It was far too vague and could quite clearly mean just about anything we wanted it to. We also knew that it would be risky to interpret this widely researched text in this way. We needed to find other texts to build the case. By broadening our research, we were more likely to come across small hints of the true method in a number of sources, especially as the truth had, in all likelihood, been partially lost.

Figure 16: Mercury (white) and Sulphur (red) putrefy
Michael Maier, *Atlanta Fugiens,* 1618

Sir George Ripley, author of the *Ripley Scroll,* gives us a clue to the truth behind the elixir in his *Twelve Gates:*

> And white appeared when all the sundry hews were passed:
> [after the venom had settled]
> Which after being tincted ruddy for ever more did last,
> [something red was added, say blood or wine]
> Then of the venom handled thus a medicine I did make;
> Which venom kills, and saveth as venom chance to take.[9]

So, in order to make the elixir the alchemist must first have something called the 'white'. This 'white' must then go through a certain process, which is said to turn it a 'ruddy' (red) colour. Finally, the alchemist turns the venom into a medicine, because although venom can kill it can also cure. Ripley is possibly being a little too obvious, but he does claim later on that his venom comes from a kind of toad, which in alchemical language suggests that the real identity of the creature is as equally repellent to most humans as the toad. It could be that Ripley was deliberately confusing the issue, especially when we consider it highly unlikely that a poisonous toad would have found its way into his possession.

The Ouroboros, as already mentioned, was extensively utilized by the alchemists from the beginning. It was also seen as the Red and White.

> Here is the mystery: The serpent ... is the composition which in our work is devoured and melted, dissolved and transformed by fermentation ... it is the cinnabar of the philosophers... The one gives the other its blood ... nature triumphs over nature.[10]

The serpent is described here as the 'cinnabar of the philosophers'. Cinnabar, which is vermilion in colour, is actually bright red mercuric oxide and thus provides a symbolic link between the snake/serpent and Mercury. The last sentence suggests that the blood of the snake (or the human) is given to the other – i.e. from snake to human, or from human to snake – while 'nature triumphs over nature' implies that it is nature's way for venom to kill, but also for venom to cure, and when it is used as a cure, 'nature triumphs over nature'.

Just as arsenic eventually took over from the snake/serpent, so Mercury (as a deity of wisdom) gradually took over from Hermes. As Charles Nicholl said in his *Theatrum Chemicum* (Chemical Theatre), 'Mercury, in short, is Alchemy itself.' Mercury is of course the serpentine god of healing. Nicholl even points out that Mercury, like the serpent, is 'self-devouring, self-generating', which alludes to the cyclical process of the third level of our Triad, as symbolized by the Ouroborus. On the first level, Mercury is described as the 'double agent', with both parts of 'the one' being brought together to create the elixir, and both being from the same source – i.e. the poison and blood of the one snake. So 'Mercury' here on this first level is the actual physical reptile we know as the snake. Mercury describes himself in the following passage from the *Aurelia Occulta*:

I am the poison-dripping dragon, who is everywhere and can be cheaply had. That upon which I rest, and that which rests upon me will be found within me by those who pursue their investigations in accordance with the rules of the Art. My water and fire destroy and put together; from my body you may extract the green lion and the red. But if you do not have exact knowledge of me, you will destroy your five senses with my fire. From my snout there comes a spreading poison that has brought death to many. Therefore you should skilfully separate the course from the fine... By the philosophers I am named Mercury ... I descend into the earth ... I am the dark and the light.[11]

The allusions in this passage perhaps need some additional clarification, although the explanation we give here does not take into account the passage's esoteric or telluric (Earth energy) implications. Mercury

Figure 17: Adam, red earth and Sulphur, mixing with Eve, who is white and Mercury, in the Grail

begins by telling us that the venom of the snake can be found almost anywhere. 'That upon which I rest, and that which rests upon me…' refers to the Earth, because the snake goes underground, and the secrets of the art and science of alchemy state that we should 'dig', for the secrets lie within the purified Earth. The 'fire and water' are opposites, as are the 'green lion and the red'. 'But if you do not have exact knowledge of me, you will destroy your five senses with my fire' is an obvious reference to the potential poisoning that will take place if one mixes the opposites in incorrect proportions. 'From my snout there comes a spreading poison…' is a clear reference to the venom that issues from the mouth of the snake. The passage ends with further references to the snake's home in the ground and the opposites, this time of 'dark and light'.

But how did this ancient 'serpent truth' find its way into the story of the Grail? Where was the link? And would this link itself provide us with any more evidence for the validity of our theory?

The Knights of St John on Rhodes had close links with the earliest alchemists and the Templars. They were also renowned for their healing skills and are said to have lived extended lives. Sir George Ripley, author of The Ripley Scroll, spent some time with the monk-knights on Rhodes, at a time when the island was said to have become the new Alexandria. Could the Knights Templar and the Knights of St John be the key to how the elixir became the Holy Grail?

The distinctive clothing of the early medical Knights Templar, a white robe with a red cross, incorporated the Red and White symbol of the ancient serpent cult. We have already described how the Templars utilized the Arthurian tales as propaganda tools for their own ends. The truth of the serpent elixir was already woven into the tales of the Celtic cauldrons and the Scythian head rituals, but the spread of Templar propaganda fused the two together to create the powerful and timeless story we now know as the 'quest for the Holy Grail'. However, we should remember that the origins of the Grail itself go back before recorded history, to the serpent people who utilized the serpent and the snake on both the third and first levels of our Triad and who encoded the metaphoric, symbolic and allegorical 'keys' to their knowledge in the myths of the second level.

During the time of the Templars, alchemists utilized an even more powerful image to symbolize their aspirations – the dragon, which must be slain to release the elixir. Dragon-slaying took on new meaning, and the story of St George (who carried the red cross of the serpent cult) and the dragon became a symbolic reference to a deeper meaning, with the red cross on the white flag providing a clue for the first level in this 'slaying of the dragon'. The story of St George is also partly of alchemical origin, but from here on alchemy becomes a whole lot more complex, as if it were not complicated enough already. Each successive generation of artisans incorporated a new language and new symbols to hide even more deeply the mystery of the serpent. So much was added and so much confusion created that in the fifteenth century Cosimo de Medici of Italy had the known world ripped apart in an attempt to rediscover the original texts.

Despite the confusion, alchemy became the unifying force behind the tattered remnants we are putting together in this book. It unified creeds, faiths and cults, and brought together Sumeria, the Americas, the ancient Egyptians, the Jews, the Rosicrucians, Freemasons, Templars, the Catholic Church and, latterly, science. In essence, alchemy was the title given to a pre-existing skill or knowledge – knowledge that appears to have been rediscovered during the Crusades.

The substance sought by the alchemists was the 'stone'. It was the tool utilized to make the 'gold'. Many understood this 'gold' literally, as already mentioned, and some even claimed to have succeeded in making it. But those who did succeed did not make gold, but instead lived extended lives – to 80 or 90 or even longer – which made them seem immortal to their contemporaries.

How did they make the elixir that gave them this immortality? The Chinese alchemist Wei-Po Yang provides the following formula:

After cooking for thirty days, a mixture of Chin 1 [gold fluid] and quicksilver is placed in a yellow earthen jar, which is then sealed with six-to-one mud and strongly heated for sixty hours. Thereupon the medicine is obtained. The swallowing of a pea-sized quantity of medicine is enough to make *hsien* [an immortal] out of any person.'[12]

Obviously the terms used here are analogous, because quicksilver (real mercury) will kill you if taken as medicine. But mercury is represented as a serpent in Arab, Chinese and European alchemical lore.

One relatively unknown alchemist comes out of the craft with startling clarity on the subject of the serpent and the elixir. He is Arnald de Villanova and we came across him quite by accident while searching through pages and pages of images of the serpent within alchemy. Arnald was born in 1245 and studied medicine at the University of Paris, where he achieved great success. Following this he spent about 20 years travelling across Europe, to Italy and Germany, picking up many secrets and medical ideas along the way. In his own lifetime he was believed to be the world's greatest physician, although it is known that, like most men of his ilk, he dabbled in alchemy and astrology. It is even said he had made considerable quantities of gold from lead. However, this simply means that he was successful at his craft: the making of gold from lead refers to the immortality he seemed to bestow on his patients.

While Arnald was travelling through Europe he made the acquaintance of Pietro d'Apone, one of the members of the craft who held similar beliefs himself. It may have been that he actually received this ancient knowledge directly from Pietro, but of this we are unsure. However, Pietro was later arrested in Italy and brought to trial by the

Church on charges of heresy and sorcery. By association, similar accusations were levelled at Arnald, who had to flee from Italy. The subsequent prestige he gained from being part of the Gnostic underground compensated for his supposed prediction of the end of the world.

Nobody knows when Arnald died. It may be that, as some Gnostics believe, he lived on in obscurity, away from ever more inquisitive eyes. His secret knowledge was much sought after, to the point that in 1311 Pope Clement V issued a circular letter to the clergy of Europe requesting information or even a copy of Arnald's now famous treatise *The Practice of Medicine*. It is said that he had promised the Holy See a copy once the work was complete, but that he died before fulfilling his promise.

Arnald's surviving texts make strange reading. He explains in a straightforward manner how one may prolong one's life for a few hundred years:

The person intending so to prolong his life must rub himself well, two or three times a week, with the juice or marrow of cassia. Every night, upon going to bed, he must put upon his heart a plaster, composed of a certain quantity of Oriental saffron, red rose-leaves, sandal wood, aloes and amber, liquefied in oil of roses and the best white wax.

In the morning, he must take it off, and enclose it carefully in a leaden box till the next night, when it must be again applied. If he be of a sanguine temperament, he shall take sixteen chickens – if phlegmatic, twenty-five – and if melancholy, thirty, which he shall put into a yard where the air and the water are pure.

Upon these he is to feed, eating one a day; but previously the chickens are to be fattened by a peculiar method, which will impregnate their flesh with the qualities that are to produce longevity in the eater.

Being deprived of all other nourishment till they are almost

dying of hunger, they are to be fed upon the broth made of serpents [or 'snakes', from the French serpents] and vinegar, which
broth is to be thickened with wheat and bran.[13]

The chickens were to be fed this 'broth' for two months, and when
eaten they were to be washed down with good white wine or claret. The
recipe concludes, 'This regimen is to be followed regularly every seven
years, and any one may live to be as old as Methuselah!' It was first
brought to light in the early sixteenth century by a Monsieur Poirier,
who claimed to have discovered it in a manuscript purported to be by
Arnald. Whether the recipe was actually written by Arnald or not, the
ideas put forward in this text are at the very least 400 years old and have
none of the fanciful alchemical symbolism that was so readily employed
in fifteenth- and sixteenth-century writings on the craft. The straightforward physician's style suggests that Arnald could very well have
written this text. In confirming that the snake can indeed be utilized to
extend life, it also provided further evidence to support our theory. But
there was more to come.

According to Longueville Harcovet, Arnald had declared that we
could restore our youth and virtually live for ever, as stags were said to
do, 'by feeding on vipers and serpents'. This declaration brings to mind
the Eastern tradition that the stag was the elixir-bringing dragon. For the
Chinese, the white stag represented Shou-hsien, the god of immortality,
while the dragon was itself called the 'celestial stag'.[14]

It was evidence like this that had been hidden under the symbolism
of 'Mercury' and 'Sulphur', names whose real significance was known to
only the few. The reason why this knowledge was so carefully concealed
becomes evident when we ask ourselves whether we too would give away
the secrets of immortality. When Philip appeared on radio recently he
asked the same question of the presenter, who was unable to give an
answer. But then, if we held the reins of power and maintained that

power through possession of secret knowledge, would we be willing to give away our secrets? How would we respond to the possibility of sharing our wealth and power with a healthy new world? Would we be able to retain our control over a growing population of ever-healthier citizens? In the past 20 years it has become evident that the world is rapidly becoming overpopulated and in the corridors of certain powers a need for radical population reduction has been expressed.[15] Conspiracy theorists are not alone in suggesting that wars have sometimes been started with the aim of reducing population and that disease has been allowed to spread – perhaps even been created – with the same end in view. In these circumstances, would we say, 'Here is the formula that will enable the population at large to achieve the health and length of life that we have'? We would probably respond as the Gnostic 'underworld' culture responded, hiding our knowledge and encoding it in such a way that it was only accessible to a few.

Once encoded in a symbolic language known only to a secret élite, new alchemical discoveries could of course be freely passed around. In fact the popularity of the written material produced by this underground stream was so great that that anything they wrote went straight into print and was distributed around the known world. This mass-marketing of ideas wrapped in symbols was perfect, for anyone with an understanding of the code could pick up a copy of the latest discoveries and interpret them, while the rest of the population continued to look up at those in power in awe and wonder, and dutifully follow as before.

However, we were constantly up against this symbolic coding as we tried to uncover what the alchemists were really up to. The conclusion we came to was that, on the first level of our Grail Triad, alchemy was the original science of the ancient world, which included knowledge of the healing snake. It could thus give us a language and a methodology to help us discover more.

Our next questions were, could modern science provide us with any means of linking the snake with the Elixir of Life? Was there any hard scientific evidence to prove – even theoretically – that the snake could extend human life?

CHAPTER FOURTEEN

Serpent Science

Our research had uncovered an abundance of mythological data, as well as historical and etymological evidence, to back up our theory that the snake/serpent lay at the literal root of the Grail, the Elixir of Life and the Philosopher's Stone. But could our theory be proved scientifically? Some scientists have raised the possibility that there could be medicinal benefits from the by-products of snakes, and others are looking at the protein structure of snake venom as an aid to boosting the human immune system, but to our knowledge no one has linked it to the 'immortality factor' as we have. Indeed, most scientific research in this area seems to have been in the realm of genetics.

In 1999 scientists claimed to have discovered a group of genes that held the key to immortality. Experiments with fruit flies identified genes that had the ability to make cells last indefinitely by simply repairing damaged cells. When these genes are activated, the fruit fly can live up to three times longer than normal. The eventual cause of death is wear and tear on the fruit fly's wings and vital organs, thus diminishing its ability to compete with other fruit flies for food. This research in itself suggests possibilities for the extension of human life if we are able to develop repairing genes similar to those of the fruit fly. But, as Professor Leonard Hayflick, Professor of Anatomy at the University of California, points out, 'There are genes that indirectly determine longevity, but if rich people could buy treatment to increase their life span it would cause chaos.'

Of course the desire to search out the Holy Grail of cure-alls is nothing new. Some people have even attempted to profit from the idea that the snake has the power to heal, as did the pedlars of the now infamous 'snake oil' back in the late nineteenth and early twentieth centuries. The very term 'snake oil' is now synonymous with quackery and fraud, but where did it originate?

Although popular belief holds that it is an entirely American phenomenon, snake oil seems to have originated in England, as evidenced by a Royal Patent issued in 1712 to Richard Stoughton's elixir, which was used in the treatment of a weak stomach or a lack of appetite. By 1750, over 200 remedies were protected by this same method. If we add to these all those remedies being touted without patents, there must have been a substantial amount of revenue created. These medicines were soon being shipped across the globe, until the American Revolution interrupted the supply chain to that particular transatlantic colony and Americans began to produce their own brand of snake oil. By 1849, men such as Perry Davies had become household names and produced remarkable painkillers and cures for such diseases as cholera. In fact, Davies' own 'all-cure' was used virtually worldwide when cholera became epidemic.

The remedy market was soon flooded with all manner of weird and wonderful concoctions, such as Kilmer Brothers' Swamp Root and Pinkham's Vegetable Compound. Men such as Doc Healy, Texas Charlie and Nevada Ned became very wealthy individuals, but the saturation of the market led to it falling into disrepute. Great medicine shows toured the nation, even the globe, pitching their tents and wares in every town. Eventually the act of selling becoming more fascinating than the product on sale, and the remedy peddlers became little more than showmen, even appearing in Barnum and Bailey's great shows.

Most of the remedies contained no snake oil at all. The name was used simply to imply that the remedy drew on the secret knowledge of

Figure 18: Clark Stanley snake oil advertisement

the Native Americans. Some did contain genuine snake oil, however. Real snake oil was highly prized, and in a newspaper article from 1880 we find John Geer, a well-known trapper, hunter and snake-tamer, telling the reporter how he killed rattlesnakes, extracted oil from their bodies and sold it for a dollar an ounce. It was said to have great curative powers.

Clark Stanley, otherwise known as the Rattlesnake King, peddled Snake Oil Liniment, which was claimed to be 'good for man and beast', and in an exhibition in 1893 he held crowds spellbound as he slaughtered hundreds of rattlesnakes, pressing their juices into vials and creating his famous 'cure-all'. His own advertising campaigns explained how his remedy was 'a wonderful pain-destroying compound; the strongest and the best', which could cure 'lame back, lumbago, contracted muscles, toothache, sprains, swellings'. Stanley claimed that he had acquired the recipe from a Moki, Pueblo Indian medicine man, which is indeed possible, since Native Americans were known to treat health problems with snake oil and even applied rattlesnake grease to afflicted areas.

By 1905, however, the rot had well and truly set in, as illustrated by an article entitled 'The Great American Fraud' in *Collier's Magazine*. Samuel Hopkins Adams, the author of the article, derided all aspects of the new 'quackery' in a hard-hitting and well-investigated piece of journalism. Because much of the content of the snake oil remedies was alcohol, there was a small resurgence in their popularity during Prohibition, but when the strict laws against alcohol were repealed there were fewer and fewer takers. As the Second World War approached, advances in modern medicine sealed the fate of snake oil and those who had profited from it.

Whereas we had previously looked at the myth and folklore traditions of the world for clues of etymology and ritual, we now needed to revisit them with a view to finding evidence of a scientific approach to the use of the snake in medicine. But where to begin? The idea of searching through millions of pages of text was daunting in itself, yet we were little prepared for the amount of evidence we were to uncover. Indeed, we soon discovered hundreds of references to the use of the snake in medicine.

Much of the scientific evidence occurs within the realm of alchemy, and we have already discussed this in previous chapters, but we found further evidence in the folklore and medical history of certain nations. With Lithuanian folk medicine, for example, we sifted through research on over 500 animal materials, all of which were utilized in the treatment of different ailments, to discover that the snake was at the very heart of their medical practice. In Egypt, the seed of the flax plant, known as 'linseed' (*lin* means 'snake') and the fat of a snake or lizard is still applied in the countryside as an ointment for rheumatic pains.[1] In Tibet, doctors divide stomach diseases into two kinds, cold and fever, and further subdivide them into seven. Recipes for the treatment of stomach disease include snake meat: 'For treatment of the "bleeding" type, use H. rham.

L., sea snail shell powder, snake meat, and ammonia salt.'[2] 'Sharp pain in the stomach, liver, chest, or lumbar region can be cured by CaCO3, H. rham. L., snake meat and Inula racemosa hook.'[3]

Ninazu, 'Lord of Physicians', was an important Sumerian healing deity. The emblem of his son, Ningishzida, was a double-headed snake, and a ceremonial double-headed snake beaker of Sumerian origin and dated c. 2000 BC[4] offers further evidence that the link between the snake and medicine was of Babylonian origin before the Greeks adapted the concept.[5] Apart from the fact that from Sumeria to China our ancestors were utilizing bee stings in the treatment of arthritis thousands of years ago (as we are rediscovering today), they were also using what they called the 'great healing properties of the snake'. They killed the creature, dried it out under the sun or over a hot fire and then immersed it in alcohol. The addition of alcohol to snake oil in nineteenth-century America would therefore seem to have been following a very old tradition. As mentioned earlier, it is said that when Jesus was on the cross he was given gall (snake venom) and vinegar (wine), a mixture that was also used by the great alchemist and physician Arnald. As far as we were able to discover, there had been no investigation into the benefits of the use of alcohol with snake derivatives. However, the alcohol may dampen the effect of the various toxins.

The reason given by most mythology experts for the serpent's symbolic link with immortality is its ability to shed old and ragged-looking skin. It does so without bleeding, and without illness or infection, which would have appeared miraculous to early human beings. In Lithuania, it is said that eating a snake would help a person to shrug off illness, much in the way that the snake sheds its skin. Indeed, in Lithuania the snake was said to cure dermatological problems: if you ate a snake, your hair, nails and skin would fall off (or out) to a certain degree and then grow back again even better than before. We have not tested this belief for ourselves and, as they warn on television, 'Don't try this at home!'

The most prolific use of the snake in medicine occurs in China. To find out more about this we contacted the Director of the Institute for Traditional Medicine at Portland, Oregon, Dr Subhuti Dharmananda, who directed us to a paper he had recently written on the subject. According to Dr Dharmananda, the earliest recorded use of snakes in Chinese medicine was the application of 'sloughed skin' described in *Shen Nong Ben Cao Jing* ('The Divine Farmer's *Materia Medica* Classic') in approximately AD 100. Athough this was the first written text, there are oral traditions that pre-date it, but even in this early text the snake was being utilized to treat superficial diseases such as skin eruptions, eye infections, sore throats and haemorrhoids.

This information provided a link to both the snake oil pedlars' claims for skin treatment and Lithuanian medical folklore. The *Ming Yi Bie Lu* ('Transactions of Famous Physicians'), from about AD 520, mentions the use of the snake's gall bladder, the meat of the pit viper and snake skin. From here on there are numerous mentions of the snake in Chinese texts, and it is widely believed that much of this information came from India. We believe it had probably originated in Sumeria. Our reason for concluding this is that there is much evidence of the use of the snake in Mesopotamian, Egyptian and Arabic cultures in ways that are similar to the usage described in Chinese texts. However, it is also possible that the Chinese developed their own system of medicine and utilization of the snake independently. The weakness with the latter argument lies in the similarity of the myths surrounding the snake, which points to a single globalized system of medicine.

According to Traditional Chinese Medicine (TCM), there are three main features about the snake that appeal to the healer: its flexibility and the speed of the cure; the shedding of its skin, which is seen as new life or resurrection; the poisonous nature of its bite. The flexibility implies that substances derived from the snake will aid those suffering from debilitating diseases of the joints, such as arthritis. Two snakes are currently used successfully in China to treat just such diseases: the *Agkistrodon* (cottonmouth snake) and the *Zaocys* (black-striped snake). The snake's shedding of its skin suggests to the traditional Chinese healer that the snake has regenerative powers, and so it is used widely for all manner of skin problems as well as a traditional method of anti-ageing.

As for the third feature, the venom, it was discovered early on that it caused paralysis and that its toxicity was greatly reduced if taken orally. Now, venom is mixed carefully and administered orally to patients who are suffering from intense pain caused by muscle contractions and convulsions.

Even the taste, or should we say 'aftertaste', of the venom has been written about. It is said to taste like sweat. A drink known as 'snake wine' has been created, and to our amazement is still served today in southern China, Hong Kong and Taiwan and in special 'snake restaurants'. One particular delicacy is rice mixed with snake bile, which is consumed before a meal as an invigorating appetizer. This may sound most unappetizing to Western ears, but there is some sense behind it. Snake bile has been shown to be good for the treatment of whooping cough, rheumatic pain, high fever, infantile convulsions, haemorrhoids and much more.

In China and elsewhere snakes are also playing an increasingly important role in the treatment of cancer, especially the *Agkistrodon*, which is said to be beneficial for leukaemia. The *Agkistrodon halys* and the *Natrix trigrina* (water snake) are converted into powder, and between three and five grams per day are taken with other herbal remedies to treat liver cancer. Recent research has also shown that snake venom itself may be of value in the treatment of cardiovascular diseases, for the anti-coagulant element of some species (others actually coagulate the blood) has been found to help with reducing blood pressure.

We also find alcohol used in conjunction with the snake in Chinese medicine. The *Agkistrodon* and the *Zaocys* are killed and soaked in alcohol, producing so-called 'snake wine', which is said to relieve problems with wind. In one particular remedy, the venom of the cobra is used as a pain-reliever. At a dosage of 0.168mg, its pain-relieving power is said to be three or four times greater than morphine and it does not induce dependence. Being a good 'immune booster', it is also effective in the treatment of tumours and heart problems. Apparently it is prepared by placing .3kg of snake meat in .18kg of wine and leaving it to infuse. The snake meat is then removed and the liquid is swallowed like a whisky-chaser!

Alcohol is also utilized in the traditional Burmese remedy for stomach-ache, burns and worms, as well as a whole host of other ailments. This time it is the Burmese python that is powdered, mixed with wine and then drunk. Sometimes it is used as a cream for its skin-healing properties.

The importation of such medicines into the West is currently restricted because Western safety guidelines are not necessarily followed in China. Only about 100 pounds of snake are now imported to the West, which is minimal in comparison to the tons utilized in mainland China. The cost of clinical trials to test for the benefits of snake substances would be prohibitive; but until such trials have been carried out, no Western government is going to authorize the use of snake as a medicine in the public realm. In the East, on the other hand, there is no shortage of financial backing for research.

Recent venom research in Taiwan has been pioneered by Tu Tsung-ming. Born in 1893, he was the first Taiwanese to become a medical doctor at a time when Taiwan was still a colony of Japan. When Tu started to teach he designated three avenues of study for his students to follow: Traditional Chinese Medicine, opium and snake venom. In the late 1920s he developed several methods to combat opium addiction and his laboratory was among the first to develop a urine test to detect traces of the drug. As for his venom research, he asked his students to collect data on the incidence of snakebite and the frequency of deaths. He then set out to discover why the venom killed, with the aim of turning it on its head and making it into a healing drug. Many have followed Tu's pioneering research into snake venom, and research continues in his laboratory to this day. At the time of writing he is still alive.

In America, recent research has shown that the protein from the venom of the copperhead viper slows the growth of cancerous tumours in mice by up to 70 per cent. There is also rapidly growing excitement about developing the use of snake venom in all sorts of cures. However, there are still old prejudices to overcome: the past reputation of snake oil salesmen, fear of the unknown, and fear of the snake and its venom.

Contrary to popular belief, however, relatively few deaths occur from snakebites, especially when compared with fatalities inflicted by other animals: in the USA there are between one and two million bites per year, but fewer than eight deaths.[6] Of course, we must take into account the modern use of anti-venom, the age of the victim, etc. Normally it is the infection created by the bite that kills, not the venom itself. Obviously there are some snakes whose venom is extremely poisonous, and all snakes should be avoided, but generally a snake will not attack you without reason, and then usually in self-defence. However, the defensive element of venom is secondary. Venom is produced in special oral glands and is an evolutionary adaptation of the saliva glands to immobilize prey, not to kill it, since it is in the interest of the attacker to keep the prey fresh. Because of the high levels of enzymes and proteins in the venom, the injected poison also tends to begin the digestive process whereby the cellular structure is broken down. Not all venom is the same, though. There are many different mechanisms involved and the diversity of the various elements that make up this unique poison are immense.

Venom generally comprises 90 per cent protein by dry weight, and most of these proteins are enzymes. Scientists have currently isolated approximately 25 enzymes – i.e. proteolyctic enzymes, hyaluronidases and phospholipases – which are proving to be of great medical worth. All these enzymes work in different ways and separating them out is an essential part of the scientist's work, much like the alchemist trying to break down the structure of his elixir. Proteolyctic enzymes are involved in the actual breakdown of tissue proteins, hyaluronidases help to speed the progress of the venom throughout the prey's tissue and phospholipases destroy muscles and nerves. There are many more enzymes, such as collagenases (which breaks down connective tissue), ribonucleases, deoxyribonucleases, nucleotidases, amino acid oxidases and lactate dehydrigenases, all of which disrupt normal cellular functions. In addition to enzymes, other elements found in snake venom include polypeptide toxins and glycoproteins. Most snakes have more than one toxin in their venom, and their accumulative effect creates a more potent poison. Generally though, most venoms can be broken down into two categories: those that are neurotoxic, which affect the nervous system, and those that are haemotoxic and affect the blood and circulatory system.

The following list separates out the various components of snake venom and describes what they do according to present scientific research:

Enzymes –   found in all snakes and speed up the destructive process of cellular breakdown.

Proteolysins –   normally found only in vipers, these dissolve the cells and tissue at the site of the bite, causing swelling and the familiar pain.

Cardiotoxins –   generally cause eventual heart failure.

Haemorrhagins – cause haemorrhaging throughout the body.

Anti-coagulants – prevent blood clots, thus enabling the venom to speed through the body.

Thrombin – causes blood clotting.

Haemolysis – destroys red blood cells.

Cytolysins – destroy white blood cells.

Neurotoxins – block the transmission of nerve impulses.

By discovering what the individual chemicals and enzymes in snake venom do, scientists are now able to utilize their beneficial effects. For instance, the anti-coagulant element of the venom can help to stop blood clotting in certain patients, whereas the thrombin element can help those who need their blood thickening. The neurotoxins in snake venom may yet be found to be excellent pain relief in a similar way to bee venom in the treatment of arthritis. A greater understanding of what are known as 'inorganic icons' will help the researchers to turn off or on the specific harmful or helpful enzymes. The potential for the medical use of snake venom is vast because of the unique diversity of its component elements.

The snake's constituent parts are already proving useful. For example, drugs used in cardiovascular treatment have been derived entirely from research into the venom of the *Bothrops* (lancehead snake). This was found to contain peptides which interrupted the enzyme involved in hypertension or high blood pressure. Scientists also found that by using a rational design based on a nanopeptide called teprotide, they were able to produce a new blood-pressure-lowering drug called Capoten, which was developed from the venom of the Brazilian pit viper. Meanwhile Cobroxin, a kind of morphine, has been derived from cobra venom and Arvin, an anti-coagulant, has been developed from the venom of the Malayan pit viper. Test results involving ingredients from the venom of the red-necked spitting cobra have indicated that they are effective in the breaking down of cell membranes, which it is hoped will eventually provide treatment for leukaemia and cancer.[7]

Components of snake venom are also being utilized in research in the fields of physiology, biochemistry and immunology. By using the specific elements that either speed up or slow down biochemical and cellular processes, researchers can more easily assess the effects of certain drugs on the individual patients. Different types of venom are also currently being investigated for use as anti-viral and anti-bacterial agents, as well for the treatment of epilepsy, multiple sclerosis, myasthenia gravis, Parkinson's disease, poliomyelitis, musculoskeletal disease, cardiovascular diseases, neuritis, conjunctivitis and cataracts. The list is widening and seemingly endless.

In 2000, *The Journal of the American Medical Association* reported on the outcome of the trial of Ancrod, a new drug made from the venom of the Malayan pit viper. Made by Knoll Pharmaceuticals, the drug acts by producing defibrinogenation in stroke patients. Fibrogen is a protein synthesized by the liver and its depletion has an anti-coagulative effect, thereby leading to improved circulation.[8] Ancrod is used in Canada and Europe in the treatment of such things as peripheral vascular disease, central retinal venous thrombosis and deep vein thrombosis. Some studies indicate that it could also be effective in the treatment of stroke patients. One particular trial involving 500 people, of whom roughly half were given the drug within three hours of a stroke while the other half received a placebo, produced positive results. Neurologic function was also assessed in both groups. The group who received Ancrod fared better than those receiving the placebo. Although Ancrod is not believed to be completely safe, it is said to offer an improved therapeutic option for stroke patients.[9]

Snake venom, as we have already described, is a multi-component system whose toxins are mostly proteins and polypeptides. Proteins are vital to the human body and increase youthful appearance. Polypeptides are amino acids derived from proteins. Although some snake venom is deadly, its effects are completely reversible with the correct anti-venom. One method of creating anti-venom is to inject venom into the bloodstream of a horse and then collect the anti-venom produced in the horse's blood. Even humans become immune to venom after small doses are administered, and it may well be that the administering of venom protected the ancients from snakebites. The Hebrews only had to look at the Brazen Serpent to be saved from the effects of snakebites!

It may be, however, that the dilution of the venom with blood – especially the blood of the same snake, which itself acts as an antidote by protecting the snake from its own venom – produced a virtual cure-all for the ancients. This would explain why the blood element in all the mythical stories we looked at was so important.

It is our belief that our ancestors were highly capable of carrying out tests on huge numbers of people in order to get the mix of venom and blood just right. Similar large-scale testing was carried out in ancient Babylon when the priests were developing their astrological forecasting systems. For now, however, we have to welcome the fact that there are some Western scientists who are willing to look at the individual elements of snake venom in their search for new medicines.

In the United Kingdom, the Cancer Research Campaign has welcomed research into Contortrostatin (CN), a protein found in the venom of the copperhead viper, which has proved effective in combating metastasis (the spread of a malignant tumour from its original site). In experiments on mice, CN reduced the spread of tumours by 90 per cent. The Cancer Research Campaign commented:

It's the spread of cancer which in the majority of cases is so devastating. This work is interesting because it's highly targeted to tumour cell behaviour. Although it's early days it's an intelligent way of dealing with cancer and clearly has therapeutic potential. Inhibiting metastatic spread of cancer and tumor blood vessel development are two of the key approaches under investigation.[10]

The US Food and Drug Administration (FDA) has already approved the drug Integrilin, which is derived from the rattlesnake, for the treatment of people suffering from chest pains, unstable angina and small heart attacks. In a recent study of 10,948 patients in 27 countries, the drug was found to reduce the risk of heart attack and death by 1.5 per cent. However, more research into the drug is needed to increase the success rate.

Another remedy derived from snake venom is Lachesis, which is used in homoeopathic medicine. It is made from the venom of a Central and South American snake, the *Lachesis mutus*, which is related to the rattlesnake. The largest venomous snake found in the New World, it can measure up to four metres in length. Only small doses of its venom are needed to totally destroy red blood cells, but with the Lachesis remedy the venom is not so much split apart into separate enzymes but diluted many times over in a lactose solution until the desired potency is obtained. Here is a medicine developed along similar lines to the message we were getting from history and mythology, but this time in a modern bottle rather than a chalice and called 'Lachesis', not 'the elixir'.

Homoeopathy works on the principle of 'like cures like', so homoeopaths recommend Lachesis for patients whose symptoms are similar to those actually created by the poison. Interestingly, the symptoms are the same as those created by sulphur poisoning, which we found quite extraordinary in view of the symbolic use of sulphur by the alchemists. (Could this be the reason why sulphur was chosen as the symbol of snake venom?) In its diluted form, Lachesis can eliminate the symptoms of full-strength venom poisoning. It is also said to aid the treatment of various symptoms, including choking coughs, croup, earache, sore throat, indigestion, throbbing headaches, insomnia, hot flushes, haemorrhoids and sciatica. It is considered to be one of the most important homoeopathic remedies and, unlike many other forms of snake cures, it is available over the counter.

Homoeopathic scientists seem to have been among the few pioneers in exploring the benefits obtainable from snake venom. For example, Lachesis was discovered by Constantin Hering. Against all orthodox and scientific advice, he travelled with his wife to the South American jungle searching for new homoeopathic remedies. The indigenous Indians informed him about a snake they called Sururuku that had terrified them for generations. They claimed that even its breath was lethal. Hering eventually persuaded them to show him the whereabouts of the snake and together they managed to trap one alive. Hering took the poison in a diluted form, but the toxins took effect almost immediately and for several hours he suffered various symptoms. Just before losing consciousness, he instructed his wife to carry on taking notes of all the reactions induced. These notes were later entered into the homoeopathic *materia medica* and have since helped cure thousands of people. Strangely, Hering never liked wearing tight collars because they gave him an unpleasant restricted feeling. One of the key symptoms of Lachesis poisoning is just that – a tight feeling on the throat – and by taking the remedy of diluted *Lachesis mutus*, Hering actually cured his own problem.

Homoeopathy is a controversial area where scientific medicine is concerned, for it works on the principle that the more the original substance is diluted, the more potent the resulting remedy becomes. As yet there is no conventional scientific evidence for the claims attributed to homoeopathic remedies, just thousands of satisfied people. However, in the context of our theory, it is significant that the most powerful homoeopathic remedy available is made from the venom of the snake.

The funding behind new homoeopathic research is minor in com-

281

parison to the huge amounts of money being invested in drugs that have far lower success rates, and there remain good scientists who are left to carry out their research with no financial backing at all. There are also scientists, who, in contrast to those who separate out the component elements of the venom, believe that the whole venom – or indeed, the whole snake – should be seen as a useful medical tool.

One such man, Peter Singfield, was known lovingly by the natives of Belize as 'Snakeman'. Many years ago this elusive man became fascinated by ancient Mayan medicine which appeared to be derived from snakes. This fascination led him to leave Canada and travel to Belize, where he began his long journey of discovery. After only a short time, he came to believe that healing was more about helping to boost the immune system than treating the affected area with modern drugs. This may be relevant in that in our modern world we seem to be losing the battle against mutating diseases and increasingly resistant strains of viruses, and ancient diseases that were believed to be almost extinct are reappearing across the globe. A localized legend in his own time, Snakeman was seen as a 'great god' of medicine. Hundreds of natives, together with the occasional Westerner, visited him for immune-boosting remedies.

Snakeman's background does not account for his remarkable rebirth as a medicine man. A mechanic and engineer at the National Research Institute in Canada, he had studied chemistry and medicine as a hobby. In the course of his studies in Belize, he became friendly with Don Eligio Panti, a Mopan Mayan healer. The last Mayan shaman to be honoured with the title 'Doctor-Priest', Panti died in 1996 at the age of 103. Following his death, Snakeman met up with an unnamed healer from El Salvador who introduced him to Cascabel (the rattlesnake), which is believed to be the source of one of the most potent medicines known to the ancient Mayans. Cascabel powder is still in use today in Mexico and Central America. However, its healing properties did not seem to be particularly effective against major ailments, and so Snakeman went in search of the right ingredients. Eventually he discovered a sub-species of the tropical rattlesnake called Tzabcan (*Crotalus durissus*) which he found to be much more potent and greatly improved the ingredients of Cascabel.

The ancient use of Cascabel is evident from its appearance in the Mayan Codices, where it is explained that no agitated rattlesnake may be used. As it turned out, the new sub-species discovered by Snakeman was more docile than the species previously used. He produced the medicine in the traditional Mayan way by skinning, drying, baking and grinding Tzabcan snakes, and natives from across the region brought dead snakes for him to convert into medicine.

Cascabel is believed to be a strong immune-booster that promotes rapid healing and aids the body to fight such diseases as AIDS, cancer, terminal diabetes and ulcers. The high levels of proteins in the venom may have some effect within the medicine, but because it is not known which element of the drug is the immune-booster, the FDA and other authorities around the world are reluctant to follow up its benefits. This reluctance to fund or even test Snakeman's theories has left him rejected by the West and now only one or two Westerners take the drug. As Snakeman himself said in a recent interview:

How you can isolate an active ingredient when you don't know what you are looking for, because we have no concept of what medicine enhances the immune system, nor what combination of compounds augmenting and reacting with each other causes it. After baking the snake dry at 320 degrees Fahrenheit no organic components are left, it's gone through the transformation, it's dehydrated, only minerals are left. It's like cement; you could mix that with sand and build with it. Well then, how can a mineral be a medicine? Well, God knows. When we put it in analysis with pharmaceutical researchers down here in the late 80s that's what they were doing, culture tests and everything … I told them from the beginning it doesn't apply to that. You can put it in a culture with a lethal disease and it doesn't kill the disease, it only works with the immune system. Well, it took them two years to figure that out. They spent more than a million dollars researching in that direction before they agreed with me.[11]

Cascabel has been proven scientifically to work. A spectacular sequence to be seen on website **www.ambergriscaye.com/pages/town/article39** shows a young drug addict who had suffered severe burns inflicted by his dealers. The burns had turned gangrenous and the standard Western method of treatment would have been amputation and antibiotics. However, Cascabel stopped the invasion of gangrene and aided the regeneration of the tissues. The man has now regained the full use of his arm without the need for any Western medical intervention.

This dramatic 'regeneration' brought to mind the myths of how the Celtic cauldrons and the Grail could heal armies of their war wounds and regenerate them to fight again another day. There is no known substance on the planet today with such remarkable and magical powers. But once there was. It was the snake.

Our own story would be incomplete without the story of the now famous Bill Haast.[2] This amazing man has been injecting himself with snake venom since 1948 and has built up such powerful antibodies that his blood, like that of the horse, has been used as anti-venom. In addition to injecting himself, he has also been bitten at least 168 times. Haast firmly believes that venom has kept him healthy and claims never to have been sick since he began taking it. Bill Haast is not a doctor. He is a lover of snakes and until recently ran one of the world's largest serpentariums. It is said that at the age of 90 he looked no older than 50, walking with a spring in his step and a secret in his veins.

In the late 1970s, a Miami physician named Ben Sheppard was

suffering from arthritis and so took some of Haast's snake drug called PROven that he had in his possession. Sheppard found the drug to be so beneficial that he started issuing it to his patients. It even became the subject of the CBS television programme *60 Minutes*. Sheppard ended up successfully treating nearly 6,000 patients, most of whom were suffering from multiple sclerosis. That is, until the FDA stepped in, shut down the clinic and banned the use of the drug because there hadn't been any clinical trials. There are still those, however, who claim that it is beneficial in the treatment of herpes simplex, herpes zoster, muscular dystrophy, Parkinson's disease, myasthenia gravis and amyotrophic lateral sclerosis. A similar drug, called Horvi MS9, has been created and is currently sold legally over the counter in Germany.

We have had confirmation closer to home of the healing power of the snake. Eddie, a friend of Gary's, told him that he had been having chest pains and other related problems. Instead of going to the doctor, he went to the local homoeopath, since both he and his wife were training to be homoeopaths at the time. The homoeopath listened to Eddie and then gave him a small cellophane pouch labelled 'Naga' with what looked like grey-brown powder inside. It was powdered cobra. Eddie said that after taking it he felt dizzy and could feel the blood rushing through his veins at an incredible rate. He felt revitalized and empowered – a feeling that lasted for several days. The last we heard from him was that the initial symptoms had gone, possibly for good.

What now needs serious investigation are the uses, the sources and the big question of 'why' snake-based medicine works. As Snakeman discovered, the degree of efficacy can depend upon the species of snake utilized. While the Tzabcan is found only in northern Belize, many other species are to be found across the globe, all of which probably provide different levels of effectiveness. It may be that different species were once used for different ailments. It seems, however, that venomous snakes in general boost the immune system, thus adding to the power of the

T-cells, the very same cells mentioned by Philip's wife which set us off on our journey of discovery.

It may be that some of the medical benefits afforded by the snake can be discovered by looking at the uses of other animals and plants in medicine. As we have already mentioned, bee venom is known to help arthritis and muscular pain, and many thousands of people across the globe subject themselves daily to bee stings in order to overcome the constant pain they find themselves in. The bee sting seems to contain an element that is a blood-borne pain-reliever. Camomile, a pungent herb of the genus *Anthemis*, has been widely used in medicinal ways. The Romans believed that camomile was an antidote to snake venom, which perhaps explains why the ancient Egyptian snake-lovers regarded it as sacred. Could camomile have been the herb used in the mixing bowl with the snake venom and blood? Later, the herb became popular throughout Europe as an 'all healer', being taken as an infused drink.

Another area suitable for investigation is the snake's apparent ability to slow down the ageing process and prolong life. One of the best known methods of anti-ageing is calorie restriction, a dietary method that emerged in the 1930s and allows for a diet rich in nutrients but low in calories. In a series of 2,000 experiments, it was found to dramatically extend the life span of mice, rats and even monkeys. Now, it so happens that the snake is very high in nutrients and low in calories, which may be one of the ways in which it aids the prolongation of life.

This brings us back to the snake as the ultimate symbol of immortality, and we have a scientific proposition to make regarding why this may be so. It is a theory that is untested and unproven, but one that we believe is backed by the surrounding evidence.

We have already mentioned that injecting a horse with snake venom activates antibodies in its immune system, thereby creating anti-venom. Its blood thus reacts with the venom in such a way as to turn a potentially harmful substance into a beneficial one. Now, when a snake attacks its prey, it injects it with a lethal dose of venom. Since the prey is usually smaller than a horse, it succumbs to the effects of the venom without developing the appropriate antibodies. The snake goes on to eat the prey while the venom is still in its bloodstream. Its blood is therefore still poisonous, but the snake devours it without any ill-effects. From this, it would seem that somewhere in the snake's blood there is an anti-venom which, when mixed with its venom, cancels out its poisonous effects. We believe that mixing the two together in the correct dosage could create an immune-system booster that could be taken orally or otherwise by humans. (Although it is believed that humans can take venom orally without too much harm, we strongly advise you not to try this at home.) It is perhaps for this reason that in many parts of the world the whole snake is used. There may be something within the process of burning and powdering the snake that hermetically fuses the venom and blood together. With the appropriate testing and trials, it should be possible to create a variety of strengths and remedies.

The myths and folklore traditions we have examined from around the globe seem to back our theory. What is required now is scientific testing. Experimental evidence is not necessarily hard to come by. As we have shown, there are people around the globe taking snake-derived medicine and being healed. What *is* difficult to come by, however, is evidence produced by scientists, since there is relatively little funding available, and not enough interest to generate funding.

Although we are personally opposed to the killing of innocent animals, we are sure that were serious research carried out into the secret formula found within the body of the snake, an artificial drug could be created to simulate its effect of boosting the immune system.

In the course of research, it became increasingly evident to us that this capacity to boost the human immune system provided a scientific explanation for the snake's association with the Holy Grail and the idea of immortality. Many people who have been closely connected with the medicinal use of the snake have lived greatly extended lives, outliving their contemporaries by decades. Could this mean that immortality is just around the corner?

According to some scientists, it is even closer than this. Dr Ben Bova, President Emeritus of the National Space Society has said, 'The first immortal beings are living among us today. You might be one of them. There are men and women alive today who may well live for centuries, perhaps even extend their life spans indefinitely. They will not become feeble and sickly. Ageing will be stopped, even reversed. You may be young and vigorous forever.' Of course, we cannot eliminate viral infections, disease, accidents and warfare. But we can boost the immune system and we can and are working hard on what is known as the 'Hayflick limit'.

The Hayflick limit was discovered in the 1970s by Leonard Hayflick, Professor of Anatomy at the University of California, who found that most types of human cells have natural limits to the number of times they divide. Once their time is up, the cells cease to divide or reproduce and this is called senesce. There are, however, 'immortal' cells – such as cancer cells – which, barring outside interference, will simply live forever: they have no Hayflick limit. Even lowly bacteria are immortal. The task at hand is twofold: to stop these harmful immortal cells from living and to make good cells immortal.

In their search to halt the ageing clock, many scientists are turning to what are known as 'telomeres'. Inside every cell in the human body are strands of chromosomes. Human cells have 46 chromosomes, except for 'sex cells', which have only half that number. The chromosomes contain the now well-known DNA – the Bible of life. At the tip of each chromosome is a kind of cap – named the 'telomere' by scientists – that stops the ends of the chromosomes from sticking together. It is believed that these caps are the 'clock of ageing'. Each time the cell divides, the telomere shortens, and when it attains a certain length the cell ceases to divide and we grow old. On the other hand, bacterial DNA does not have telomere caps and therefore the ends stick together in a kind of circle, as Ben Bova says, 'like a snake swallowing its tail'.

By 1998, researchers had announced that they had managed to extend the life of human cells indefinitely by adding 'telomorase', an enzyme (a protein which assists chemical processes; a catalytic protein, reducing toxins) that had been found to build new telomeres. Cancer cells had been found to produce telomerase in plentiful supply, and this is what gave the researchers the clue. Telomerase is present in normal human cells, but for reasons as yet unknown it is deactivated. By adding it to a cell in abundance it was found that activation occurred. However, scientists have also pointed out that this may increase the rate of cancer in certain individuals.

Psychoactive Substances

It is widely known that the trance state and the enlightenment experience were sometimes initiated by, or facilitated by, certain psychoactive drugs or substances that stimulated the pineal gland. One such substance was *Soma*, otherwise known as *rue* or *haoma*, for which the Latin name is *Pergunam harmala*. It is said that the term 'Essene' came from another name for this drug, the assena bush, which suggests that these early teachers of Christ (the archetypal shaman) were well in touch with the pharmacology of the plants and animals around them. According to alchemical tradition, rue is said to neutralize snake poison via its beta carbolines. The name 'rue' is similar to the Egyptian word RU, which is depicted as the oval of the ankh and was originally a serpent oval. It is also the root of 'rose', which is associated with the gateway into the World Mother and the Underworld. Perhaps the drug was named 'rue' because it was used to facilitate shamanic entry into the Underworld, which is really one's conscious access of the collective subconscious.

As we have already mentioned more than once, when Jesus was on the cross he was given a mixture of gall and vinegar. The gall was snake venom and it was believed that the vinegar was just stale wine. However, according to the Nag Hammadi Gospels and other alchemical texts, this vinegar was called the 'Vinegar of the Four Thieves', one of whose ingredients was *Perguman harmala* (also known by its Syrian name as 'rue'), which neutralizes poison. It is interesting that *Soma* means 'eat my body'. Was this a subtle allusion to the Eucharist of Christ?

It has been said that taking *Perguman harmala* together with a subtle mixture of snake venom causes trance-like visions of snakes, leading people to believe that they are experiencing other worlds or even enlightenment. They may well be, but we suggest that this psychedelic effect may be partly caused by the mixture of drugs triggering the pineal gland into releasing 'happy hormones'. These include melatonin, a potent antioxidant that scientists have shown to be beneficial in combating anti-ageing and cancer as well as a number of other problems. We also suggest that this unique mixture of poison and hallucinogenic drugs must have made the ancient 'user' feel that they were in contact with their god, for it would have boosted their immune system and left them on a high for several days, giving them a feeling of being 'born again'. It is perhaps no coincidence that in the subtle language of symbolism the pineal gland is known as the 'cup' or 'chalice' and Mandean Christians perform a ritual taking of these substances to this very day. It is therefore a distinct possibility that the so-called 'Grail journey' – the quest for enlightenment, which sometimes involved visiting magical and dream-like places – could have been facilitated by these trance-inducing mixtures of drugs.

Those who undertook the Grail journey also held the secret elixir – the venom of the snake – within themselves. The practice of meditation would have boosted this psychedelic trip. When meditating, the initiate synchronizes their brainwaves to 8Hz, and by closing their eyes they actually prevent the leakage of melatonin from the brain into the greater body, thus saturating the neo-cortex, which in turn boosts the cycle and increases the yield of melatonin and another hormone called pinoline. It is believed that this extra pinoline actually helps the cells in our body to replicate, thus extending life and boosting the immune system by 2.6 fold, as well as activating the brain by as much as 40 per cent more than normal. In other words, both the science of the Grail and the mystical idea of enlightenment could have been facilitated by, or possibly have been the result of, a chemical- and drug-induced trip.

The implications of this are enormous. It means that when the snake/serpent is fully understood according to the three levels of our Grail Triad, we will be able to improve greatly our health, boost our immune system, become more alert, live much longer and enjoy the whole of our journey through life.

CHAPTER FIFTEEN

The Serpent Grail

There are many different versions of the Grail story. Among the oldest are the French *Le Conte du Graal* (1188–1190) by Chrétien de Troyes, *Perlesvaus* (1190–1212) by an anonymous author, the German *Parzifal* (before 1220) by Wolfram von Eschenbach, and a pagan Celtic version, *The Mabinogion* or *Mabinogi* of Peredur. These peculiar stories have mesmerized generations of people, who remain mystified as to what they all mean. However, many are now coming to the view that the Grail romances allegorize an initiatory experience, as indicated by the authors of *The Holy Blood and the Holy Grail*:

> As the *Perlesvaus* suggests, the Grail, at least in part, would seem to be an experience of some kind. In his excursus on the Grail's curative properties and its power to ensure longevity, Wolfram would also seem to be implying something experiential as well as symbolic – a state of mind or a state of being. There seems little question that on one level [our third level] the Grail is an initiatory experience, which in modern terminology would be described as a 'transformation' or 'altered state of consciousness'. Alternatively it might be described as a 'Gnostic experience', a mystical experience', 'illumination' or 'union with God'.[1]

The authors of *The Holy Blood and the Holy Grail* are also right to suggest that this experience is associated with what has been described in the

Kabbalah as 'a series of rituals – a structured sequence of successive initiatory experiences leading the practitioner to ever more radical modifications of consciousness and cognition'.[2] The Kabbalah itself is the 'Judaic equivalent of similar methodologies or disciplines in Hindu, Buddhist and Taoist tradition – certain forms of Yoga, for example, or of Zen'.[3] We would agree, while placing more emphasis on the Hindu descriptions of this experience (i.e. Kundalini), but all of the above would indeed apply. The lack of emphasis on the experiential aspect of the Grail is probably because few people have experienced the altered state of consciousness for which the Grail is the symbol. They therefore have difficulty in relating to the mystical implications of the Grail, and instead go in search of a literal cup or chalice. On the other hand, those who have had this experience know that it cannot easily be conveyed through everyday language, for they have broken through the limitations of time and space and become one with the Placeless and the Timeless. In this context, the Grail is the epitome of the mysteries and the goal of all experience, wisdom and knowledge. At their highest level the Grail and the enlightenment experience are one and the same thing: to drink from the Grail is to drink the wine of the fountain of all knowledge.

The extensive corpus of Grail legends and myths belongs to the second level of our Grail Triad. By following the symbolic clues in a synthesized summary of these second-level stories, we can see how they apply to both the third and first levels of the Grail.

The hero of the story is known as Perceval or Parzifal. He is the 'son of a widow' and begins his adventures as the archetypal fool. Leaving his mother behind, he sets out on a journey to seek his fortune. He encounters a damsel who gives him a jewelled finger-ring and soon afterwards he is initiated into warriorhood after a fight with a red knight who had stolen the queen's golden cup. Our hero slays the knight and takes his red suit of armour. He then goes to the aid of a maiden named Blanchefleur ('White-flower'), with whom he falls in love and whom he will one day marry.

Here we see the theme of the Red and the White representing the nerve channels that are 'wedded' together during the initiatory experience. What we are being told here is that Perceval has already experienced this internal union at some time in his life, but does not yet know this.

Next, our hero arrives at the court of King Arthur. Later he sets out from the court and comes across the castle of the Fisher King. He is greeted by the king's courtiers and shown to a square hall where the Fisher King is reclining on a couch. He has been wounded in the thigh (some say in the groin, while others say through both thighs) by a spear, making him infertile. Because of his incurable wound, he spends his days out on the lake fishing. His kingdom has fallen into ruin and become a wasteland. A squire gives Perceval a sword that will not break.

Our hero then witnesses a strange procession outside the hall, headed by a young man carrying a white lance dripping with blood. He is followed by two more squires carrying a gold candelabrum. In turn, these are followed by a damsel carrying in both hands the Grail, which radiates a light so bright that the lights of the candles are swallowed up by it. We are not told what the Grail is. In some versions it is a vessel or cup of some kind, inlaid with jewels; in others it is a 'stone'. The maiden carrying the Grail is followed by another maiden who carries a round silver platter or dish. In Eschenbach's version, Perceval sees the bloody lance being held over the dish or platter so that it catches the drips of blood. In the Celtic version of the story, the dish carries a decapitated head, swimming in blood. The procession moves slowly into another chamber.

Later, Perceval is invited to sit with the king at supper. A cornucopia of rich food is placed before the diners and the Grail is again passed before them. Although mystified, Perceval does not ask what the Grail is used for, nor whom it serves. We are led to understand that his silence is a big mistake.

When Perceval rises the next morning, he finds the castle deserted.

He mounts his horse to search for his host and after he has crossed the drawbridge the castle disappears behind him. Later, he is reprimanded by an old hag who tells the young fool that if he had asked what the Grail was for and whom it served, the Fisher King would have been healed and the land restored to its former glory.

The strange items carried in the procession – the sword, lance/spear, the Grail and the platter/dish – are highly symbolic and have found their way into the Tarot as Swords, Wands, Cups and Disks/Coins respectively, and also into packs of playing cards, where they have become the suits of Spades, Clubs, Hearts and Diamonds. The candelabra carried by the two squires seem to be associated with the tree and therefore the spine, with the candles (usually seven) symbolizing the seven chakras associated with the seven endocrine glands that align the spine. This imagery is indeed ancient, for it features on Mesopotamian cylinder seals as a candelabra-like tree with several appendages and flanked by two figures.

Significantly, the Grail appears twice in the story. This double appearance possibly refers to the two crucial points in each and every cycle – 'where' and 'when' a pulse of energy is delivered from the source-centre of creation. As explained earlier, we are mostly unaware of this dynamic point in the cycle and therefore blind to its significance. It is possible that our ignorance of this contact with the very source of our being is represented by Perceval's failure to ask about the mysterious Grail when it passes directly in front of his eyes. This failure means that he spurns the possibility for enlightenment and wisdom, and so remains a young fool.

In writing this book we have tried to include every relevant aspect of human history. There may be some areas we should not have strayed into and there may be others that we have set aside for inclusion in future books. We apologize if we have crossed a bridge we should not have or not wandered into a field where we should have been. But our search goes on. Our hope is that by releasing these discoveries into the public arena there may be others out there who have a similar desire to get to the truth. By working together, we may once again be able to utilize the lost secret of the Elixir of Life.

As many scholars and authors have discovered, the snake has appeared in myths, legends and folklore for thousands of years and may have featured in ancient esoteric initiation ceremonies whose original meaning has now become so obscured that modern misunderstandings have been overlaid on old ideas.

At the beginning of this journey we asked a simple question: how do you visualize the Holy Grail? A cup? A jewelled chalice? Can you recall what your answer was? And what about the Philosopher's Stone? Has your answer changed? Do you still see a sparkling diamond of green? Or a small white pearl? Then, of course, there is the Elixir of Life …

When we now imagine the Grail our minds go back in time on a fanciful journey, to the man (or woman) who first discovered it. On the first level of our Triad, what might this discovery have been like?

Imagine a dark cave, wind raging outside and rain beating a confused melody at its entrance. The cave is lit from one corner by a small flickering flame of orange, producing ghostly spectres on the dripping and uneven walls.

The shaman, dressed in animal skins, with red-ochred face and wild eyes, is standing before his assembled disciples. He is grasping a rattlesnake tightly by the neck. The all-male audience sits uneasily, gazing intently upon the snake as the poisonous fangs are pressed against the top section of a sacred staff. A thick liquid slowly oozes down the shaft into a stone bowl decorated with strange pictoglyphs. The shaman counts each drip of the venom.

When his counting reaches a certain number, he takes up a flint knife and decapitates the snake on a stone platter or dish. There is a spurt of blood as the body writhes from the effect of nerves on the muscular system. The head of the snake is left at the centre of the bloody platter or dish, its mouth wide open.

As the flow of blood slows to a trickle, the shaman wraps the body of the snake in a spiral around the shaft of the sacred wooden staff. Clasping the staff and the snake's body close to the open wound, he squeezes the last drops of blood from the body. Like the venom before it, the blood now runs down the staff into the stone bowl. Using the staff as though it were a measuring rod, the shaman again counts each drop of blood.

When he is satisfied that the right mix has been attained, he throws the body of the snake into the audience, and his disciples scramble to win this sacred prize. Taking a shining stick from his medicine pouch, the 'high snake-priest' stirs the two ingredients together … and the true elixir is born.

This is a fanciful image, with a lot of artistic licence, but it is based on archaeological and historical evidence.

As can be seen, the four items of the Grail romances each have their place in the creation of the elixir. We have the flint knife, later replaced by a knife or sword, and the platter or dish, with a serpent's head swimming in blood. We also have the staff, later symbolized by a spear or lance, dripping blood into the mixing bowl or Grail. The point at which the staff was bitten by the snake would be replaced by an orb (Ab or Oub) or ornate knob. This design has come down to us as the gentleman's cane or walking stick. Ideally, the bowl would also have been a skull or skullcap – possibly the skull of a shaman or even a 'serpent being' who had experienced enlightenment in both the higher worlds and the Underworld.

And last but not least, we have the 'serpent energies' of the most important ingredient, the snake sacrificed on the staff. Later, the snake entered the world's mythological traditions in the form of a 'serpent being' or 'serpent god', nailed to a symbolic tree, from whom flowed an Elixir of Life that granted us the gift of rebirth and immortality.

Appendices

The Three Levels of the Grail Triad

First Level

The first level of the Triad is the mixing of the venom and blood of the snake, usually inside a skull or skull cup. This practical application of the serpent energies is symbolic of the Kundalini enlightenment experience. One snake is used, but the two properties of the venom and the blood provide a magical correspondence with the fiery male *Pingala* channel (venom) and the 'watery' female *Ida* channel (blood). The mixing of these two physical opposites in the skull cup corresponds to the union of the two opposing energies in the centre of the head. The curative elixir is then administered, promising a revitalized mind and body, youthful ness, longevity (with perhaps a sense of one's immortality) and spiritual release via hallucinogenic experiences.

Second Level

This level embraces the legends, mythical stories, folk tales, allegories and true events that have been altered to reveal their symbolic meaning. It thus contains the necessary clues for discovering and understanding both the first and third levels of the Grail Quest.

Third Level

This is the enlightenment experience known by the Hindus as *Kundalini*. For the sake of physical existence the *aether*-like 'serpent energy' (the son) of the Godhead or source-centre of creation is divided in two: male and female, positive and negative, mind and matter, conscious self and subconscious, left brain and right brain, etc. In the individual, the *Pingala* and *Ida* nerve channels that align the spine represent these two opposites and are themselves represented by the two entwined serpents of the Caduceus. During the Kundalini 'enlightenment experience' one is conscious of these two opposite energies as they ascend the spine via the spinning wheel-like vortices of the chakras.

If successful, the two energies will rise together, uniting within the head as pure bright light. The fusion of these two opposites results in enlightenment. However, during the more spontaneous cases the fiery male energy will rise through the *Pingala* channel first, sometimes causing a burning sensation around the spine. After some time the female energy will ascend, extinguishing the 'fire' and finding balance with it at the level of one or other of the chakras. If successful, both energies will unite together in the centre of the head, again resulting in enlightenment.

This experience brings confirmation of one's own immortality and grants a higher level of knowledge and intelligence. One feels as if one has been reborn or 'resurrected', with a whole new view on life and existence. The answers to the enigmas and mysteries of life and death begin to present themselves.

To understand the very thing that is at the core of all our religions and that has provided the religious impulse of humankind through history, we would ask that the reader consult books about Kundalini.

The Quantum Grail and the Quantum Serpent

In light of the evidence we have uncovered during our years of research, we believe that the ancients understood the 'quantum state' long before quantum theory was formulated in the early part of the twentieth century.

According to shamans this quantum state was something that could be experienced through the shamanic trance state, which was often described as being simultaneously alive and dead. It was observed that the two properties of the snake – the venom and blood – corresponded to the opposites of life and death. The venom was associated with death, as observed in the white bloodless cadaver (some venom can also turn the skin pale white) and the red blood was associated with life, the lifeblood, thus presenting us with the theme of the Red and White as expressed in the Eucharist.

We suggest that the snake itself was seen as something neutral, much like the quantum subatomic entity we know today, which, depending on how we observe it, expresses itself as either a particle or a wave. Similarly, the snake can either inflict death or be used as a cure-all, thereby sustaining life and even extending it. For those who knew of its healing qualities, the snake was therefore seen as a paradox in that it both contained within it and expressed these contradictory opposites, just like the node-point in all cycles, where the positive and negative phases of an electromagnetic 'serpentine' wave become neutralized.

Whichever of these two properties we apply to the snake depends on how we perceive it or experience it. It was observed that as one's body adjusted to the mixed snake elixir one was in a paradoxical state of existence: at the same time both dead and alive and neither, just like the suspended alive/dead state of Schrödinger's Cat, the hypothetical animal used to illustrate the fundamental quantum paradox known as the Uncertainty Principle. This is exactly the same state one is in during the enlightenment experience: caught between the opposites, suspended between life and death. This neutral state is also alluded to in cauldron myths and in the universal myth of the dying and resurrecting god. It is also the crucial point in all cycles – the alpha-omega.

As the snake was seen as containing these opposite properties while being something neutral in itself, it became a symbol for the life-force, the 'ground-state energy' of the universe, once known as the *æther*, the source of which is known to mystics as the Void. It is this energy that one experiences during the enlightenment experience described in the Hindu scriptures. This experience is also the 'Stone' – the zero-point at which one's conscious and subconscious minds merge with the collective unconscious and one becomes superconscious.

The Realm of the Snake
in Mythology

The snake is intricately linked with magic and mythology in almost every culture. It is seen as the personification of wisdom and goodness and as the personification of evil, thus revealing its implicit duality. Snake worship is a worldwide phenomenon, which many experts believe can be traced back via India to Persia, Babylonia and earlier civilizations.

According to scholars of mythology, the erect posture adopted by the snake when threatened led to it being seen as phallic and therefore male. Through its association with the watery elements, it was also seen as female. However, we disagree with much of what is generally assumed about this association of the snake and human sexuality. Many instances in which a serpent god is linked with the phallus are due to the correspondence between the sexual act and the creative processes of consciousness in which there is a similar fusion of opposites. The phallus may itself also be a symbol of the power and fertility of the snake, which is what most experts would seem to believe. In our view, however, the snake was more than just a symbol of fertility. Like the male sperm, which is itself serpentine in form, the snake was a carrier of fertility.

It is widely acknowledged that the ancients believed that caves, wells and other openings in the Earth were entrances to the womb of the World Mother or Earth Goddess, from whom all life emerged and into whom all things returned at death. The snake lives within the Earth, the body of the Goddess, and is thus aware of her wisdom and her secrets, including those of life, death and rebirth.

Water, which is one of life's essentials, was also considered to be sacred, and the shrines erected at the site of wells or springs were later replaced by temples, churches and mosques. Because the snake's movements are sinuous and wave-like, similar to the course of a river, the letters 'M', 'W' and 'S' are associated with the snake. (These letters need to be approached with caution when they appear in snake mythology or alchemy, however, since they do not always allude to the snake.) In many cultures it was believed that a pool, pond or well harboured a resident guardian in the form of a spirit-serpent. These serpent guardians were linked implicitly with water cults and, especially in Celtic culture, the gods and goddesses of sacred wells and healing. The twelfth-century cleric Giraldus Cambrensis (Gerald of Wales) wrote that one particular well in Pembrokeshire contained a golden torque guarded by a hand-biting serpent. (The torque is widely accepted as a serpent symbol, but we would add that it also symbolizes the toroidal vortex and cycles, with the 'end-beginning' point in the cycle being represented by the open part of the torque.) The Maiden's Well in Aberdeenshire was reputed to be the dwelling-place of a winged serpent and similar stories are reported elsewhere in Europe.

According to some authorities, the snake was originally the symbol of the Virgin Goddess who gave birth to the cosmos, unaided by any masculine principle, in a virtually androgynous act of creation. We would add that the serpent also embodied this androgynous act in that it was a symbol for the neutral energy which transcends the duality of opposites.

The association of the snake with both male and female thus meant that the serpent was simultaneously a symbol of a) duality and b) the creative act by which the neutral energy divides itself in two, thus giving birth to the duality which it itself transcends. The coiled or spiral symbol of the serpent also represents the vortex or womb of the Virgin Goddess, with the opening into the vortex symbolizing the vagina of the Goddess.

In some early myths the Goddess gave birth to the universe, but later the primordial singularity of the Goddess split into a god and goddess (the neutral energy dividing in two), and it was from the sexual union (fusion) of these two that creation was thought to arise. This creative process of fission (division) and fusion (union) occurs at every instant in all oscillating periodic cycles and systems – even our own consciousness is doing this every fraction of a second.

In the Pelagian creation myth, the Goddess created the first living creature, the giant serpent Ophion, from air. She then became a female serpent, mated with Ophion and gave birth to the World Egg or Cosmic Egg. Next she became a dove and floated on the primordial ocean, while Ophion coiled around the egg three times – like the Kundalini serpent at the base of the spine – until the egg hatched, and from it emerged the heavens, the Earth and the Underworld. (The dove later became a symbol for the Spirit of God and the human, both of which are often seen as female.)

Lightning was known as the 'sky serpent' or 'lightning snake', while thunderstorms were believed to be the mating of the Sky Father and the Earth Mother, which brought the fertilizing rain. The lightning strike itself was a male thrusting and fertilizing power, comparable with the ejaculation of the Sky God. The site of a lightning strike was thus considered to be a place so full of power that it was designated an *abaton*, an abyss or forbidden place. The lightning flash corresponds to the flash of bright light in the centre of the head during the enlightenment experience.

In the Dionysian mysteries, a serpent (representing the god) was carried in a box called a *cista* on a bed of vine leaves. This may be the *cista* mentioned by Clement of Alexandria, which was said to contain the phallus of Dionysus. The *cista* mentioned in the mysteries of Isis is also said to have held a serpent, the missing phallus of Osiris. The fertility festival of the women of Arretophoria included cereal-paste images 'of serpents and forms of men'.

The claim made by several ancients that they had been fathered by a god in serpent form links with the royal lineages of India who claimed to be descended from the Naga serpents of antiquity. It also links with the idea of Christ being the 'serpent king' and with later European kings claiming descent from his bloodline. The Emperor Augustus was said to have been fathered by a snake, and his mother never lost the marks of its embrace. (Some authorities suggest that the mythical aspects of the life of Augustus were taken from the same pre-existing myths that influenced the biblical accounts of the life of Jesus.) A serpent was said to have been found beside the sleeping Olympias, mother of Alexander the Great, whose life story was also based in part on the pre-existing myths just mentioned. Her husband, Philip of Macedon, is reputed never to have coupled with the 'Bride of the Serpent' again. Alexander himself is sometimes connected with the horned serpent. Aesculapius, the god of healing, is said to have fathered a son by a woman who is depicted in Aesculapius' temple at Sicyon as sitting on a serpent. Barren women who sought help at the temples of Aesculapius often slept in the precincts of the *abaton*, the abyss or womb of the World Mother.

Serpent Seasons

In classical mythology, the year was divided into three seasons to represent the three aspects of the Goddess. These three divisions were ruled by the totems of lion, goat and serpent. The serpent, which represented the autumnal death of the Goddess, is sometimes seen as ruling the winter half of the year. The python at Delphi is said to have been slain by the sun-ray arrows of the sun god Apollo; however this may be a myth depicting the ascendancy of the patriarchal gods over the snake Goddess and her priestesses.

The snake may also be seen as the Lord of the Waning Year, the dark twin of the Sun Lord, with the two lords fighting for rulership of the land at the beginning of summer and again at the beginning of winter. This may have given rise to the later debased myths of the hero (for example St George) who slays the dragon instead of merely defeating him for the summer months. According to the Pagan worldview, the slain lord rises again every year, and the light and dark (winter and summer, day and night) rule in balance. Later myths portray death as a final ending and the light and dark in opposition to each other. The Sun Lord also dies nightly, and passes through the Underworld realm of the serpent or dragon. Ra, as the solar cat, was seen as battling the serpent of darkness, Zet or Set. Similar stories are told in many myth systems of sky gods fighting serpents, as for example the myths of Marduk and Tiamat, Apollo and the Python, Zeus and Typhon. The sea monster Leviathan, which appears in the Old Testament, was probably the original totem deity of the Levite clan, whose name means 'son of Leviathan'. Medallions from the first century AD portray Jehovah as a serpent god, and so Leviathan may have been a dual deity with Jehovah, each ruling half of the year.

In Greek myth Ge, the Earth goddess, gives the Tree of Immortality as a wedding gift to Hera. The tree is located in the Hesperides, an island in the far west, and guarded by the daughters of night and the serpent Ladon. The apples of the tree represent the sun, which sets or dies nightly in the west and journeys through the Underworld lair of the serpent or dragon to be reborn each dawn in the east. The story of Adam and Eve is said by some to be a degeneration of a similar myth.

As we have seen, the serpent was initially the great creator god, who brought about life itself. Slaying the serpent originally represented winter, but the same symbolic image was eventually seen as representing the triumph of light over dark or one religion triumphing over another. Apollo slew the snake at Delphi, while St Michael and St George slew dragons. St Patrick is said to have banished snakes from Ireland. The Virgin Mary is often depicted as trampling the serpent underfoot. This change of meaning led to the serpent's life-giving symbolism being replaced with the attributes of Satan, and the serpent duly became a symbol of evil.

The Mithraic god of time, Zervan, is depicted as having the body of a man and the head of a lion and being wrapped in the cosmic serpent. The snake is depicted with Mithras, along with his horse and dog, travelling with the god and licking up the blood of the sacrificial bull.

Prophecy

Snakes are associated with divination throughout the world. The Greeks kept oracular snakes at temples and the Arcadian word for priest literally meant 'snake charmer'. Accoring to Philostratus, the Arabs could foretell omens through the sound of birds, as these had eaten the heart or liver of a snake. Both Arabs and Hebrews derive their word for magic from the word for serpent. The Druids used 'snakestones', said to be formed by adders breathing on hazel wands, for healing and divination.

Worship of the serpent goddess was widespread in pre-dynastic northern Egypt. The asp had the title of *uzait* (meaning 'the eye') because of its otherworldly sight and wisdom. The goddesses Hathor and Maat were both called 'the eye'. The Uraeus headdress worn by the pharaohs symbolically gave the wearer the power of the 'third eye'. The snake was meant to strike at any enemy coming into the presence of the ruler. All Egyptians queens were given the title of 'Serpent of the Nile'.

The Indigenes of America, on occasion, chose a warrior to undergo the ordeal of allowing a snake to bite him several times during a sacred dance. If he survived, he was considered to have gained great wisdom and insight into the workings of the cosmos. This is typical of the trials of shamanic initiation.

Many so called 'serpent plants' (plants given the title of 'serpent' or 'snake' for their ability to alter consciousness) have been used shamanically to bring about trance states and engender otherworldly journeys. These plants include several mushrooms.

The Triple Realm

In its simplest form, the Triple Realm refers to the tripartite division of the world and the cosmos into the celestial, earthly and subterranean realms. It is an extremely ancient concept identical to the Three Cosmic Zones described in Chapter 2 (*see page 30*).

The serpent is intricately linked with the Triple Realm by the Egyptian Pyramid Texts in which the snake/serpent itself is spoken of as being celestial, earthly and subterranean. As the 'divine phallus', it was in perpetual copulation with Mother Earth and represented the *axis mundi*, which passes through all three realms.

Because the serpent lives underground, it is seen as a link with the Underworld, the land of the dead. This link was further reinforced by the fact that snakes were often found in graveyards, where they were thought to communicate with the dead.

The serpent or dragon is often the guardian of Underworld treasure that is kept hidden in a variety of circumstances, such as under a lake or river, in a cave or on an island in the west. Cherokee legends tell of the great wisdom that will come to the warrior who takes the jewel from the head of the serpent king Uktena. This brings to mind the myths and legends from across the world which say that the snake has a jewel set in its head and the idea that the Elixir of Life was an emerald jewel that fell from the forehead of Lucifer, the serpent angel. The great treasure guarded by the serpent is often identified as the Goddess's secrets of life, death and rebirth. The 'jewel' in the serpent's head is a reference to the thalamus at the centre of the brain, the gland through which we perceive and create our reality. The risks inherent in this process are symbolized by Lucifer's fall from heaven and the fall of the jewel from his head, which illustrate the 'evil' that befalls us when we become trapped in delusions of our own making.

The healing power of the snake is often attributed to the fact that it sheds its skin. The ancient Chinese saw the human process of rejuvenation as a person splitting their old skin and emerging once more as a youth. The Buddha is said to have taken the form of a snake to stop disease among his people. Likewise, Cadmus and his wife were turned into snakes to cure the ills of mankind. Snakes were also associated with Aesculapius, who is said to have been a serpent in one of his previous human incarnations. His daughter, Hygeia, is sometimes depicted with a serpent at her breast.

A temple dedicated to the Earth goddess Bona Dea on the slopes of the Aventine (one of the seven sacred hills on which Rome was built) was said to be a kind of herbarium. Here, in this sacred place of healing, snakes were kept as symbols of the healing art, and possibly for other, more practical reasons that are ignored by historians. The blind Emperor Theodosius is said to have recovered his sight when a grateful serpent laid a precious gem upon his eyes.

The Melanesians said that to slough one's skin meant eternal life, and we find a similar theme in Judaism and Christianity. Siegfried bathed in the blood of the dragon he had slain and became invulnerable.

During the mediaeval period, the snake was generally regarded as a symbol of evil through its association with the creation of reality and illusion, yet it still had links with healing. Adder stones, thought to be formed from the skins of fighting adders, were used to heal cataracts; dried snake heads were used to cure snakebites, and snake skins were worn about the head to prevent headaches or around parts of the body to ward off rheumatism. Adder venom was even used to induce abortions. It was believed that by eating part of a snake one assimilated the snake's healing qualities and gained medical skill.

The ancient serpent tribes of Kashmir, who were famous for their medical skill, attributed this to their health-giving snakes. The ancient Psylli of Africa and the Ophiogenes of Cyprus were worshippers of the serpent, and this association alone enabled them to heal people as though they too were imbued with the healing properties of the serpent.

Galen, the famous Greek physician and scholar, admitted to having requested help from the Marsi people who inhabited the central mountainous area of Italy. The Marsi were snake hunters, charmers and excellent druggists. They were said to have immunity from snake poison and sold antidotes to snake venom. Galen eventually produced many prescriptions that included viper's flesh.

Aristotle claimed that the Scythians used a deadly poison made from decomposed snake tissue and human blood on their arrowheads. As we have seen, it was these same people who were responsible for bringing the origins of the Arthurian tales and the Grail to mainland Europe, having themselves received this knowledge from the serpent people.

There is no doubt that the snake/serpent is deeply rooted in the mythology of the world. There is no other creature on the planet with such a powerful and widespread tradition that embraces everything from mythology and folklore to medicinal value. From ancient pre-civilization to modern medicine, the serpent is ever present, either as a symbol or through its practical use. As we have shown, it is also discernible in the stories associated with the great resurrecting gods of the world's religions.

There must be more to all this than the snake's simple ability to slough its skin. In our view the explanation is very simple: the snake has within it the ability to heal and extend life. It has been used for this purpose for thousands of years. It was the first in this field, and when science catches up, it will be the last.

Notes

Chapter 1: Alpha-Omega

1 Linda A. Malcor, 'What is a Grail?', from the dissertation *The Chalice at the Cross*, http://www.chronique.com/Library/Knights/Grail.htm

2 Ibid.

3 Walter Skeat, *The Concise Dictionary of English Etymology* (DIANE Publishing Co., 1900), p.184

4 Laurence Gardner, *Bloodline of the Holy Grail: The Hidden Lineage of Jesus Revealed* (Element Books, 1996)

5 Michael Baigent, Richard Leigh and Henry Lincoln, *The Holy Blood and the Holy Grail* (Jonathan Cape, 1982)

6 Graham Phillips, *The Search for the Grail* (Century, 1995)

7 C. Austin, *Song of the Otherworld is Heard in the Balance of Spring*, http://merganser.math.gvsu.edu/myth/march98.html

8 Carl G. Jung, *A Study in the Process of Individuation*, translated from *Zur Empire des Individuationsprozesses* (Gestaltungen des Unbewussten, Zurich, 1950)

9 C. Austin, *The Soul's Myth Guides Those Who Search*, http://merganser.math.gvsu.edu/myth/nov01.html

10 Quoted ibid.

11 Ibid.

Chapter 2: The Mixing of Opposites

1 Quoted in Anyara, *The Self in Astrology*, http://koti.mbnet.fi/neptunia/astrology/selfx1.htm

2 Gary A. David, *The Orion Zone: Ancient Star Cities of the American Southwest*, Chapter 2, http://azorion.tripod.com/high_desert.htm

3 Ibid.

4 David Ovason, *The Zelator: The Secret Journals of Mark Hedsel* (Arrow, 1999), p.420

Chapter 3: The Mixing Bowl

1 Michael Baigent, Richard Leigh and Henry Lincoln, *The Holy Blood and the Holy Grail* (Jonathan Cape, 1982)

2 Christopher Knight and Robert Lomas, *The Second Messiah: Templars, the Turin Shroud and the Great Secret of Freemasonry* (Century, 1997). In his sermon to prelates, Bernard of Clairvaux said, 'Show affection as a mother would... Why will the young man, bitten by a serpent, shy away from the judgement of the priest, to whom he ought to run as to the bosom of a mother?' (*See also 'Lactating Goddesses' in Chapter 8.*)

3 Alan Pert, 'Glossary entry for the Holy Grail' from *The Grail Legend: A New Translation*, http://www.harbour.sfu.ca/~hayward/van/glossary/grail.html

4 What we mean by 'extra energy', is the energy that we can gain when our mind is not focused on either 'this' or 'that' (the polarities). If we are able to adopt a neutral state of mind, we acquire another kind of energy – one which, for want of a better description, is of a 'higher frequency'. We remain unaware of this extra energy until we learn about it from someone else or experience it for ourselves. Our habitual dualistic division of the mind is an integral part of our experience of existence on the physical plane and actually 'blocks' the extra energy that enables us to experience those 'other worlds' which correspond to other planes of existence.

Chapter 4: The Seed at the Centre

1 Wolfram von Eschenbach, *Parzifal* (Random House, 1961)

2 Ibid.

3 This theme of the fruit and seed has been pursued in some depth by Stan Tenen of the Meru Foundation. *See Continuous Creation*, http://www.meru.org/contin.html. The reader will find much here that relates to the central themes we are presenting.

4 Richard Cavendish, *The Magical Arts* (Arkana, 1984, first published as *The Black Arts*, 1967), p.157

5 Ibid.

6 Quoted in Peter Marshall, *The Philosopher's Stone: A Quest for the Secrets of Alchemy* (Macmillan, 2001), p.323

7 Matthew 13:31–2

8 Chandogya Upanishad, trans. Juan Mascaro, *The Upanishads*, Penguin, 1965, p.114

9 Lynn Picknett and Clive Prince, *The Templar Revelation: Secret Guardians of the True Identity of Christ* (Transworld, 1997)

10 J. C. J. Metford, *Dictionary of Christian Lore and Legend* (Thames and Hudson, 1983), p.89

Chapter 5: The Hidden Wisdom in Arthur's Grail

1 *The Well and the Cauldron,* http://www.angelfire.com/ma3/mythology/thewell.html

2 J. R. Church, *Guardians of the Grail* (Chambers,1942)

3 Julius Caesar, *Book VI,* (Oxford University Press, 1978), p. 14, and Robert Graves, *The White Goddess* (Faber & Faber, 1961), p. 91

4 http://www.morien-institute.org/caersidi.html

5 SPACE.com staff, *Ancients Could Have Used Stonehenge to Predict Lunar Eclipses,* 19 January 2000, http://www.space.com/scienceastronomy/astronomy/stonehenge_eclipse_ 000119. html

6 *Secrets of the Dead,* television programme by the Educational Broadcasting Corporation, Thirteen/WNET New York, 2002

7 Ibid.

8 http://www.greatserpentmound.org

9 Walter J. Friedlander, *The Golden Wand of Medicine: A History of the Caduceus Symbol in Medicine* (Greenwood Press, 1992)

10 Dr. Keith T. Blayney, MBChB, *The Caduceus vs the Staff of Asclepius,* http://drblayney.com/Asclepius.html

11 Ram Kumar Rai, *Ajna Chakra.* http://www.namaste.it/kundalini/kundalini_eng/ajna.html

12 Harold Bayley, *The Lost Language of Symbolism,* Vol. II (Bracken Books, 1912)

13 The information provided by Malory's *Sangraal* and a number of popular folk traditions add up to Joseph coming to Britain around AD 75. They also suggest that various Grail Knights were descended from Joseph – age never seems to matter in these 'fairy tales'.

14 Wolfram von Eschenbach, *Parzifal* (Random House, 1961)

Chapter 6: The Cauldron of the Head of the Underworld

1 Euripides, *Heracles*

2 Wm. Michael Mott, *Echoes of the World Cauldron: Legendary, Mythic and Religious Belief in Lands Beneath the Earth,* http://www.hollowplanets.com/journal/J0001Echoes.asp, 2000, originally published in slightly shorter form in *Principium Paradoxi* magazine, vol. I, no.1, Spring 1999

3 Shapeshifting is an ability attributed to the shaman who, it is claimed, is able to alter his body by first altering his consciousness. He is

thus able to take on the guise of different creatures, of which the dog or the wolf are the most common.

4 John Bathurst Deane, *The Worship of the Serpent* (London, 1830)

5 *Glossary of Gnostic Terminology.* See www.gnosis-usa.com/Glossary/glossary-n.html

6 C. W. King, *The Gnostics and their Remains: Ancient and Mediaeval* (second edition, 1887; reprinted by R. A. Kessinger Publishing Co. Ltd, 1998), p.145

7 Alice Ouzounian, *The Mystery of Janus the God of Gateways,* http://www.plotinus.com/janus.htm

8 Job 40:25

9 Quoted in Kenneth Grant, *Nightside of Eden* (Skoob Books, 1995)

10 H. Bayley, *The Lost Language of Symbolism* (Bracken Books, 1912)

11 The 'serpent in water' metaphor is seen by some to be connected to the serpentine and spiralling double-helix strands of the DNA molecule, which resides in the nucleus of the cell and is mostly made up of salt water. This may have some validity. Both may come together in the 'otherworldly' trance experiences of the shaman who claims to be able to access the Underworld, which is possibly an ancient term for the underlying 'quantum-potential field. (*See* Jeremy Narby, *The Cosmic Serpent,* Georg Editeur SA. Geneva, 1995; English translation Victor Gollancz, 1998.)

Chapter 7: The Serpent in Classical Myth

1 Adolf Erman, *The Ancient Egyptians: A Sourcebook of their Writings* (Harper and Row, 1966)

2 See http://www.sanskrit.org/Sanskrit/sanskritterms.htm

3 Beatty Longfield, *The Garden of the Golden Flower: The Journey to Spiritual Fulfilment* (Rider, 1938)

4 See www.occultopedia.com/b/bacchus.htm

5 J. M. Roberts, *Antiquity Unveiled,* Health Research, 1970

6 Ibid.

7 Martin A. Larson, *The Story of Christian Origins,* Village, 1977

8 Roberts, op. cit.

9 J. G. Frazer, *The Golden Bough: A Study in Magic and Religion* (Macmillan Press, 1922), p.428

10 Deuteronomy 33:17 (King James version) refers to 'horns of unicorns'.

11 *See* Ecclesiasticus 24:18 (Vulgate) or 24:14 (Greek).

12 W. Roberts, *Printer's Marks*

13 Revelation 21:11

Chapter 8: Asian Myths

1 Aelian, *De Natura Animalium*

2 W. J. Wilkins, *Hindu Mythology: Vedic and Puranic* (reprinted D. K. Printworld, New Delhi, 2003)

3 Charles Gould, *Mythical Monsters* (W. H. Allen & Co. 1886)

Chapter 9: Celtic and European Myths

1 F. Graham Millar, The Gundestrup Cauldron (Halifax Center, Royal Astronomical Society of Canada). See http://www.lexiline.com/lexiline/lexi85.htm

2 Ibid.

3 See http://www.unc.edu/celtic/catalogue/Gundestrup/e.html

4 Ophiolatreia (1889), anonymous. See http://www.sacred-texts.com/etc/oph/oph09.htm

5 Thomas Pennant, *Tour in Wales* (Benjamin White, 1784)

6 Ibid.

7 M de Longueville Harcovet, *Histoire des personnes qui ont vecu plusieurs siecles, et qui ont rajeuni*

8 Song of Solomon 7:8

9 Ibid. 2:3

10 Wolfram von Eschenbach, *Parzifal* (Random House, 1961)

Chapter 11. The Serpent in Religion

1 www.biblehistory.net/Chap15.htm

2 The title 'Immortal Race' is mentioned in several books on Jews and Jewish history, including *The Trail of the Serpent* by Inquire Within, published in the 1930s and probably written by the Rosicrucians.

3 Numbers 21:6–9

4 Josephus, *Antiquities of the Jews*, Indypublish.com

5 Helena Petrovna Blavatsky, *Isis Unveiled* (Theosophical University Press, 1999)

6 Jean Doresse, *The Secret Books of the Egyptian Gnostics: An Introduction to the Gnostic Coptic Manuscripts Discovered at Chenoboskion* (Inner Traditions International Ltd., 1986)

7 Murray Hope, *The Temple of Set FAQ*. See http://www.snakeskin.net/sonsof.htm

8 *See* http://istina.rin.ru/eng/ufo/text/108.html

9 Robert M. Grant with David Noel Freedman, *The Secret Sayings of Jesus according to the Gospel of Thomas* (Fontana Books, 1960), p.69

10 This information was kindly provided in an e-mail from Andrew Collins.

11 Deuteronomy 32:32–3

12 Michael Baigent, Richard Leigh and Henry Lincoln, *The Holy Blood and the Holy Grail* (Corgi, 1983), pp.192–3. The authors also say that the 'M' in the name Ormus is the glyph for the astrological sign of Virgo, the Virgin, which we say is composed of both the ram's head and the fish. The remaining letters make the word 'ORUS', which brings us back to the ancient Egyptian god Horus. As we have already mentioned, Jesus and his mother Mary were based on Horus and his mother Isis.

13 Revelation 2:17

Chapter 12: Archaeology and Imagery

1 Wolfram von Eschenbach, *Parzival* (Random House, 1961)

2 Aeschylus, *Prometheus Bound*, ed. Mark Griffith (Cambridge University Press, 1983)

3 Robert T. Mason, PhD, *The Divine Serpent in Myth and Legend* (1999). See http://www.geocities.com/Athens/Delphi/5789/serpent.htm

4 C. J. S. Thompson, *Mysteries and Secrets of Magic* (Causeway Books, 1973)

5 Mason, op. cit.

6 This information was kindly provided by Raj D Sheth, MD, Director Comprehensive Epilepsy Program and Chief Professor, Departments of Neurology and Pediatrics, University of Wisconsin

7 *W. Pastor Kila at Goaribari* (Oral History, 1977), p.24, quoted in Vittorio Di Cesare and Adriano Forgione, *Malta: The Skulls of the Mother Goddess*, http://andrewcollins.com/page/articles/maltaskulls.htm

8 Di Cesare and Forgione, ibid.

9 Ibid.

10 *See* http://www.angelfire.com/home/thefaery/sceptics.html

11 Forgione, op. cit.

12 Ibid.

Chapter 13: Serpent Alchemy

1 Geoffrey Chaucer, *The Canterbury Tales*, trans. Nevill Coghill (Penguin USA, 2003)

2 Sebastian Brant, *The Ship of Fools*, trans. Alexander Barclay (William Paterson, Edinburgh; Henry Sotheran & Co., London, 1874)

3 Louis Figuier, *L'alchimie et les alchimistes: essai historique et critique sur la philosophie hermétique* (Publication Num. BNF de l'éd. de Paris: L. Hachette, 1860)

4 Kurt Seligmann, *The Mirror of Magic* (Pantheon Books Inc., 1948)

5 Arthur E. Waite, *The Hermetic Museum Restored and Enlarged*, 2 vols. (London, 1893).

6 Seligmann, op. cit.

7 Sir George Ripley, *The Ripley Scroll*, http://www.levity.com/alchemy/rscroll.html

8 *Emerald Tablet of Hermes Trismegistus*, eds Patrick J. Smith, J. D. Holmes (Holmes Publishing Group, 1997)

9 Sir George Ripley, *Twelve Gates*, modernized by Adam McLean from the 1591 edition of *The Compound of Alchymy*, http://www.levity.com/alchemy/ripgates.html

10 Marcellin P. E. Berthelot and Charles Emile Ruelle, *Collections des anciens alchimistes grecs*, 1888, reprinted 1963; R.Patai. Adam va'Adamah, Jerusalem, 1942, 1:159–61

11 'Aurelia Occulta' from *Theatrum Chemicum* (1613)

12 See 'What is Alchemy?' http://www.alphachisigma.org/alchemy/whatisit/

13 Arnald de Villanova, *Boke of Wine*, 1438, translated into English from Wilhelm von Hirnkofen's German version by Henry Sigerist, MD (Shuman, New York, 1948)

14 J. C. Cooper, *An Illustrated Encyclopaedia of Traditional Symbols* (Thames and Hudson, 1978) p.158

15 Documents on population control, including 'negative growth', can be found at www.optimumpopulation.org

Chapter 14: Serpent Science

1 Sameh M. Arab, MD, *Medicine in Ancient Egypt*. See http://www.arabworldbooks.com/articles8b.htm

2 See www.icrts.org/multipurpose/tibet.htm

3 Ibid.

4 A picture of the beaker can be seen at http://www.hmc.org.qa/hmc/heartviews/ H-V-v2%20N4/7.htm#King%20Esarhaddon%20and %20his%20doctors

5 Hajar A. Hajar Al BinAli, MD, FACC, *History of Medicine*, http://www.hmc.org.qa/hmc/ heartviews/H-V-v2%20N4/7.htm

6 Reptile House, www.thesnake.org

7 *The Cold Blooded News*, newsletter of the Colorado Herpetological Society, vol. 28, no.3, March 2001

8 *Life Extension* magazine, May 2000

9 Ibid.

10 www.cancerresearchuk.co.uk

11 See www.ambergriscaye.com/pages/town/article39

12 *The Miami Herald*, 10 May 2001

Chapter 15: The Serpent Grail

1 Michael Baigent, Richard Leigh and Henry Lincoln, *The Holy Blood and the Holy Grail* (Corgi, 1982), p.318.

2 Ibid.

3 Ibid.

Bibliography

Abdalqadir as-Sufi, Shaykh, *The Return of the Khalifate*, Madinah Press, 1996

Ableson, J., *Jewish Mysticism*, G. Bell and Sons Ltd, Dover Publications, 2001

Aeschylus, *Prometheus Bound*, ed. Mark Griffith, Cambridge University Press, 1983

Andrews, Richard, and Schellenberger, Paul, *The Tomb of God*, Little, Brown and Co., 1996

Anyara, *The Self in Astrology*, **http://koti.mbnet.fi/neptunia/astrology/selfx1.htm**

Apollodorus, *The Library of Greek Mythography*, trans. Robin Hard, Oxford Paperbacks, 1998

Ashe, Geoffrey, *The Quest for Arthur's Britain*, Pall Mall, 1968

Austin, C., *Song of the Otherworld is Heard in the Balance of Spring*, **http://merganser.math.gvsu.edu/myth/march98.html**

Austin, C., *The Soul's Myth Guides Those Who Search*, **http://merganser.math.gvsu.edu/myth/nov01.html**

Bacher, Wilhelm, and Blau, Ludwig, *Shamir*, n.d.

Baigent, Michael, *Ancient Traces: Mysteries in Ancient and Early History*, Viking, 1998

Baigent, Michael, and Leigh, Richard, *The Elixir and the Stone*, Viking, 1997

Baigent, Michael, Leigh, Richard, and Lincoln, Henry, *The Holy Blood and the Holy Grail*, Jonathan Cape, 1982

Balfour, Mark, *The Sign of the Serpent: The Key to Creative Physics*, Prism Press, 1990

Balfour, Michael, *Megalithic Mysteries*, Collins and Brown, 1998

Barrett, David V., *Sects, Cults and Alternative Religions: A World Survey and Sourcebook*, Cassell, 1996

Barrow, John D., *Theories of Everything*, Clarendon Press, 1991

Basham, A. L., *The Wonder that was India*, Sidgwick & Jackson, 1985

Bauval, Robert, and Gilbert, Adrian, *The Orion Mystery*, William Heinemann, 1994

Bayley, Harold, *The Lost Language of Symbolism*, Bracken Books, 1912

Beatty, Longfield, *The Garden of the Golden Flower: The Journey to Spiritual Fulfilment*, Rider, 1938

Begg, Ean, *The Cult of the Black Virgin*, Arkana, 1985

Begg, Ean and Deike, *In Search of the Holy Grail and the Precious Blood: A Traveller's Guide to the Sites and Legends of the Holy Grail*, Thorsons, 1995

Berthelot, Marcellin P. E., and Ruelle, Charles Emile, *Collections des anciens alchimistes grecs*, 1888, R.Patai. Adam va'Adamah, Jerusalem, 1942

Blaire, Lawrence, *Rhythms of Vision*, Warner Books, 1975

Blavatsky, Helena Petrovna, *Theosophical Glossary*, R. A. Kessinger Publishing Co. Ltd, 1918

Blavatsky, Helena Petrovna, *Isis Unveiled*, reprinted Theosophical University Press, 1999

Borchert, Bruno, *Mysticism: Its History and Challenge*, Weisner, 1994

Bord, Janet and Colin, *Earth Rites: Fertility Practices in Pre-Industrial Britain*, HarperCollins*Publishers*, 1982

Bouquet, A. C., *Comparative Religion*, Pelican, 1942

Brant, Sebastian, *The Ship of Fools*, trans. Alexander Barclay (William Paterson, Edinburgh; Henry Sotheran & Co., London, 1874)

Brine, Lindsey, *The Ancient Earthworks and Temples of the American Indians*, Oracle, 1996

Broadhurst, Paul, and Miller, Hamish, *The Dance of the Dragon*, Pendragon, 2000

Bryant, Nigel, *The High Book of the Grail*, D. S. Brewer, 1996

Brydon, R., *Rosslyn: A History of the Guilds, the Masons and the Rosy Cross*, Rosslyn Chapel Trust, 1994

Budge, E. A. Wallis, *An Egyptian Hieroglyphic Dictionary*, Volume I, Dover Publications, 1978

Butler, E. M., *The Myth of the Magus*, Cambridge University Press, 1993

Caesar, Julius, *Book VI*, Oxford University Press, 1978

Callahan, Philip S., *Nature's Silent Music*, Acres, USA, 1992

Callahan, Philip S., *Paramagnetism: Rediscovering Nature's Secret Force of Growth*, Acres, USA, 1995

Callahan, Philip S., *Ancient Mysteries Modern Visions: The Magnetic Life of Agriculture*, Acres, USA. 2001

Campbell, Joseph, *Transformations of Myth Through Time*, Harper and Row, 1990

Cantor, Norman F., *The Sacred Chain: The History of the Jews*, HarperCollins*Publishers*, 1994

Carpenter, Edward, *Pagan and Christian Creeds: Their Origin and Meaning*, R. A. Kessinger Publishing Co. Ltd, 1992

Carr-Gomm, Sarah, *Dictionary of Symbols in Art*, Duncan Baird Publishers, 2000

Castaneda, Carlos, *The Teaching of Don Juan*, Plaza & Janes, 1984

Cavendish, Richard, *The Magical Arts*, Arkana, 1984; first published as *The Black Arts*, 1967

Cavendish, Richard, *Mythology*, Little, Brown and Co., 1999

Chadwick, N., *The Druids*, University of Wales Press, 2000

Childress, David Hatcher (ed.)., *Anti-Gravity and the World Grid*, Adventures Unlimited Press, 1993

Church, J. R., *Guardians of the Grail*, Chambers, 1942

Churchward, Albert, *The Origin and Evolution of Religion*, R. A. Kessinger Publishing Co. Ltd, 1996

Clarke, Hyde, and Wake, C. Staniland, *Serpent and Siva Worship*, R. A. Kessinger Publishing Co. Ltd, 1996

Coles, John, *Field Archaeology in Britain*, Methuen, 1972

Collins, Andrew, *From the Ashes of Angels: The Forbidden Legacy of a Fallen Race*, Michael Joseph, 1996

Collins, Andrew, *Gods of Eden*, Headline, 1998

Collins, Andrew, *Gateway to Atlantis*, Headline, 2000

Collins, Andrew, *Twenty-First Century Grail: The Quest for a Legend*, Virgin, 2004

Cooper, J. C., *An Illustrated Encyclopaedia of Traditional Symbols*,
    Thames and Hudson, 1978

Croker, Thomas Crofton, *Legend of the Lakes*, Collins Press, 1829, out of print

Crooke, W., *The Popular Religion and Folk-lore of Northern India*,
    R. A. Kessinger Publishing Co. Ltd, 1996

Cumont, F., *The Mysteries of Mithra*, Dover Publications, 1956

Currer-Briggs, N., *The Shroud and the Grail: A Modern Quest for the True Grail*,
    St Martin's Press, 1988

David, Gary A., *The Orion Zone: Ancient Star Cities of the American Southwest (Part 2)*,
    http://www.100megsfree4.com/farshores/amorion2.htm

David-Neel, Alexandra, *Magic and Mystery in Tibet*, Dover Publications, 1971

Davidson, H. R. Ellis, *Myths and Symbols of Pagan Europe*, Syracuse University Press,
    1988

Davidson, John, *The Secret of the Creative Vacuum*, The C. W. Daniel Company Ltd,
    1989

Davies, Rev. Edward, *The Mythology and Rites of the British Druids*, J. Booth, 1809

de Longueville Harcovet, M., *Histoire des personnes qui ont vécu plusieurs siècles*,
    et qui ont rajeuni, Paris chez la veuve Charpentier et chez Laurent Le Compte

De Martino, Ernesto, *Primitive Magic*, Prism Unity, 1988

de Villanova, Arnald, *Boke of Wine*, trans. Henry Sigerist, MD, Shuman, New York 1948

Deane, John Bathurst, *The Worship of the Serpent*, London, 1830

Devereux, Paul, *Shamanism and the Mystery Lines*, Quantum, 1992

Devereux, Paul, *Symbolic Landscapes*, Gothic Image, 1992

Devereux, Paul, *Places of Power: Measuring the Secret Energy of Ancient Sites*,
    Cassell Illustrated, 1999

Devereux, Paul, *Secrets of Ancient and Sacred Places: The World's Mysterious Heritage*,
    Caxton Editions, 2001

Devereux, Paul, and Thompson, Ian, *Ley Guide: The Mystery of Aligned Ancient Sites*,
    Empress, 1988

Dodd, C. H., *Historical Tradition of the Fourth Gospel*, Cambridge University Press, 1976

Doel, Fran and Geoff, *Robin Hood: Outlaw of Greenwood Myth*,
    Tempus Publishing Ltd, 2000

Doresse, Jean, *The Secret Books of the Egyptian Gnostics: An Introduction to the
    Gnostic Coptic Manuscripts Discovered at Chenoboskion*, Inner Traditions
    International Ltd, 1986

Duckett, Shipley, Eleanor, *The Gateway to the Middle Ages: Monasticism*, Diane
    Publishing Co., 1988

Dunford, Barry, *The Holy Land of Scotland: Jesus in Scotland and the Gospel of the
    Grail*, Sacred Connections, 2001

Dunstan, V., *Did the Virgin Mary Live and Die in England?*, Megiddo Press, 1985

Eliade, Mircea, *Shamanism: Archaic Techniques of Ecstasy*, Princeton University Press, 2004

Ellis, Ralph, *Jesus: Last of the Pharaohs*, Edfu Books, 2001

The Emerald Tablet of Hermes Trismegistus, eds Patrick J. Smith, J. D. Holmes, Holmes Publishing Group, 1997

Epstein, Perle, *Kabbalah: The Way of the Jewish Mystic*, Shambhala Classics, 2001

Erman, Adolf, *The Ancient Egyptians: A Sourcebook of their Writings*, Harper and Row, 1966

Ernst, Carl H., *Venomous Reptiles of North America*, Smithsonian Books, 1999

Evans, Lorraine, *The Kingdom of the Ark*, Simon & Schuster, 2000

Feather, Robert, *The Copper Scroll Decoded*, Thorsons, 1999

Fergusson, Malcolm, *Rambles in Breadalbane*, 1891

Figuier, Louis, *L'alchimie et les alchimistes: essai historique et critique sur la philosophie hermétique*, Publication Num. BNF de l'éd. de Paris, L. Hachette, 1860

Fontana, David, *The Secret Language of Symbols*, Chronicle Books, 2003

Ford, Patrick K, *The Mabinogi and other Medieval Welsh Tales*, University of California Press, 1977

Fortune, Dion, *The Mystical Qabalah*, Weiser Books, 2000

Foss, Michael, *People of the First Crusade*, Caxton Editions, 2000

Frazer, Sir James, *The Golden Bough: A Study in Magic and Religion*, Macmillan Press, 1922

Freke, Timothy, and Gandy, Peter, *Jesus and the Goddess*, Thorsons, 2001

Friedlander, Walter J., *The Golden Wand of Medicine: A History of the Caduceus Symbol in Medicine*, Greenwood Press, 1992

Gardiner, Philip, *Proof: Does God Exist?* www.radikalbooks.com

Gardiner, Philip, *The Shining Ones*, www.radikalbooks.com

Gardiner, Samuel R., *History of England*, Longmans, Green and Co., 1904

Gardner, Laurence, *Bloodline of the Holy Grail*, Element Books, 1996

Gascoigne, Bamber, *The Christians*, Jonathan Cape, 1977

Gerber, Richard, *Vibrational Medicine*, Bear & Company, 2001

Gilbert, Adrian, *Magi*, Bloomsbury, 1996

Gilbert, Adrian, *The New Jerusalem*, Bantam Press, 2002

Goldberg, Carl, *Speaking with the Devil*, Viking, 1996

Gould, Charles, *Mythical Monsters*, W. H. Allen & Co., 1886

Grant, Kenneth, *Nightside of Eden*, Skoob Books, 1995

Grant, Robert M., with Freedman, David Noel, *The Secret Sayings of Jesus according to the Gospel of Thomas*, Fontana Books, 1960

Graves, Robert, *The White Goddess*, Faber & Faber, 1961

Gray Hulse, Tristan, *The Holy Shroud*, Weidenfeld and Nicolson, 1997

Hagger, Nicholas, *The Fire and the Stones*, Element Books, 1991

Halifax, Joan, *Shaman: The Wounded Healer*, Thames and Hudson, 1982

Hanauer, J. E., *The Holy Land*, Merchant Book Company, 1995

Hancock, Graham, *The Sign and the Seal*, Arrow, 2001

Harrington, E., *The Meaning of English Place Names*, The Black Staff Press, 1984

Hartmann, Franz, *The Life of Jehoshua the Prophet of Nazareth: An Occult Study and a Key to the Bible*, Kegan, Trench, Trubner & Co., London, 1909

Harvey, Clesson, *The Great Pyramid Texts*, www.pyramidtexts.com

Heathcote-James, Emma, *They Walk Among Us*, Metro, 2004

Hedsel, Mark, *The Zelator*, Century, 1998

Howard, Michael, *The Occult Conspiracy*, Rider & Co. Ltd, 1989

James, E. O., *The Ancient Gods*, Weidenfeld and Nicolson, 1962

Jean, Georges, *Signs, Symbols and Ciphers*, Thames and Hudson, 1999

Jennings, Hargrave, *Ophiolatreia*, R. A. Kessinger Publishing Co. Ltd, 1996

Johnson, Buffie, *Lady of the Beast*: The Goddess and her Sacred Animals, 1988

Jones, Alison, *Dictionary of World Folklore*, Larousse, 1995

Josephus, *Antiquities of the Jews*, Indypublish.com

Jung, C. G., *A Study in the Process of Individuation*, Gestaltungen des Unbewussten, Zurich, 1950

Kauffeld, Carl, *Snakes: The Keeper and the Kept*, Doubleday and Co., 1969

King, C. W., *The Gnostics and their Remains: Ancient and Mediaeval*, second edition, 1887; reprinted by Kessinger Publishing Company, 1998

King, Serge Kahili, *Instant Healing: Mastering the Way of the Hawaiian Shaman Using Words, Images, Touch, and Energy*, Renaissance Books, 2000

Knight, Christopher, and Lomas, Robert, *The Second Messiah: Templars, the Turin Shroud and the Great Secret of Freemasonry*, Century, 1997

Knight, Christopher, and Lomas, Robert, *Uriel's Machine: Reconstructing the Disaster behind Human History*, Arrow, 2004

Laidler, Keith, *The Head of God*, Weidenfeld and Nicolson, 1998

Larson, Martin A., *The Story of Christian Origins*, Village, 1977

Layton, Robert, *Australian Rock Art: A New Synthesis*, Cambridge University Press, 1992

Leakey, Richard, and Lewin, Roger, *Origins Reconsidered*, Abacus, 1993

Lemesurier, Peter, *The Great Pyramid*, Element Books, 1999

Leone, Al, 'The Totality of God and the Izunome Cross: Unlocking the Secret Riddle of the Ages', unpublished at time of writing this but can be read in full at **www.gizapyramid.com/Leone1.htm**

Levi, Eliphas, *Transcendental Magic*, Red Wheel/Weiser, 1968

Lincoln, Henry, *Key to the Sacred Pattern*, The Windrush Press, 1997

Loomis, Roger S., *The Grail: From Celtic Myth to Christian Symbol*, Columbia University Press and Wales University Press, 1963

Loye, David, *An Arrow through Chaos: How We See into the Future*, Inner Traditions International, 2000

Maby, J. C., and Franklin, T. Bedford, *The Physics of the Divining Rod*, Bell, 1977

MacCana, Proinsias, *Celtic Mythology*, Hamlyn, 1970

Mack, B. L., *The Lost Gospel*, HarperSanFrancisco, 1994

Magin, U., 'The Christianisation of Pagan Landscapes', *The Ley Hunter* (1992), no. 116

Mann, A. T., *Sacred Architecture*, Element Books, 1993

Marshall, Peter, *The Philosopher's Stone: A Quest for the Secrets of Alchemy*, Macmillan, 2001

Matthews, John, *Sources of the Grail*, Floris Books, 1997

Matthews, John, *The Quest for the Green Man*, Godsfield Press, 2001

Mcij, Harold, *The Tau and the Triple Tau*, H. P. Tokyo, 2000

Metford, J. C. J., *Dictionary of Christian Lore and Legend*, Thames and Hudson, 1983

Michell, John, and Rhone, Christine, *Twelve-Tribes and the Science of Enchanting the Landscape*, Phanes Press, 1991

Milgrom, Jacob, *The JPS Torah Commentary: Numbers* The Jewish Publication Society, New York, 1990

Morton, Chris, and Thomas, Ceri Louise, *The Mystery of the Crystal Skulls*, Thorsons, 1997

Mott, Wm. Michael, 'Echoes of the World Cauldron: Legendary, Mythic and Religious Belief in Lands Beneath the Earth',
http://www.hollowplanets.com/journal/J0001Echoes.asp, 2000, originally published in slightly shorter form in *Principium Paradoxi* magazine, vol. I, no.1, Spring 1999

Muggeridge, Malcolm, *Jesus*, Fount, 1976

Narby, Jeremy, *The Cosmic Serpent*, Georg Editeur SA. Geneva, 1995; English translation Victor Gollancz, 1998

Newton, Janet, *Ancient Board Games*, www.goddesschess.com/chessays/janigk.html 2001

O'Brien, Christian and Barbara Joy, *The Shining Ones*, Turnstone Press, 1983

Oliver, Rev. George, *The History of Initiation*, R. A. Kessinger, 1841

Oliver, George, *Signs and Symbols*, R. A. Kessinger, 1999

O'Neill, John, *Nights of the Gods*, publisher unknown, 1893

Oppenheimer, Stephen, *Eden in the East*, Weidenfeld & Nicolson, 1998

Ouzounian, Alice, *The Mystery of Janus the God of Gateways*,
http://www.plotinus.com/janus.htm

Ovason, David, *The Zelator: The Secret Journals of Mark Hedsel*, Arrow, 1999

Pagels, Elaine, *The Gnostic Gospels*, Weidenfeld and Nicolson, 1980

Paterson Smyth, J., *How We Got our Bible*, Sampson Low, Marston & Co Ltd, 1856

Pennant, Thomas, *Tour in Wales*, Benjamin White, 1784

Pennick, Nigel, *Sacred Geometry*, Capall Bann Publishing, 1994

Pert, Alan, *The Grail Legend: A New Translation*,
http://www.harbour.sfu.ca/~hayward/van/glossary/grail.html

Phillips, Graham, *The Search for the Grail*, Century, 1995

Picknett, Lynn, and Prince, Clive, *The Templar Revelation: Secret Guardians of the True Identity of Christ*, Transworld, 1997

Piggot, Stuart, *The Druids*, Thames and Hudson, 1985

Pike, Albert, *The Morals and Dogma of Scottish Rite Freemasonry*, L. H. Jenkins, 1928

Plichta, Peter, *God's Secret Formula*, Element Books, 1997

Powell, T. G. E., *The Celts*, Thames and Hudson, 1983

Radin, Dean, *The Conscious Universe*, HarperCollinsPublishers, 1997

Randles, Jenny, and Hough, Peter, *Encyclopaedia of the Unexplained*,
    Brockhampton Press

Rees, Alwyn and Brynley, *Celtic Heritage*, Thames and Hudson, 1989

Reid, Howard, *Arthur: The Dragon King*, Headline, 2001

Roberts, Alison, *Hathor Rising: The Serpent Power of Ancient Egypt*,
    Northgate Publishers, 1995

Roberts, J. M., *Antiquity Unveiled*, Health Research, 1970

Roberts, J. M., *The Mythology of the Secret Societies*, Secker & Warburg, 1972

Roberts, W., *Printer's Marks*, publisher unknown, n.d.

Rolleston, T. W., *Myths and Legends of the Celtic Race*, Mystic P, 1986

Russell, Peter, *The Brain Book*, Routledge, 1980

Sinclair, Andrew, *The Secret Scroll*, Sinclair-Stevenson, 2001

S. Acharya, *The Christ Conspiracy: The Greatest Story Ever Sold*, AVP, 2003

Schaya, Leo, *The Universal Meaning of the Kabbalah*, University Books, 1987

Schele, Linda, and Miller, Mary Ellen, *The Blood of Kings: Dynasty and Ritual in
    Maya Art*, George Braziller, 1992

Scholem, Gershom G., *On the Kabbalah and its Symbolism*, Routledge & Kegan Paul,
    London, 1965

Schonfield, Hugh, *The Essene Odyssey*, Element Books, 1984

Schonfield, Hugh, *The Passover Plot*, Element Books, Hutchinson, 1965

Schwartz, Gary, and Russek, Linda, *The Living Energy Universe*,
    Hampton Roads Publishing, 1999

Seife, Charles, *Zero: The Biography of a Dangerous Idea*, Souvenir Press, 2000

Seligmann, Kurt, *The Mirror of Magic*, Pantheon Books Inc., 1948

Seligmann, Kurt, *The History of Magic*, Gramercy Books, 1998

Sharper Knowlson, T., *The Origins of Popular Superstitions and Customs*,
    Merchant Book Company Limited, 1994

Skeat, Walter, *The Concise Dictionary of English Etymology*, Diane Publishing Co.,
    1900

Smith, Morton, *The Secret Gospel*, Victor Gollancz, 1974

Snyder, Louis L., *Encyclopaedia of the Third Reich*, McGraw-Hill, 1976

Spence, Lewis, *Introduction to Mythology*, R. A. Kessinger Publishing Co. Ltd, 1997

Stephen, Alexander M., *The Journal of American Folklore*, January/March 1929

Stone, Nathan, *Names of God*, Moody Press, 1944

Sullivan, Danny, *Ley Lines*, Piaktus Books, 1999

Talbot, Michael, *The Holographic Universe*, HarperCollins*Publishers*, 1991

Temple, Robert, *The Crystal Sun*, Arrow, 2001

Temple, Robert, *Netherworld: Discovering the Oracle of the Dead and Ancient Techniques of Foretelling the Future*, Century, 2002

Thiering, Barbara, *Jesus the Man*, Corgi, 1993

Thompson, C. J. S., *Mysteries and Secrets of Magic*, Causeway Books, 1973

Thomson, Ahmad, *Dajjal the Anti-Christ*, Ta-Ha Publishers Ltd

Toland, John, *Hitler*, Wordsworth, 1997

Tolstoy, Nikolai, *The Quest for Merlin*, Little, Brown and Co., 1988

Tull, George F., *Traces of the Templars*, The King's England Press, 2000

The Upanishads, trans. Juan Mascaro, Penguin Books, 1965

Vadillo, Umar Ibrahim, *The Return of the Gold Dinar*, Madinah Press, n.d.

Villanueva, Dr J. L., *Phoenician Ireland*, Dublin, 1833

von Eschenbach, Wolfram, *Parzifal*, Random House, 1961

Waite, A. E., *The Hermetic Museum Restored and Enlarged*, 2 vols, London, 1893, reprinted Red Wheel/Weiser, 1990

Waite, A. E., *The Hidden Church of the Holy Grail*, Fredonia Books, Amsterdam, 2002

Wake, C. Staniland, *The Origin of Serpent Worship*, R. A. Kessinger Publishing Co. Ltd, 1996

Walker, Benjamin, *Gnosticism Its History and Influence*, HarperCollins*Publishers*, 1983

Wallace-Murphy, T., and Hopkins, M., *Rosslyn: Guardian of the Secrets of the Holy Grail*, Element Books, 1999

Waters, Frank, *The Book of the Hopi*, Viking, 1963

Watson, Lyall, *Dark Nature: A Natural History of Evil*, Hodder & Stoughton, 1996

Weber, Renée, *Dialogues with Scientists and Sages: Search for Unity in Science and Mysticism*, Arkana, 1990

Weisse, John, *The Obelisk and Freemasonry*, R. A. Kessinger Publishing Co. Ltd, 1996

Wheless, Joseph, *Forgery in Christianity*, Health Research, 1990

Williamson, A., *Living in the Sky*, Oklahoma Press, 1984

Wilson, Colin, *The Atlas of Holy Places and Sacred Sites*, Dorling Kindersley, 1996

Wilson, Colin, *Frankenstein's Castle: The Double Brain – Door to Wisdom*, Ashgrove Press, 1980

Wilson, Colin, *Beyond the Occult*, Caxton Editions, 2002

Wilson, Hilary, *Understanding Hieroglyphs*, Caxton Editions, 2002

Wood, David, *Genisis*, The Baton Press, 1985

Woods, George, Henry, *Herodotus: Book II*, Rivingtons, London, 1897

Woolley, Benjamin, *The Queen's Conjuror: The Science and Magic of Doctor Dee*, HarperCollins*Publishers*, 2001

Wylie, Rev. J. A., *History of the Scottish Nation*, Volume I, publisher unknown, 1886

Zollschan, Dr G. K., Schumaker, Dr J. F., and Walsh, Dr G. F., *Exploring the Paranormal*, Prism Unity, 1989

Other Sources

Dictionary of Beliefs and Religions, Wordsworth
Dictionary of Phrase and Fable, Wordsworth
Dictionary of Science and Technology, Wordsworth Edition
Dictionary of the Bible, Collins
Dictionary of the Occult, Geddes and Grosset
Dictionary of World Folklore, Larousse

The Apocrypha, Talmud, Koran, Bible, Dead Sea Scrolls - Damascus Document, The
Community Rule, War of the Sons of Light with the Sons of Darkness, Messianic Rule
of the Congregation, The Temple Scroll, The Writings of Pliny the Younger, Flavius
Josephus, Pythagoras, Plato, Hippolytus of Rome, Ephraim the Syrian, Carl Jung,
Jeremiah Creedon (Guardian), Foundation for the Study of Cycles, The I Ching
(Richard Wilhelm translation), The New Scientist, Nag Hammadi Gospel of Truth,
Gospel of Mary, Gospel of the Egyptians, On Baptism.
Documents received from the following and used by their permission, Scientologists,
Jehovah's Witnesses, Mormons, Jewish Pentecostal Mission, Rosicrucians, Freemasons,
Inner Light. Websters Encyclopaedia, Encarta Encyclopaedia, The Unexplained
(Focus), Encyclopaedia of History (Dorling Kindersley), Staff at Lichfield Cathedral,
The New Scientist (21 March 1998 and 11 July 1998), Bible Explorer (Expert
Software), Faith in Every Footstep (The Church of Jesus Christ of Latter-Day Saints –
press Information CD-Rom).

www.gardinerosborn.com
www.serpentgrail.com
www.theshiningones.com
www.radikalbooks.com
www.elfhill.com
www.handstones.pwp.blueyonder.co.uk
www.angelfire.com/ma3/mythology/thewell.html

Index